New Feminism in Ch

Jiaran Zheng

New Feminism in China

Young Middle-Class Chinese Women
in Shanghai

Jiaran Zheng
Beijing Institute of Technology
Beijing
China

ISBN 978-981-10-0775-0   ISBN 978-981-10-0777-4   (eBook)
DOI 10.1007/978-981-10-0777-4

Jointly published with Foreign Language Teaching and Research Publishing Co., Ltd.

Library of Congress Control Number: 2016934013

Printed on acid-free paper

This Springer imprint is published by Springer Nature
The registered company is Springer Science+Business Media Singapore Pte Ltd.

Acknowledgements

This research is about social change in contemporary Chinese society and its impact on the lives of urban young women. It has been designed and undertaken by a young Chinese woman who is experiencing such a change. In this sense, this project is also a report of a personal history, an autoethnographic study of my own feminist adventure and small victory: from a spoilt only daughter in a middle-class family in China's capital who is always dreaming about 'making some change in the future', to a grown-up young lady who is today realising her dream of completing her doctorate degree in the best university across the globe.

This research project was funded by Cambridge Overseas Trust (COT), China Scholarship Council (CSC) and Funds for Women Graduates (FfWG), and supported by Springer Press and Foreign Language Teaching and Research Press (FLTRP).

For their helpful comments and advice, I thank Dr. Rob Moore, my doctorate supervisor and mentor in Cambridge University, who has offered me patience, support and understandings as well as intellectual inspirations; Professor Madeleine Arnot, Dr. Hilary Cremin and Dr. Jo-Anne Dillabough in the Faculty of Education, Cambridge University; Professor Lisa Hall in Queens' College. I especially thank Professor Becky Francis and Dr. Nigel Kettley, for commenting on the full manuscript: many of the book's best arguments and clever formulations come from their comments.

Elsewhere, I give my sincere gratefulness to my parents, who taught me to be strong and diligent. Thanks also go to Keith Lawn and Jannie Lawn, who have offered me consistent love, care, support and encouragement during my stay in Cambridge, UK. In addition, I would thank Foreign Language Teaching and Research Press and Springer Press for their kind and generous support for publishing.

Contents

Abbreviations

ACWF	All-China Women's Federation
AR	Autonomous Regions
CASS	Chinese Academy of Social Sciences
CCP	Chinese Communist Party
ECOSOC	Economic and Social Council
FWCW	Fourth World Conference on Women
LAT	Living Apart Together
NBSC	National Bureau of Statistics of China
NGO	Non-government Organisation
PRC	People's Republic of China
ROC	Republic of China
SAR	Special Administrative Regions
SEZ	Special Economic Zones
WTO	World Trade Organisation
UN	United Nations

List of Figures

Introduction

Rosy Future for Girls

It's an exciting time to be Chinese. While in the West the first decade of the 21st century was defined by pessimism due to 9/11, the Iraq War, and the Great Recession, Chinese people are very optimistic that the 21st century will be the 'Chinese century'. The fruits of China's three decades of rapid economic growth are there for all to see: by 2010, the People's Republic of China (PRC) had the fastest computer in the world and the smartest students in the world, and it was enthusiastically entering the space age—just as the United States was retiring its fleet of Space Shuttles.[1]

The idea of this book originates from my doctoral thesis on the social transformation of China and its influence on the lives of young women. It was taken from 2008–2012, when I was one of thousands of young Chinese women seeking for a foreign education in the UK. At that time, China had just successfully organised the 29th Olympic Games in Beijing and was preparing to gear herself up as a global giant under the leadership of Hu Jintao and Wen Jiabao. As a young Chinese student studying and living abroad, there is a strong sense of mission and obligation from the bottom of my heart to serve as a cross-cultural communicator by writing something about the socio-cultural change of China and her people in contemporary times. Also, as a young woman, I strongly agree with Roces and Edwards (2000:1) regarding their view that women possess the substantial power of serving as 'an indispensable societal component establishing dynamic new conceptions of contemporary cultural practice'. To some extent, it is a faith and determination that encourages me to overcome all difficulties and obstacles during the process of pursuing my doctorate in another language in a foreign country.

Undoubtedly, the overwhelming social transformation experienced in China's modern history has exerted great impact on the lifestyle and ideologies of her people. In this book, I am particularly interested in the changes manifested on the

---

[1]"China's Leap in Supercomputer Rankings," Bloomberg Businessweek Online, October 5, 2010; Dillon, S. "Top Test Scores from Shanghai Stun Educators," New York Times, December 7, 2010.

single-child generation of Chinese women who are living in the urban context. The 'Single-Child' generation was a young generation of Chinese people who were born in the 1980s when China had established the 'Single-Child' policy to control the nation's population. Thus, Chinese scholars and researchers usually call it the 'Post-80' Generation. It is this cohort of city-dwelled young Chinese women that turns to be the focus of this book. Here, I relate issues of Chinese sexuality and the female body, urban employment, women's affect and belonging, sense of citizenship and national identity to contemporary feminist debates on the discursive production of female subjectivity and local/global feminisms. By carrying out a four-year qualitative research, I attempt to examine how these 'promising' young Chinese women's self-perceptions have reflected the 'going to market' of contemporary Chinese culture, and how these meanings have reflected on the 'gender turn' in the context of China.[2] In so doing, I illuminate some interesting concerns about a new kind of feminism which may be developing amongst young Chinese women who were born in middle-class and affluent urban families. Throughout the book, two questions are to be answered:

(a) How do the urban-dwelling middle-class young women construct their meanings of young womanhood in the age of marketisation and globalisation in China?
(b) What are the potential values of women's success in education to the ongoing women's emancipation in China as well as to global feminism in contemporary times?

Overall, this research topic is based on my own research interest, the understanding of relevant literature (including literature of Western feminist youth studies, Women's/Gender Studies, Chinese cultural studies as well as some modernity and 'post' thesis which shed light on this research), the identification of the research gap in the field, as well as the realisation of the socio-cultural background and the status quo of the academic field of Chinese Women's/Gender Studies. I also use international and domestic news as well as the latest business and management reports to enrich my analysis of the impact of social change on the reconstruction of gender and class in contemporary China.

While making an effort on exploring the life experience of the younger generation of Chinese women, the ultimate concerns for me in this book is to establish a better cross-cultural understanding with English readers regarding the changing ideologies and mentalities of contemporary Chinese young people.

---

[2]Feminist scholar Frader (2003) examines how the cultural and linguistic productions of gender have impacted on gender relations in labour history in different Western societies. She coined the term 'gender turn' to argue that the tendency to thinking of gender as a synonym for women has obscured the more radical potential of gender as an analytical tool.

Gender Equality Matters

Feminists should always keep in mind their ancestors' efforts in fighting for equality between men and women over the years. When we traced back the history of the gender equality issue, it suggested that the battles for gender equality had been promoted by grassroot feminist movements in many Western countries. For example, the contraceptive revolution starting from about 1965 has been evaluated as a huge success for feminists, who, for the first time in history, won the rights for sexually active women to get reliable and independent control over their own fertility. Later, the equal opportunities revolution, for the first time, ensured that women in many Western societies obtained equal access to almost all positions, occupations and careers in the labour market. France and the USA, for example, pushed the revolution to cover more widely beyond just the labour market by giving women equal access to housing, financial services and other public services via legislation.

Being different from Western societies, Chinese activists initiated socialist revolutions to help their women to achieve their social and economic liberation under the support of the state. For example, the Women's Emancipation Movement led by the Chinese Communist Party (CCP) in the late 1950s–1960s is evaluated as the first contemporary socialist movement aiming at empowering homebound Chinese women with political, social, educational and financial resources (Li 2000). Along with the implementation of the market-oriented economic reform and the opening-up policy in the late 1970s, Chinese women have been provided with greater opportunities to get access to higher education and to participate in a wider range of social production activities in the public domain. Since then, it is possible for Chinese women to run their own business or to manage their community activities.

It has to be admitted that all these changes in the labour market and in other social sectors have produced a qualitatively different and new scenario of options and opportunities for women. The implication is profound, either in the West or in China. More than a decade ago, sociologists and feminist researchers began to focus on the younger generation of women under social transitions and their gendered experiences of new economic options available to them. To what extent is their capacity of seeing themselves as 'tomorrow's women' (Wilkinson et al. 1997) or as 'choice biographers' (Aapola et al. 2005)? In a classic feminist work of *Growing Up Girl: Psychosocial Explorations of Gender and Class*, Walkerdine Lucey and Melody (2001) have powerfully analysed the role that social class plays in relation to gender in present British society, arguing that the category of 'class' still exists in the midst of its social remaking in the UK and massively divides girls and young women in terms of their educational attainment and life trajectories. In their words, '[w]hile new discursive, economic and social organisations intervene—in the form of the new individualism, globalism and the transformed labour market—old practices of subjectivity continue to exist and yet are transformed materially and

discursively' (Walkerdine et al. 2001:19). And this conjunction and its consequences has profound implications on their people's lives.

Agreeably, under the influence of individualisation, globalisation and labour
market transition, traditional gendered practice has once again experienced
remarkable changes. This required us to draw much attention to the impact of social
changes on femininities and masculinities within different societies and cultures and
to re-frame the changing gender relations as a part of the 'crisis' in late modernity
(see also Arnot and Mac an Ghaill 2006; Lingard et al. 2009). As Mac and Ghaill
and Haywood (2007:253) stated, 'we are at a particular cultural moment where
gender no longer carries the understandings and feelings that have prevailed in
modern societies'.

Let us see a new scenario! Under the sway of global economic and social forces,
the traditional education-to-work transitions are going through a radical revision.
Especially for young women, while many have reaped the benefits of the 'feminisation' of the labour market, taking up rewarding positions in the new economy, a
large number of others, however, have been deeply affected by the rise in youth
unemployment and therefore have negative experiences of the new emphasis on
training and skills. Greatly and continuously, gender relations are being re-shaped
within this new scenario.

Contextual Overview

It is time to have a close look at the regional context, which is the scenario in this
book—China. To most Western readers, China is a vast country, densely populated
with several ethnic minorities and characterised by a communist political system
(see Fig. 0.1). In fact, what is commonly called 'China' is mainly a cultural concept
that describes different agents and areas born from the same cultural matrix and
populated by different ethnic groups spread all over the world. The concept of
'China' is bound to a population, a history and a culture that goes beyond the

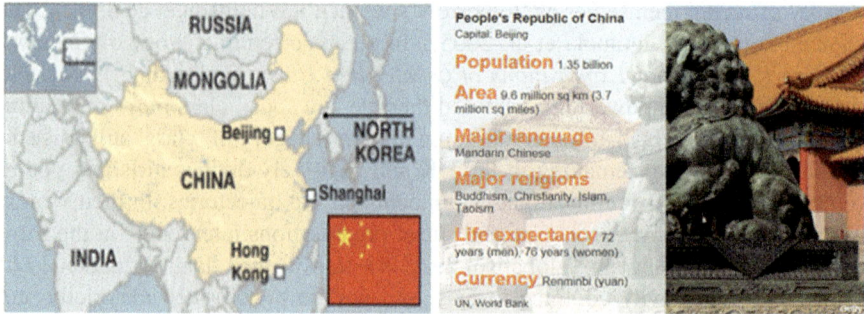

Fig. 0.1 China Country Profile. *Source* http://www.bbc.com/news/world-asia-pacific-13017877

Fig. 0.2 Locations of SEZs and SARs of PRC. *Source* Administrative divisions of the PRC

physical limits of its geographical areas. Most commonly, the geographical areas of 'China' could be divided into seven main sub-groups: Mainland China (People's Republic of China of the countryside/inland), Special Economic Zones of the People's Republic of China (SEZs), Special Administrative Regions of the People's Republic of China (SARs) (Hong Kong and Macao) (see Fig. 0.2), China of the ethnic minorities groups, the Autonomous Regions of People's Republic of China (Xinjiang, Tibet, Guangxi, Ningxia, Inner Mongolia) (see Fig. 0.3), Taiwan and Chinese people of the Diaspora (*huaqiao*). In this book, however, I will only limit my experiences within Mainland China, which I hereafter refer to as China.

Ethnically, China serves as home to 56 official ethnic groups. The largest group, the Han, makes up over 92 % of China's vast population, and it is the element of Han civilisation that the world considers as the so-called 'Chinese culture'. Yet, the 55 ethnic minorities, nestled away on China's vast frontiers, maintain their own rich traditions and customs, and are all part of Chinese culture. Both in common sense terms and by scholars, 'Chinese culture' has been widely regarded as strongly

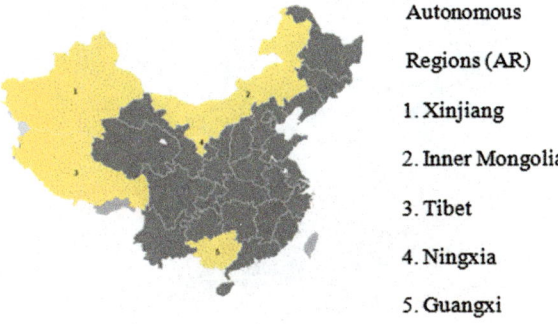

Autonomous

Regions (AR)

1. Xinjiang

2. Inner Mongolia

3. Tibet

4. Ningxia

5. Guangxi

Fig. 0.3 Locations of ARs of PRC. *Source* Administrative divisions of the PRC

Fig. 0.4 Olympic slogan at Beijing airport. *Source* Jiaran Zheng

traditional, especially in terms of family, gender and even (despite decades of communist rule) Confucian influences (see Meskill 1973).

In the late 1970s, the Chinese reformer Deng Xiaoping implemented the market-oriented economic reform. Since then, China has transformed quickly from a position of 'socialism' in name, but in actual fact, to a hybrid form of 'capitalism'. After years of economic reform ranging from the political relaxation of foreign direct investments to the promotion of entrepreneurship, China has emerged as one of the world's top economies and is well on track to transform herself to a central force in the global capitalist system. If the Beijing Olympics in 2008 serves as a new chapter milestone that signifies the beginning of China's third wave of economic growth—industrial consolidation (see Fig. 0.4), the official establishment of the slogan of the 'China Dream' in 2012 could be seen as a climax for China's determination to become a strong and powerful nation under the leadership of President Xi Jinping (see Fig. 0.5).

For self-development, the Party and the State have all along put a premium on education. Since the founding of the People's Republic of China, the entire Party and society have worked hard to blaze a road to develop socialist education with Chinese characteristics, establish the world's largest education system, and

Fig. 0.5 The slogan of China Dream for publicity. *Source* Jiaran Zheng

guarantee the right to education for billions of Chinese under the leadership of the Party's three generations of central collective leadership with Mao Zedong, Deng Xiaoping and Jiang Zemin at the core, and the Party's Central Committee with Hu Jintao as General Secretary. Education funding is growing by huge margins, which enables school-running conditions to have dramatic improvement; education reform is going steadily in-depth, which contributes to the consistent rise of school-running proficiency. Since the beginning of the twenty-first century, while free compulsory education has become the norm in both urban and rural areas, vocational education has made fast headway. In the meantime, higher education reached a new stage of popularisation as rural education grew in strength. Besides that, remarkable progress has been made in achieving education equity. For example, in rural areas, girls have equal opportunities to get access to education as boys. In universities, increasing number of girls nowadays get enrolment in many traditional 'male's subjects', such as computer sciences, physics and engineering. While education has been greatly emphasised by the nation over years, there is no doubt that educational development has vastly enhanced the quality of the entire nation, and stimulated innovation in science, technology and cultural prosperity, thereby making irreplaceable and significant contributions to China's economic growth, social progress, and the betterment of people's livelihood in recent years.

Successful Chinese Girls

Apparently, education in China is endowed with the mission of transiting the nation from a populous one to a nation with a larger scale of human resource. It increasingly becomes a most important social institution which could shape young people's everyday lives, identities as well as their understandings of their future life chances. Particularly for women, in the case of China, it also seems that China has a unique and globally influential political history in which the status of women has been a high-profile issue over the past century (see Chap. 1). Since the economic reform in 1974, it has been commonly observed that increasing number of Chinese women could get access to higher education and were making impressive academic achievements in university and colleges. For example, on August 21, 1996, a widely read national newspaper, the *China Youth Daily*, published a report titled, 'Is It Good or Bad that Females Occupy More Top Places in the National Entrance Examination?' It said that in Beijing in 1996 (the same as in 1995), the Number-Ones in university entrance examination both in liberal arts and science were all female students. In Shaanxi province, three Number-Ones in liberal arts and science (two Number-Ones in science) were female students. In Shanghai, seven of ten top-ranked students were females. The report also wrote, Number-One places in liberal arts were taken up by female students in the vast majority of Chinese provinces, and the number of female students was extremely large as a proportion of all students who had passed the admission score line.

Although the above-mentioned statistics are mainly based on local observations and reports in the media, it is undeniable that the news indeed gained countrywide public attention at that time. Some Chinese scholars have expressed their concerns that the phenomenon of 'female prosperity and male decline' does exist in Chinese higher education (Hu, 2001). Later, two Chinese educationalists Liu and Wang (2009) carried out a research project of studying the gender ratio of freshman admission in universities. They studied data from 1978–2005 at an elite university in Beijing, finding that female student enrolments had already grown from nil to a considerable size during that period of time. Yet, although the exclusion of women from college had been overcome to achieve gender balance, there still was obvious sex segregation in the selection of specialties. They conclude that the progress of gender equality in higher education is limited in that class exclusion and the urban–rural gap is still significant in contemporary university enrolment in China (Liu and Wang 2009).

Moreover, despite the fact that the number of Chinese female students who achieve higher scores in the national entrance examinations to enter elite universities is rising today, it remains problematic in terms of their employment after graduation. On graduation, as some local news reported, the reality is that society still needs more males, and as such, there will be an overabundance of female labour and of the impossibility of putting this female labour resource to full use. Equality in higher education from the perspective of female–male ratio alone is a 'lame equality' (Liu and Wang 2009). It seems that there is a need to re-examine what equality means to young Chinese women when both sexes have approximately equal opportunities to higher education nowadays.

Against the current social background of China, I am interested in exploring to what extent young Chinese women could change the conditions for their future selves as they begin to demand more equal rights in careers, interpersonal relations and individual development. Yet, whilst I critically explore the gender identity of young women in the context of China, I have no intention to simply reproduce the generational split that has characterised much of the framing of feminist debates in the West. Rather, I would like to call the issue of 'young women' into question. I suggest that we should expand the concept of feminism. 'Feminism' ought not to be seen only as legitimate when it takes the form of recognised activism; rather, it can have an important place in the 'micropolitics' of young women's everyday lives. In addition, I argue that we should not deny differences and contradictions of the complex grounded experiences when we attempt to understand the everyday life of contemporary girls and young women living in different socio-cultural contexts. I suggest that we should provide very careful and sophisticated analyses of the meaning of culture and religion, which complicates fixed notions of privilege and discrimination. Thus, in this book, I make use of feminist ideas which focus on the relationship between the two sexes, and carefully apply feminist theory developed in the West to the Chinese condition. I make no claim whatsoever to be comprehensive—no single study could possibly do that—nor even to be representative; yet, I do hope to arouse more academic interests on further exploring the richness of the scope of contemporary feminism developed both within and outside Western cultures.

Throughout the book, terms such as 'gender role' and 'gender identity' are used to refer to 'gender role/identity as a woman or as a man'. However, these terms are never satisfactory because I do not want to be essentialist about gender. It is for convenience and for the purpose of this book that I decide to use them to distinguish between 'gender' and 'sex'. Also, terms such as 'female' and 'male', 'women' and 'man', 'girl' and 'boy' are used interchangeably. Here, the term 'young women' is used to refer to Chinese women between the ages of 18 and 26, or as defined by social terms, those who are going through the transition period from a teenage daughter to a young daughter-in-law.

Book Organisation

The rest of the book comprises eight chapters. Chapter 1 sets out the socio-cultural and political background of China in order to facilitate Western readers to understand the gender equality issue in China and the development of Chinese Gender/Women's Studies. It begins with a review of the history of women's movements in China and its unique characteristics. I argue that although Western feminist thoughts exert much influence on the development of Chinese feminism, Chinese women's movements have indicated great difference from Western feminism; and accordingly, the academic field of Women's/Gender Studies in China has been developed under dual influences of local thinking on women and Western theoretical perspectives on gender.

Chapter 2 reviews contemporary Western feminist youth studies and feminist theorising of young women's activism, aiming to conceptualise a new conceptual framework for exploring women's life experiences and contemporary feminism in China. Four aspects are reviewed, including young women's understandings of the female body, women's access to education and workplace, girls' position in their parental families, and their political ambition. I argue that the current Western feminist debate on the 'successful young women' discourse have both theoretically and methodologically informed this research of studying young women in the context of China.

Chapter 3 justifies the research methodology and then lays out the procedures of this research project. I first suggest that qualitative research methodology should be more open to adaptation in terms of flexible design, mixed paradigms and varied use of tools and methods. I further argue that a small-N ($N = 20$) multiple-case study adopted in this research has its strength to gain an in-depth understanding of the ongoing women's emancipation and the potential social movement led by a growing number of young urban Chinese women. By explaining how my fieldwork has been conducted in China, I finally discuss the ethical issues, validity and reliability of this research.

Chapters 4–7 ask two research questions represented above. Chapter 4 focuses on young women's responses to fashion and beauty culture in the age of the flourishing global consumerism. In this chapter, I argue that young women construct their different meanings of Chinese femininities discursively and practically. Chapter 5 focuses on the interesting work-marriage philosophy held by young Chinese women. I use qualitative data to argue that young women envisage their marriage and plan for their future motherhood in an individualised manner. Chapter 6 asks how these young women redefine inter-generational power relations in the domestic sphere nowadays, and the external and social causes that might contribute to the shifting power balance in their private life. To answer the question, I analyse the pros and cons of the Single-Child Policy issued in 1978, arguing that the Single-Child Policy has produced 'unexpected' consequences for an absolute privilege of being the only daughter in urban families. Chapter 7 tries to find how young Chinese women perceive political issues and how they understand feminism. I argue that modern Chinese girls have indicated a strong inclination to take themselves as not only Chinese citizens but also global citizens. I also relate their individual ambitions to my interpretation of 'China Dream'. Overall, the aim of these chapters is to illuminate interesting concerns for the development of a new kind of feminism among the emerging middle-class young women in Chinese urban areas.

By bringing up these issues together, I make my efforts in integrating the concepts of Western feminism, Chinese culturalism and the development of individual autonomy into a new theoretical framework. I finish this book by inviting more cross-cultural feminist discussions on young women in future research. Although I see it as an end of this book, I believe there will be no end of such an invitation.

Chapter 1
Chinese Women and Feminism

The very subject of 'Chinese feminism' is ambivalent and controversial linguistically and conceptually. There are two common renditions of the English term 'feminism' in Chinese. Feminism as *nuquan zhuyi* (women's rights or power-ism) connotes the stereotype of a man-hating he-woman hungry for power; hence it is a derisive term in China today except for a small circle of scholars and activists. Feminism as *nuxing zhuyi* (female or feminine-ism), in turn, appears far less threatening... Although few in the Anglophone world would consider this position 'feminist,' this 'soft feminism' enjoys more purchase than *nuquan zhuyi* among Chinese scholars who identify themselves as 'feminists.' (Ko and Wang 2007: 1)

The Purpose of this chapter is to identify the difference between Chinese feminism and feminism developed in the West, and to emphasise the unique characteristics of Chinese feminism and Chinese feminists' concerns. I argue that in the context of China, although Marxist theory used to serve the political interest of the Chinese Communist Party government in keeping women's concerns under state/party control at different historical times, it should also be appreciated as a scientific inquiry and intellectual theory with analytical power since it has the capability for macro, systematic analyses of women's liberation. Therefore, I suggest that Chinese elites should neither abandon the Marxist theory of women entirely nor accept Western feminist theory immediately. Neither should we treat these two theoretical frameworks as monolithic or static. Any categorical labelling of scholars and their works should be avoided. Rather, in the context of China, Marxist and feminist theory should not be treated as an either-or approach which juxtaposes one against the other in order to develop new gender theories in the field of Chinese Women's/Gender Studies.

Here I mainly draw upon publications and research written in Chinese with the aim of translating and transmitting local knowledge to a non-Chinese-speaking readership in the international Women's Studies community. Also, I would draw on English materials deemed relevant for discussion, aiming to illustrate how the field of Women's Studies in the socio-political condition of China has evolved in the dynamic process of theoretical knowledge production.

© Foreign Language Teaching and Research Publishing Co., Ltd
and Springer Science+Business Media Singapore 2016
J. Zheng, *New Feminism in China*, DOI 10.1007/978-981-10-0777-4_1

Women's Movements in Progress

The first sign of dawning: Chinese society has enjoyed a long pre-modern history, in which a patriarchal relationship has been untouchable and unchallenged for more than 2000 years. Under the feudal system, there has also been a long silence for women's movements. It was only until the mid-nineteenth century when the largest peasant movement (*Taipin Tianguo* Movement) broke out that Chinese women's oppression was brought into scrutiny for the first time (Lu 2004). Hong Xiuquan, the leader of this peasant movement, advocated that both men and women were children of *Shang Di* (God) and they were brothers and sisters. Women were encouraged to participate in the revolution as much as men (see Fig. 1.1).

This could be construed as the first time in modern Chinese history that there is the idea of equality between men and women. However, Hong's idea of equality between men and women did not generate Chinese feminism at that time because women's status was given importance only under the circumstances of meeting the demands of the war (Zhou 2006). Gasster (1969: 230) also points out that it is only when Chinese people encountered Western and Japanese imperialism in the nineteenth century that bred the seeds of Chinese feminism. The first Opium War in 1841, although being seen by the Chinese as the most humiliating defeat, did force China to open its door to other cultures for the first time.

After the Opium War, Western culture, including feminism, began flowing into China through the influence of Western missionaries. These Western missionaries were opposed to the tradition of women's footbinding and began to shift their religious and educational concerns to social reforms (Siu 1982). Under such Western influence, some Chinese activists and reformists also realised the weakness and inefficiency of the government. In 1898 Kang Youwei (1858–1927) and Liang Qichao (1873–1929) initiated the Hundred-Days Reform with the aim of pushing the Chinese government to change its political system.[1] As one of the reform measures, Chinese students were sent to Japan and European countries to study Western science and technology. These overseas students finally initiated the modern Chinese women's movement and the revolution of 1911 (Siu 1982).

In the Hundred-Days Reform, Kang inspired a new generation of Chinese women to strive for their natural rights. By recognising that the footbinding custom was a cruel treatment of women, he organised natural-foot societies and established a modern education campaign to propose a footbinding abolishment law (Siu 1982). With the failure of the reform, the proposal lost the official support and finally failed in 1904. Some succeeding movements related to women's rights were accordingly stagnated. For example, Qiu Jin, a woman's activist and revolutionary, was

---

[1]The Hundred Days' Reform in China was a 104-day national cultural, political and educational reform movement from 11 June to 21 September 1898, undertaken by the young Guangxu Emperor and led by his reform-minded supporters Kang Youwei and Liang Qichao. Yet, the movement proved to be short-lived, ending in a *coup d'etat* by powerful conservative opponents led by Empress Dowager Cixi (Schirokauer 1991).

Fig. 1.1 *Taiping Taiguo* movement (1851–1864). *Source* http://www.qulishi.com/huati/taipingtianguo/

executed by the Qing government in 1907. Thus, the advocacy and practice of feminism at that time were still limited within a small intellectual circle in the east coast cities which were opening up to the West (Ono 1978).

In this reform, Kang and Liang viewed women's liberation as a part of the nation's liberation. By advocating liberating women from the family to working at machines and mills, the reformers attached more emphasis on the aspect of women's duty to strengthen China's economy. Thus, although the Late Qing Dynasty saw China approaching the eve of the women's movement, it still did not witness the first wave of Chinese feminism (Zhou 2006).

Along with the realisation that everyone, including women, was responsible to make China stronger, the Revolution of 1911 also resulted in increasing attention to women's rights. It was led by Sun Yet-sen, the first president of the Republic of China (ROC), who received a Western education and organised the former Nationalist Party *Tong Meng Hui*.[2] Sun systematically advocated democratic principles, arguing that it was not enough to acknowledge the sovereignty of the country without a democracy. Under Sun's leadership, the Nationalist government made another achievement by abolishing the custom of foot-binding which had lasted for thousands years (Siu 1982). It also recognised women's right to vote, to have knowledge of laws and politics and freedom and equality. For example, the revolution created the Suffrage Alliance in Shanghai in order to allow women to become vocal and active in gaining their rights (Siu 1982). In a word, this Revolution opened up a way for Chinese women's liberation.

The Revolution of 1911 legally ended the Chinese feudal political system, and transformed it into the republican government. Although it ended with failure due to the restoration of the monarchical system by Yuan Shih-kai in 1916 (see Schirokauer 1991), it did awaken the Chinese people, especially the Chinese elites,

---

[2]Sun Yat-sen has been likened to George Washington in more than a few Chinese textbooks over the years.

who began to devote themselves to upcoming social movements. Since the Republican government even had not yet built up a new constitution which included women's rights, a further promotion of women's liberation was postponed. After the Revolution of 1911, Chinese intellectuals and reformists reflected upon the failure and urged the break out of the first meaningful cultural revolution in China's modern history—the May Fourth Movement.[3] This cultural revolution promoted a real women's movement for the first time.

May Fourth as the first wave: During the Revolutions of 1911, most Chinese scholars had confirmed the importance of democracy and science in China. They reached a consensus that science could make China strong and democracy could establish equality between men and women. Some Chinese elites also began to seek the root of China's problems from the Confucian Chinese cultural tradition. For example, Chen Duxiu (1879–1942), who later became one of the founders of the Chinese Communist Party (CCP), argued that Confucianism was responsible for China's weakness and women's oppression, and therefore Confucianism must be put down first in order to make China and its women strong. In 1915 he founded the journal *New Youth*, setting up the first intellectual forum for criticising Confucianism and proclaiming a new culture (see Fig. 1.2). In the first issue of *New Youth*, Chen highlighted individual freedom and in the second issue he introduced American liberalism. Being seen as the flag of the May Fourth Movement of 1919, *New Youth* guided Chinese people to call for a new culture. *New Youth* also trained a new generation of culturalists and radicalists, including Mao Ze-dong and Li Dazhao (see Appendix 1 for the spelling of Chinese names), the other founders of the Communist Party. With a strong passion to proclaim a new culture, these culturalists began to introduce a variety of Western scholars' work into China, among which they had translated many work on women. The most influential one is an English socialist philosopher Edward Carpenter's work *Love's Coming-of-Age*: *A Series of Papers on the Relations of the Sexes* (Siu 1982).

Since 'the May Fourth Movement called into question the very basis of Chinese society' (Bianco 1971: 28), it was not at all surprising that the goals the intellectuals sought to achieve were frightening to the traditional-minded. By challenging the mainstream of Confucianism, this cultural movement is commonly regarded as being the first wave of Chinese feminism (Zhou 2006). Yet, the women's movement in this period demonstrated its weakness: it was not independent, but dependent on nationalism. In other words, the women's movement in the May Fourth period was set forth by nationalists rather than feminists. What nationalists

---

[3]The broader use of the term 'May Fourth Movement' often refers to the period during 1915–1921. The May Fourth Movement is an anti-imperialist, cultural, and political movement growing out of student demonstrations in Beijing on May 4, 1919 in order to protest against the Chinese government's weak response to the Treaty of Versailles, especially the Shandong Problem. Sparking the massive national protests, these demonstrations mark the upsurge of Chinese nationalism, a shift towards political mobilisation and away from cultural activities. Since this is the first move towards the populist base rather than the intellectual elites, the May Fourth Movement is more usually called the New Culture Movement.

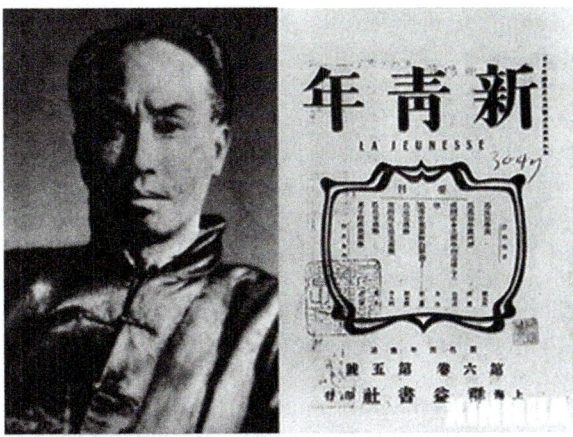

Fig. 1.2 Chen Duxiu and his *New Youth*. *Source* National Library

highlighted was that 'women were human beings' rather than 'there were differences between the sexes' (Zhou 2006). Therefore, at that time, the central concern was that a strong nation needed women who were strong. In practice, many different reforms demanding equal rights for women focused on women's education, female chastity codes and the inhumanity of arranged marriage. Although the nationalist government began to establish the legislation to protect women's rights of property, politics, education and marriage during the May Fourth Movement, women's liberation in China had still not reached the grassroots level. In the context of China, women's liberation could only be further achieved through a communist revolution.

Communist Revolution and 'women hold up the half sky': The term of the Communist Revolution of 1949 could be used to refer to the communist movements from its beginnings up to the founding of the People's Republic of China. Unlike previous revolutions, the Communist Revolution of 1949 accomplished China's transformation from a semi-feudal and semi-capitalist society to a socialist country. The communist party also particularly gave their attention to the women's issue in order to generate women's enthusiasm to support the communist revolution before 1949. For example, the Party organised different associations, including women's organisations to recruit party members, opened various public forums to promote socialism, and mobilised students' and workers' movements in big cities, such as Beijing, Shanghai and Wuhan (Gilbert 1973). The Chinese Soviet Republic proclaimed the first marriage law in 1931 to ensure freedom of marriage. This law was further developed so that women in the liberated areas could have the right to step out of the home and join the revolution (Gilbert 1973). Moreover, the Party encouraged women to participate in social production and produce more food, clothing and weapons in order to support the military. For example, Cai Chang, the top leader of the women's organisation in the Border Region government, pointed out that production work was the most important for women to do (Stranahan 1981).

After the founding of the People's Republic of China in 1949, large-scale political campaigns were launched to remove the 'feudalist mountain' that oppressed millions of Chinese women. To provide protection to Chinese women, many policies were taken into effect, such as putting an end to polygamy, allowing women to have rights to vote, and abolishing prostitution and gambling (White Paper 1994). The new government also established the All China Women's Federation (ACWF) as the national women's organisation with the dual mission of representing both state and women. It declared that Chinese laws guaranteed that women and men enjoyed the same rights and status and had equal personal dignity (White Paper 1994). The first Marriage Law was promulgated in 1950 and established to smash the feudal marriage system and guarantee freedom of marriage for Chinese women.

Almost at the same time, the government fundamentally altered the situation of economic inequality between men and women by launching the land reform that distributed land to all peasants including women. In 1953, the Electoral Law of the People's Republic of China was promulgated to empower Chinese women to have the same rights to vote and stand for election as men (White Paper 1994). The Women's Emancipation Movement in late 1950s and 1960s, in particular, empowered homebound women with political, social, educational, and financial resources to walk out of their homes into the larger society to assume new social roles alongside men (Li 2000). Women were organised to run small businesses, manage community events, hold government office positions, and participate in decision-making. According to Zhou (2006), there were about three million urban women and seventy percent of rural women being encouraged by the party to engage in social production work in 1957. Furthermore, the new government improved the educational level of Chinese women. Before 1949, ninety percent of Chinese women were illiterate because education used to be a wealthy family's privilege in pre-modern China. By 1958, however, there were sixteen million women (about 38 % of the total) who had learned to read, representing an initial step in eradicating the illiteracy of Chinese women (Zhou 2006).

Moreover, Mao stressed that Chinese women should 'hold up half the sky' and began to promote women's self-empowerment and the image of the 'Iron Girl' nationwide.[4] Although today this gender ideology is commonly criticised for disregarding women's physiology by forcing women to take on 'men's jobs,' this official ideology has provided women of that era with the possibility to challenge the traditional gendered division of labour. As Li (2005: 129) observed, 'not to differentiate females from males served as a challenge to the unequal social status between men and women and a challenge to the traditional ideology of men being superior to women.' Also, since most women who joined the 'Iron Girl' brigades

---

[4]The 'Iron Girl' is both a heroine created during the Cultural Revolution and a sign of the state ideology that 'men and women are the same.' In the article of 'Rethinking the "Iron Girls:" Gender and Labour during the Chinese Cultural Revolution,' Jin (2007) examines multiple dimensions of this gender ideology and pays particular attention to the relationship between the official gender discourse and women's practices during the Cultural Revolution period and its aftermath.

during the Cultural Revolution were from the lower echelons of society and had to perform heavy physical labour, it especially provides new discursive space for working-class women, who were at the lowest level of the social stratum, to express themselves (Li 2005).

Unfinished task: After Mao's death, the new generation of Chinese leaders began to revise the communist ideology. Setting the national economy as the top priority in China, the economic reform took place in 1978. Chinese reformer Deng Xiaoping led this communist revolution by opening up China's doors to the rest of the world and making China a part of the global village. Over the past thirty years, China has achieved some of the fastest economic growth rates in the world.

The achievement of the Chinese economy has also exerted a great impact on Chinese women in terms of releasing women's potential talents, offering women more opportunities for competition in a variety of areas, and providing additional employment opportunities for women in many areas (Li 2000). Since the 'Iron Rice Bowl' was smashed under the economic reform, Chinese women have had to develop themselves in order to compete with men in the labour market.[5] More and more women began to run their own private business as a way of living. All of these are impelling the formation and expansion of a civil society, and offering a space for women to raise their individual consciousness. In order to perform a fundamental strategic task in the protection of women's rights and interests, the ACWF also launched a campaign to promote the 'Four-selfs'—self-respect, self-confidence, self-reliance and self-strengthening at the Sixth National Congress of Chinese Women (Li 2000).

Having benefited from the economic improvement, Chinese women 'are becoming women' and, are acting on their own to make a unique lifestyle (Li 2000). By having equal rights to possess property and being granted the rights to take part in productive activities, Chinese women are no longer appendages of their husbands. About 286 million Chinese women were employed in the 1990s, making up about 44 % of the total work force in China, higher than the world rate of 34.5 % (Zhou 2006: 60). According to the 2001 survey conducted by the ACWF and the National Bureau of Statistics of China (NBSC), the majority of the women respondents in both rural and urban areas said that they had an equal voice or a decisive vote in making decisions on the family's investments (60.7 %—a 10.2 % increase from 1990), home purchase (70.7 %—a 15.1 % increase), or agricultural production (67.4 %—a 17.3 % increase). Most women (82.4 %) said that they had confidence in their own abilities, and 80 % of them declared that they could not be reconciled to achieving nothing. Two-thirds of the women were against the statement 'Men are more able than women by nature;' and 88 % expressed that they would choose to work even if their husbands could earn enough money or if their families had a large fortune (Zhou 2006).

[5]'Iron rice bowl job' is a Chinese term used to refer to an occupation with guaranteed job security, as well as steady income and benefits. Military personnel, members of the civil service and employees of various state-run enterprises (through the mechanism of the work unit) are usually considered to have 'iron rice bowl jobs.'

With these achievements, many Chinese scholars have confirmed that under the leadership of the communist party, the new government made impressive progress in women's liberation in the first decade of the new China. For example, Li Xiaojiang, the founder and pioneer of Women's Study in China, claimed that Chinese women enjoyed a large degree of economic freedom after the Communist Revolution of 1949. It was the communist revolution that liberated them from the feudal society (Li 2000). By presenting a comprehensive review of the history of women's liberation in the People's Republic of China, Li (2000) concluded that in post-Mao China, Chinese women's liberation could be categorised into two stages. The first stage was from 1949 to 1976, in which Chinese women as a whole had achieved social equality. From 1976 onwards, Chinese women's liberation entered the second stage, where women began to enjoy more economic freedom. Wang (1998), a diasporic scholar dedicated to Chinese Women's Studies, also confirms that presently, women in Mainland China are more likely to see their diverse views, aspirations and needs expressed in public discourse than at any point since 1949.

While there is no doubt that the Chinese government has made big progress in terms of improving women's situation, we should also notice that gender inequality still widely exists, such as the unequal pay in general and the imbalanced number of women in top leadership positions, and this happens in both urban and rural areas. For example, in the 1990s the average monthly incomes for male and female workers in urban areas were 193.15 yuan and 149.60 yuan respectively, with women receiving only 77.4 % of the pay given to men. In rural areas the average annual incomes for men and women were 1518 yuan and 1035 yuan respectively, with women getting 68.2 % of the earnings of men (ACWF Research Group 2001). In the past ten years the income gap between men and women has increased 19.3 % (ACWF Research Group 2001). Moreover, women are underrepresented in the top leadership positions even though they became the majority in many organisations in the late 1990s. In this respect, even Chinese officials have acknowledged that 'the condition of Chinese women is still not wholly satisfactory' (ACWF Research Group 2001) and it remains an arduous task for the government to tackle in order to further achieve gender equality and promote women's development nationwide to a satisfactory level. Presently, it has been witnessed that more and more cross-cultural dialogues have been established between Chinese scholars and their Western counterparts in terms of the women's issue.

Women's/Gender Studies: An Emerging Field

Accordingly, Women's/Gender Studies in China have become increasingly popular. Yet, given the specific socio-cultural and political context, the academic field of Chinese Women's/Gender Studies has its own theoretical perspectives and practical concerns. As mentioned previously, the May Fourth Movement is commonly regarded as the first wave of women's movements in China. This New Cultural Movement could also be seen as the first wave of Chinese Women's Studies. In the words of Chow et al. (2004: 167), 'this anti-imperialist, anti-Confucian, nationalist and intellectual movement aimed at rejuvenating the nation makes women's issues one of the central foci for public and scholarly discourse.' Just as male nationalists promoted gender equality in China, so the first wave of carrying out research on women was also led by Chinese male scholars. In this section, however, I only focus on the current wave of Women's Studies after the founding of People's Republic of China in 1949.

The current wave of Women's Studies in China has originated in the mid-1980s in the emerging urban-based women's movement (Wesoky 2002; Zhang and Wu 1995). While inheriting the legacy of predecessor efforts, the current wave of Women's Studies attempts to give a direct response to the old and new problems faced by women in the economic reform. This wave is characterised by the rise of women's consciousness about themselves as women, the formation of women's organisations, and the creation of new forms of activism to protect women's rights and interests and to embark on a new discourse on women (Li 2000).

With a more diversified economy and a relaxed political, social, and intellectual climate, the current field of Women's Studies is different from those of earlier years. Firstly, the current field is initiated and has been strongly advocated for by women themselves rather than male scholars. Secondly, it has resulted more from efforts by women from below than by the party/state from above, with an emphasis on women's own identity and interests as a social group. Thirdly, the present concern distinctively establishes Women's Studies as an academic discipline and challenges traditional knowledge about women and their social world (see Chow et al. 2004).

The current development of Women's Studies in China is the outcome of a combination of the global and local impact. In less than two decades, it has even become one of the most dynamic influences on various academic fields including sociology and on the women's movement in China. According to Yi (2000), the current wave of Women's Studies could be divided into two periods, with a first stage of initiation and consolidation from the 1980s to the early part of 1993, and a second stage of expansion and internationalisation from the second half of 1993 onward.

In the first period, the initial effort to study women's issues was made by research-oriented organisations within and outside of the ACWF (Yi 2000). Under the ACWF's leadership, various research associations were established at the provincial level and some municipal levels, bringing interested scholars and professional women together to study women's issues. As the national women's organisation, the ACWF began with the study of marriage and the family in the early 1980s. Within the academy, the first Women's Studies group was formed in 1985, led by Li Xiaojiang of Zhengzhou University, who later established China's first Women's Studies centre at her university in 1987 (Yi 2000).

There were also many NGOs being established by 1993 in order to support networks for Women's Studies. More than 40 women's magazines and newspapers, mostly within the ACWF system, were published; among these are the *Chinese Women's News* and *Collection of Women's Studies*. *Collection of Women's Studies* is China's only journal focusing on research on women. In the same period, efforts were made to study women's practical issues, informed by the CCP's 'Marxist perspective on women.' Practical research had been done in response to many problems women faced, such as unemployment, migration, maternity benefits, divorce, domestic violence, crime, and sex trafficking of women (see for example Chow 2003; Liu 1999). There are also a few works (ACWF 1986, 1988, 1989; Tao 1991) on examining the history of the Chinese women's movement and critiquing the Marxist perspective on women being published during this period.

Since 1993, more emphasis has been attached to Women's Studies when China began to prepare for hosting of the United Nations's Fourth World Conference on Women (FWCW) in 1995. In less than two years' time, from September 1993 to May 1995, 18 Women's Studies centres were added to the original 5, with another 13 established by December 1999 (Chow et al. 2004). Moreover, Women's Studies centres began to find their places in the Chinese Academy of Social Sciences (CASS) and other social research institutions. This expansion signalled a shift in the pattern of development of Women's Studies organisations in China, from concentration in the ACWF system in the 1980s to growth in academia in the 1990s (Du 2000; Yi 2000). Since then, China began to make efforts with the development of Women's Studies in order to connect itself to the international track (*yu guoji jiegui*) and incorporate the Chinese women's movements into the transnational women's movement.

Compared to the first period, the second was distinguished by the increased influence of the international women's movement and organisations. Direct exchange intensified between Chinese scholars and activists with their counterparts and institutions such as the Chinese Society for Women's Studies. The world concerns of women specified by the Beijing Declaration and the United Nations Platform for Action introduced new research topics for Women's Studies in China, framed by the theoretical and analytical perspectives in the international documents (i.e., the new language and perspective of gender) (Chow et al. 2004). Concepts and perspectives such as gender, development, reproductive health, human rights, environment, and poverty alleviation also provided rather new analytical categories for examining women's issues in a changing China. Increased external funding also came into China to direct Chinese women scholars and activists to carry out empirically based projects on these topics (Du 2001; Liu 1999).

Being the prime movers of the development of Women's Studies in China, the ACWF and scholars in academia are dedicated to re-examining women's past experience and to carrying out social investigation in order to improve women's social status.

Unique Characteristics

Developed as an integral part of the Chinese women's movement, the field of Women's Studies in mainland China is not an outgrowth of the women's movement as in the West and therefore it embraces unique characteristics and related issues.

Meanwhile, it also has much in common with the international Women's Studies community. Here I summarise three major characteristics. These characteristics provide meanings for how women and gender knowledge are produced in various social settings and are embedded in the ideological framework that supports existing power relationships between the two sexes and the state.

The first characteristic is their dynamic relationships with the state, in which the state supports and exerts control over women's organisations and their research activities. As Chow et al. (2004: 174) have described, '[t]he fluidity of the state-women power relationship is best reflected by the ACWF as a state apparatus mediating between the state and women.' Being politically situated, the ACWF plays a critically important role in officially legitimising women's research and making the state accountable for women's interests and concerns. In the meantime, the state uses the ACWF to advance its political agenda to make the masses comply with state policy and its implementation (e.g., the family plan policy limiting women's reproductive rights) (Chow and Chen 1994). By the early 1990s, the Marxist assumption that economic growth simultaneously brings women's liberation had come under criticism. When the state switched its full attention away from the gender issue during economic reform, the market economy, however, only resulted in women's marginalisation (Chow et al. 2004). Some women researchers then reverted to the state policy directive, claiming that government intervention is necessary for women's betterment (Lin et al. 1998). The ACWF, rather as a monolithic entity, consists of both conservative leading figures, who often represent the official line on women's issues, and feminist researchers, who use the ACWF as a site of women's agency, promoting scholarship in and public policy for women. In a similar manner, discipline building can be seen as both an academic and a political process in China. It can been seen that Chinese scholars and activists are actively engaging in negotiation and manoeuvring, both within and outside of the ACWF system, in order to promote women's research from both below and above.

The second characteristic is that the variations in institutional settings—inside and outside academia—combine to form a broad organisational base that affects the nature, content, resources and outcomes of Women's Studies in China. Within each setting, there are differences and commonalities in the way that they operate independently and collaboratively with each other (Du 2000). On the one hand, as governmental research arms, the ACWF and CASS tend to hold to the Marxist theoretical orientation and the official lines on women and offer the most funding to support research and inform public policy. On the other hand, the NGOs and other grassroots-based research groups in general must cope with meagre funds, resources and trained personnel, and this has limited what they can study. Inside academia, the scholars adopt two different approaches—multidisciplinary and interdisciplinary to promote discipline building of Women's/Gender Studies. In order to warrant its own resources, faculty, institutional support and due recognition of its scholarly work, further efforts should be made on calling for disciplinary integration and autonomy simultaneously (Du 2000).

The third characteristic of Chinese Women's Studies is that in the process of local-global interaction through international women's movements, the Chinese indigenous nature and perspective are maintained in China. As Musil (2000) pointed out, the first Centre for Women's Studies was established in 1987, obviously not a result of the FWCW in 1995. Thus, the field of Chinese Women's Studies has its local roots, rather than being totally imported from the West. In China, Chinese scholars use *bentu* (indigenous) to refer to studies originating in China in contrast to those coming from *wailai* (outside). *Bentuhua* (literally, to make it indigenous) is used to refer to the process of critically applying overseas scholarship to the Chinese context. On the one hand, after the reopening of China, Chinese scholars are urgent to find out what there is in Western feminist scholarship. On the other hand, Chinese scholars are conscious of the threat of China's burgeoning Women's Studies being limited, marginalised, and/or colonised by well-developed, well-financed international Women's Studies or by movements dominated by Western feminism. While *bentu/bentuhua* helps illustrate the dynamic of local and global exchanges, the two should not be dichotomised and essentialised (see also Chow et al. 2004).

Owing to some distinctive characteristics of Chinese Women's Studies, the construction of the discipline in China follows its own path. When research on women's issues took off in the early 1980s, the term 'women's studies' was introduced to China from the West in three different versions of Chinese translation: *funuxue* (women's studies), *funu yanjiu* (women's research or research on women), and *nuxingxue* (literally, female studies) (Du 2001). The interest in this new field sparked a debate over whether to establish this discipline in China (Wang 1998). Since the CCP government has established its official theories and ideology on the women's liberation in China, the adoption of *funuxue* is originally objected by some high-ranking theorists in the ACWF who disdained its Western, bourgeois origin. Later, under the continuous efforts by Chinese feminist scholars, women's studies began to be perceived as a new academic discipline that promised a modern, scientific approach to women's issues, and '*funuxue*' began to become the preferred term to refer to not only studies done in academic settings but also the collective effort to research women's issues in China generally. Women's studies centres (*funu yanjiu*) were established in universities and research institutions to carry out research on women.

According to Chow et al. (2004), from the outset of women's studies in China, there has been a heated discussion in terms of the discipline building. The focus of this new discipline was to envision and conceptualise: what would this discipline be like, what should its guiding theoretical framework be, and what should be included in it? Li Xiaojiang, the founder of this discipline, initiated this discussion by perceiving women's studies as a cluster of existing disciplines with women added as a subject of study (e.g., women's history, women's sociology) (Li 1988). Also, Li (1988) considered women's studies as a way to examine the whole existence of humanity from the perspective of a 'sexed being' (*youxing*), viewing the discipline building in China as part of the 'human science' guided by Marxist theory on women. She edited more than a dozen volumes in the Women's Studies Series, with the first volume appearing in the year 1988.

Since the 1980s, the ACWF edited a collection of essays reflecting a decade's theoretical research on women under the title 'female disciplines.' These essays include women's anthropology, female population study, women's sociology, women's psychology, women's literature, women and sexology, and women and law (Xiong et al. 1992). Some scholars began putting these ideas into practice, trying to bring women's studies into their own discipline or subject of study. However, at that time, the teaching of women's studies did not get much emphasis.

In the mid-1990s, the field of Women's Studies experienced some growth and project support since a conference organised by Beijing University Women's Studies Centre in 1998 and a series of conferences afterwards (North-eastern Normal University 2002; Wang 2001). In this period, the teaching of Women's Studies in tertiary education was a major concern. Degree-/diploma-conferring programmes began to be set up. For example, China Women's College is now running a four-year B.A. degree and a pre-master's degree programme in Women's Studies department in conjunction with the Chinese University of Hong Kong and the University of Michigan (Gu 2001). Across the country, there are 65 colleges and schools with 2000 faculty and staff, recruits an average of 20,000 students, and trains 30,000 female cadres annually (Gu 2001).

Starting from 2000, Du Fangqin, a Chinese feminist historian and Wang Zheng, a diasporic scholar in the United States, initiated the multiyear Developing China's Women's/Gender Studies Project, aiming to bring discipline building of Women's Studies in Mainland China into a new phase. This project gave special emphases from four aspects:

(a) a commitment to make feminism and gender the theoretical bases and the principal analytical concepts of women's studies;
(b) an engagement with scholarship from outside China through a series of reading/discussion seminars to evaluate the relevance of this scholarship to the Chinese context;
(c) curriculum building and faculty development by combining scholarship with teaching practice inside and outside China for theory building, curriculum development, and pedagogy; and
(d) multidisciplinary and interdisciplinary approaches targeting three disciplines: history, sociology and education (see more Chow et al. 2004).

Critique of Marxist Theory on Women

Marx (1968) analyses the role of capitalism in human oppression, arguing that the first priority of human beings is the production of their means of subsistence through labour. While humans produce food, clothes and all manner of tools with which to share their living environment, they create their positions and status in societies. Thus, the central categories of Marxism are labour and forms of social organisation where material production takes place. The organisation of a model of material production is not simply a matter of coordinating objects; rather, it is inherently tied up with relations between people. These relations are not only co-operative and coordinated but also matters of power and conflict. Given the priority according to production, other aspects of human relations—consciousness, culture and politics—are structured by economic relations (Barker 2008). Therefore, Marxism emphasises the class dynamics of capitalist society, believing that the inequality in society arises from processes which are intrinsic to capitalism as an economic system.

Marxism has been used as a state ideology to serve the political interest of the state in China. The CCP government represents the proletarian class, arguing that material production should be prioritised in order to realise socialism, which is what the CCP has called 'socialism with a Chinese character' (Jiang 1990). A Marxist perspective on women is taken as the theoretical foundation of the Chinese communist state ideology and the political discourse on women. Within an official theoretical framework, the leaders of the CCP and the ACWF are taking charge of the articulation of views and assumptions about women and women's liberation. Gilmartin (1995) examines that Chinese officials set up this framework from three sources: Chinese feminism from the May Fourth Movement, Marxist-Engels' critique of the family, and the nationalist discourse. As mentioned in the previous chapter, the May Fourth Movement initiated the first wave of feminism in China. During that time, the oppression of women became emblematic of the 'old society.' In the face of Western imperialism, liberal ideas of individualism and modernity, the nationalist government has to urgently change the situation of women. Wang (1999) points out that in China, individuals are always subordinate to the larger collectivity. Thus, at that time, whether for a nationalist or a communist ruling party, the survival of the nation was assumed a higher priority than a real sense of women's liberation.

After the founding of the People's Republic of China in 1949, the CCP formally institutionalised women's liberation for the 'new society' within the Marxist theoretical framework on women. In 1978, this stance was specified as 'Chairman Mao's theory and line on women's liberation' by then-ACWF Chair-woman Kang (1978), and it was renewed in 1990 by former CCP general party secretary Jiang (1990) as the Marxist perspective on women (Marxist '*funuguan*'). The equal rights advocators at that time related the roots of women's subordination and oppression to private ownership and the class system, arguing that public ownership, state power, women's participation in production outside the home, and collectivisation of housework were necessary conditions for eradicating the roots of women's oppression and realising human liberation (Jiang 1990; Kang 1978). They set up women's organisations under CCP leadership for addressing women's needs and interests in an attempt to mobilise women to participate in the revolutionary struggle for the realisation of socialism and communism.

Taking Marxist perspective on women, the state claims that Chinese women's liberation and gender equality, which began with a proletarian class struggle, have been achieved with the arrival of Chinese communism. Women's problems, if any, were often considered to be residual of the old society. This ends the official discussion of the need for political struggle for gender equality. However, while the political path of national liberation allowed the CCP and the state to play a major role in improving women's status, it also limited the abilities of the women's movement to achieve its goals by leaving women's cultural, psychological, and individual liberation not fully addressed (Li 1995).

Against this historical backdrop, Chinese women scholars and activists begin to critically examine the CCP's theoretical and practical approaches to women. They notice that the Marxist perspective on women should not be simply seen as an official, state ideology that is under the discussion of being abandoned or not in China. Rather, this framework should be viewed as complex, fluid, and viable for both political/ideological and academic/theoretical purposes (see Li 1988, 1989, 1995; Wang 1998).

At the political/ideological level, the Marxist perspective on women has to be upheld as the banner of women's liberation, and discourse on women has been and still is a state-sponsored dominant theme for the CCP and the leadership of the ACWF. The idea of 'socialism with a Chinese character' requires the CCP government to support women's rights and entitlements. Thus, as the most important negotiator with the state on behalf of women in order to guarantee the material base of women's equality in employment, political participation, and social benefits, the ACWF should maintain its institutional and ideological continuities as a state bureaucracy, and uphold the Marxist banner of women's liberation, by which it could serve both the state and women's interests simultaneously (Chow et al. 2004).

At the theoretical/academic level, as the official line to provide scholars with theoretical resources (*lilun ziyuan*) for guiding Women's Studies in China, the Marxist perspective on women is under discussion. On the one hand, trained in this theoretical tradition, the cohort of women's movement pioneer in Mao's era, particularly those in the ACWF and scholars in academic settings, have produced a rich social and historical legacy on women in China, and this has exerted positive effects on the practice of solving women's problems at that time (Chow et al. 2004). Since the ACWF legitimised this official theoretical position academically and mainstreamed it into everyday discourse and practice, socialist revolutions have become part of Chinese women's lived experiences (Li 1995). On the other hand, the singular theoretical tradition of the Marxist perspective on women also brought about negative effects on opening up the theoretical/academic discussion. For example, Chinese scholars who still hold to this orthodoxy regard the Marxist perspective as a standpoint for resisting a postcolonial impact on Women's Studies in China (see Chow et al. 2004). In this sense, the Marxist perspective on women largely limits a thorough understanding of women's oppression. Chinese feminist scholar Li (1989) once initiated a heated debate about ACWF's functions, openly questioning the necessity for its existence. She contends that there are 'three forbidden areas' of discussion in Women's Studies at that time: class (separating women's from class oppression); sex (incorporating sexuality in research on women); and feminism (including feminist thoughts) (Li 1989). Without entering these areas, women's self-consciousness could not be effectively raised. Other Chinese intellectuals also contend that the persistence of the ACWF has closed up the social space for Chinese women's spontaneous activism and demand that it should be re-opened (for example Lin et al. 1998).

Along with the free-market rationality of capitalist development in China, a gender-related inequality and problems in relation to women's social, economic and political life becomes more obvious. For example, although women's conditions have been largely improved in education and employment as a result of the economic reform, Chinese women still lag behind in many aspects of social life, and this has either contradicted or cancelled the CCP's early policy of gender equality. Lin et al. (1998) point out that while the logic of a capitalist market and commercial values has altered social attitudes that have once championed equality, state control does not leave much room for individual freedom, self-realisation, or voluntary organisations. The Marxist assumption of the material base of women's liberation has thus been faced with challenge and criticism.

In the early time, voices and writings on women did not carry a feminist label in China. After the economic reform in 1978, more and more Western feminist thinking has been gradually transmitted into the ACWF, academic institutions, and other women's organisations in China (Li 1988, 1989; Wang 1998). Chinese women scholars who embrace moral voices of social conscience are increasingly aware of Western feminism and begin to become intellectual interrogators of gender-blind Marxism. By arguing that Western feminist thinking should be added onto a Marxist analytical framework, they advocate a revolutionary stand of promoting women's identity, self-realisation, and equality (Lin et al. 1998). For them, without a sense of self-realisation, women cannot be fully liberated.

Thus, although Marxism has provided an analytical framework, which contributes greatly to supporting Chinese women's liberation and research on women in the early development of Women's Studies in China, it is deemed that this state-sponsored theory and practice remains a site of women's struggle for fuller liberation, equality and advancement in China.

Theoretical Re-construction

When Western feminism and theories are first imported into China, Chinese intellectuals, officials and activists have indicated varied responses. Some perceived it to be a homogeneous entity, while others saw its diversity. Some disdained its hegemonic, imperialist and bourgeois nature, arguing that Western feminism will only promote 'war between the sexes,' which has 'nothing to do with the reality of hardworking socialist women;' while others recognised that it could be used as a new theoretical challenge to the validity of a Marxist perspective on women (see Papic 1992).

With the increasing understanding of Western feminism, more and more Chinese women scholars have realised that the views of Chinese and Western feminists actually have achieved some consonance on the following four issues (Chow et al. 2004). First, Marxist economic determinism gives primacy to class analysis that includes women's issues. However, in a prolonged socialist revolution, although considerable efforts have been made on eliminating private property, overthrowing the bourgeois class, and installing the proletarian class as leader of the state, Chinese women's liberation has still not been fully achieved.

Second, Western feminism emphasises the importance of studying patriarchy, both public and private, as it shapes gender power relationships and their hierarchical structure that oppresses women. In China the Maoist slogan 'women holding half the sky' once created a myth of sameness between men and women. Women in China used to believe, and some still do, that they are rather liberated in comparison to previous generations of women living under a patriarchal-feudal system. Yet, they still face traditional gender role ideology and sexism (Li 2000).

Third, Western feminism's critical analysis of the state-gender relationship parallels Chinese scholars' critique of Chinese women's liberation under socialism as a state-sponsored project which is underlined by a paternalistic discourse. As Li (1988, 1989) argued, Chinese women's liberation under socialism has fostered women's dependency on the state and hindered their self-development, and this will further reinforce the ruling ideology and power relationships.

Finally, like their Western feminist counterparts, Chinese scholars and activists have engaged in feminist consciousness-raising. A feminist awakening from within and from outside the ACWF makes Chinese scholars to question the ruling role of the state and of women's interests enmeshed within it, particularly when the state lowers the priority which had been giving women in favour of economic expediency, modernisation and development (Chow et al. 2004).

Since the 1980s, there has been an emerging interest among many Chinese feminists in essentialising gender differentiation and discourses on femininity. Many Chinese scholars begin to conduct research on young women, exploring the ways in which they could separate women's issues from class analysis and combine feminism with Marxism (see Du 2001; Jin 2000). Chinese feminists are also working towards a new theoretical framework to coincide with Chinese Women's Studies for the present day. For example, Li (1988) has conducted the first Chinese feminist work, representing this new theorising about women and gender in China. Wang (1998) analyses women's resentment of the de-sexed approach in the Maoist era, arguing that the official version of gender equality plays a large role in the zeal for a 'feminisation of women,' but this, in fact, holds up men as the standard for women. As pioneers in the field of Women's/Gender Studies in China, Li and Wang have made an early effort to challenge the Marxist and Maoist theoretical status quo in order to foster female consciousness and self-realisation.

However, Western feminism and gender theory could only be partially adopted in the Chinese context for further developing this new academic field; otherwise, Western feminist ideas would be perceived as a potential threat in the People's Republic of China. As some Chinese scholars noted, there is also a need to explore other theoretical frameworks in order to resist the Westernisation of Chinese Women's/Gender Studies (Bao 1995). By exercising its legitimate power, the ACWF has also reinserted the Marxist theory of women in the CCP agenda. On March 8, 1990, Jiang Zemin, then the general secretary of the CCP, reiterated that the entire party and society should establish the Marxist perspective on women in promoting social development in China (Jiang 1990). This proclamation culminated in a joint publication by the ACWF and the Shanxi Women's Federation in 1991, *An Introduction to the Marxist Theory of Women* (1991). This book, which represents one of the most important theoretical works on the Marxist theory of women in contemporary China, devotes one chapter to the Marxist theory of women and feminism. Thus, for both political and strategic reasons, Chinese women scholars, officials, and activists should neither abandon the Marxist theory of women entirely nor accept Western feminism instantaneously. Rather, they are awaiting an opening of intellectual space at an appropriate time and place.

When Western feminist theory is imported to China, the term 'gender' firstly appears to be difficult to translate, as it has no direct Chinese equivalent and is often confused with 'sex' and 'femininity.' Also, the term 'feminist sociology' has not been widely adopted, and 'sociology of women' has been accepted and translated as 'female sociology.' Chinese Society for Women's Studies publications have clearly recommended translating 'gender' as *'shehui xingbie'* (literally meaning 'social sex') in order to separate it from 'sex' and 'femininity' linguistically (Bao 1995; Hom and Xin 1995; Wang 1998). *'Nuquan zhuyi'* (women's rights-ism) and *'nuxing shuyi'* (female-ism) in Chinese have been argued by Chinese scholars to be used distinctively in order to refer to Western feminism for Chinese women's experience and to emphasise the differences in agenda and context of the two women's movements. There are also some Chinese scholars who prefer to use neither term, or have chosen to put them together with a slash.

Since 1992 there have been more direct, intense scholarly exchanges between Chinese and Western feminists, and this further opens the intellectual space for Western feminism and a gender analysis in China. In 1992, a group of Women's Studies scholars from China participated in an academic conference of Engendering China held at Harvard University, and that was the first overseas conference Chinese scholars attended (Gilmartin et al. 1994). At that conference, Chinese scholars found that they shared the same interests with their Western counterparts in critiquing ethnocentrism, orientalism and the cultural imperialism of conventional knowledge in the West. The success of that conference actively promoted the second crucial event, which took place in the following year.

In 1993, the Chinese Society for Women's Studies and the Centre for Women's Studies at Tianjin Normal University organised an International Conference entitled 'Chinese Women and Development-Status, Health, and Employment.' At that seminar, 'gender,' as a key concept for discussion, greatly aroused the interest of Chinese scholars (Du 1993).

The third momentous event occurred in 1995, when FWCW and the NGO Forum were held in Beijing. That event had several significant outcomes for developing women's research and studies in China in the 1990s. First, the official use of the feminist concept of gender was legitimised internationally, not restricted to Western use in terms of language and perspective. This concept mainstreamed into feminist discourses in the academic disciplines and grassroots activism. Two ACWF publications, *China Women's News* (*Zhogguo Funubao*) and the journal *Collection of Women's Studies* (*Funu Yanjiu Luncong*), adopted the feminist concept of gender. Second, the ideas and agendas of the international women's movement embedded in the FCWF documents have shaped the official Chinese gender rhetoric and policy. Huang (1996: 14) explicitly stated that 'in order to incorporate gender into policy making, we have to begin gender analysis before a policy, a law, a programme, and a project are made.' Third, new concepts of women's empowerment, sustainable human-centred development, women's rights as human rights, women and the environment, and gender-based violence against women were inspired by global feminisms. Fourth, while hosting the FWCW was a politically expedient opportunity for the Chinese government to showcase its supposedly progressive policies, the positive effects on women included government funding, resources and support for women's projects and programs internally and externally, which furthered the development of Women's/Gender Studies and the production of gender knowledge in China (Chow et al. 2004).

All these events successively encouraged Chinese scholars to practise a Western gender theorising in its local context. More and more Chinese scholars and researchers began to embrace the feminist concept of gender as a social and cultural construction, negating the narrowly focused discourse on femininity, as well as broadening and repositioning research concerning women in the gender context for analysis (see Lin et al. 1998; Liu 1999). Feminist works also began to emerge in Chinese academia since then. For example, in 1993, Chinese scholar Du (1993) took a 'gender-woman angle of view' in her research. Her gender theorising did not only reduce bias and prejudice against women but also enriched human understanding of self and society and hence produced an inclusive system of knowledge. In her later work, Du (1998) theorised the historical formation of gender systems in China. Jin (2000) studied the impact of 'depeasantisation' of rural women and men in Jiangsu Province.[6] These Chinese scholars have turned to gender and development theory to dispel the myth of equating economic growth with women's liberation and class struggle with women's issues, shifting the blame from women for lagging behind in the market economy to gender bias. Their works are regarded as the prime example of combining Marxist class with gender analyses.

To conclude, influenced by Western feminism and feminist ideas, Chinese scholars begin to interrogate gender-blind Marxism. As for now, Marxism is increasingly appreciated as a scientific inquiry with analytical power and capabilities for providing macro, systematic analyses of women's liberation. While this intellectual theory remains central in women's research in China, more Chinese feminist scholars have realised that future work is needed to be done in studying patriarchy and masculinity. They begin to recognise that women's positioning in society depends greatly on their relative situations in gender relations vis-à-vis men,

---

[6]'Depeasantisation' is a self-created word, which means 'to liberate rural women peasants from agricultural work'. Many rural women are encouraged and supported to enter cities and set up their small-scale business (*dagongmei* or *wailaimei*).

forming a gender hierarchy that is often compounded by class, ethnicity, age, religion, sexual orientation and disability.

Currently, the incorporation of a gender perspective is still in transition in China. With the adoption of the concept of 'gender,' Chinese scholars have begun to show a tendency toward a Western theoretical framework and embrace a gender analysis in Chinese Women's/Gender Studies. Liu (1999) commends that gender analysis has now become a powerful analytical tool and a critical perspective for a large number of scholars, and this immediately results in some highly regarded scholarly work in Chinese academia. Along with incorporating the concept of 'gender' and Western feminist perspectives in China, Chinese scholars have also drawn new questions and implications for gender theory, method, analysis and even praxis in its local context. For example, many Chinese scholars continuously pose some important questions, such as: 'What is (are) Chinese feminism(s) and what are their indigenous characteristics?' 'How has nationalism, and now socialism with a capitalist twist, benefited or not benefited Chinese women?' 'How do gender interests intersect with class and other interests, and in what way does patriarchy enter into gender analysis?' 'Is the CCP's Marxist perspective on women a form of Marxist feminism?' 'Is the marriage between Marxism and feminism a happy or unhappy one and why?' These questions remain unsolved and are still under debate and exploration in China (see also Li 2000; Chow et al. 2004).

Conclusion: An Unusual Way for Chinese Women

There was a saying in old China: marry a man and get food and clothing. It means that marriage for women was to get room and board in the husband's home. Yet, the mentality of lazybones and idlers must criticised. If women wanted to liberate themselves, they must participate in productive labour to increase family income and improve the livelihood of the family. Only in this way could women raise their economic and social status in society and achieve equality between men and women. If a woman only attended to her children and stayed around the pot, the kitchen stove and the bed, she would never get liberated even though she worked so hard and worked herself to death. True liberation came from taking part in socialist production, which was the only way out.

In China, women's liberation originates and develops in a different way from Western feminist movements; and correspondingly, the theoretical foundation of women's studies in China is grounded in its specific historical and socio-political context, which is suggested as a continually changing interplay between Marxism and feminism over time.

When I provided a historical review of the development of Chinese women's liberation, I started with the first idea of gender equality by Chinese male revolutionaries in the 1850s and ended up with China's economic reform in the 1970s.

Some main national reforms during this time period were touched upon since they were closely related to Chinese women's liberation. An interesting point I would like to emphasise is that: the first indigenous Chinese idea of gender equality comes from Chinese male nationalists with the purpose of encouraging women to participate in the war. This also contributed to a major difference between Chinese women's liberation and Western feminist movements. I categorised the first wave of Chinese women's movement promoted by Chinese men as 'nationalist feminism.' From late Qing Dynasty onwards, Chinese people began to encounter Western feminist ideas, but feminism in China was still mainly conducted by male intellectuals. During this period, Chinese scholars translated a great deal of Western feminist work and Chinese feminism is mostly attending to cultural issues, such as foot-binding, concubinage, arranged marriage, female chastity and sexual segregation. By gradually integrating Western feminist ideas into the local context, Chinese feminism in this period could be categorised as 'cultural feminism.' From 1949 the CCP government began to launch the large-scale political campaigns in order to remove the 'feudalist mountain' that oppressed millions of Chinese women. After a series of institutionalisation and legislation to promote gender equality in China, modern Chinese women have made significant strides toward their equality status with men. Thus, in strict sense, Chinese women's movements were intertwined with national liberation. It was the encounter with Western feminism and feminist values from the 1980s onwards that culturally nourished Chinese feminists to re-think the women's issue.

I have also reviewed the development of Chinese Women's/Gender Studies under the global and local influences and some unique characteristics of this emerging academic field. I argue that being developed as an integral part of Chinese women's movements, the field of Women's/Gender Studies in China is not an outgrowth of women's movements in the West. It has different theoretical perspectives and practical concerns. In other words, there has been historical interplay between Western feminist ideas and the Chinese Marxist tradition in Chinese context. Although Marxism has been seen as the state ideology and theoretical mainstay of almost all disciplines, Chinese feminists once pose challenge to Marxism on solving women's problems. For the disciplinary construction, Chinese Women's Studies is gradually incorporating a gender's perspective in the local research on women by taking in Western feminist ideas. Given that, I suggest that Chinese scholars, officials and activists need to strategically adopt Western feminist theories and models, and explore new theoretical framework to conduct research projects in the future.

For me, it is fair to affirm the achievements made by Chinese women in terms of the gender equality issue; yet, it also deserves to draw an attention that women's cultural, psychological and individual liberation has not yet been fully addressed, and gender inequality is still perpetuated in present society, which would further limit the abilities of Chinese women to achieve their goals. Moreover, the academic field of Women's/Gender Studies (and its overlapping field of 'the sociology of women/gender') is still in its early formation in present China in terms of the theory development and curriculum construction. Therefore, it requires Chinese scholars in this field to make ongoing efforts to venture out on the theoretical frontiers to explore diverse perspectives on women's issues by continually transmitting and incorporating Western feminist theories within the local context.

Chapter 2
Feminism in the Third Wave

'Unlike power feminism, [the third-wave feminism] is committed to a view of the personal (sexuality, body image, relationships, the impact of cultural representations) as political ... it seeks to represent young women as angry, in charge and taking action.' (Aapola et al. 2005: 203)

'The kind of feminism which is taken into account in this context is liberal, equal opportunities feminism, where elsewhere what is invoked more negatively is the radical feminism concerned with social criticism rather than with progress or improvement in the position of women in an otherwise more or less unaltered social order.' (McRobbie 2009: 14)

The 'third-wave feminism' emerged around the 1990s in the Western world, seeing itself as building on and expanding previous waves of feminism in contemporary times. It marks a shift away from second wave feminisms adherence to the notions of shared interests among women.[1] Feminists in the third wave are particularly careful to acknowledge and thank second wave feminists, but in the same breath, they argue that young people today live in times and under conditions that make political activity and cultural critique difficult to engender. Instead, they consider that the politics of issues such as beauty, sexuality, fashion and popular culture are more complex than what has been presented by earlier feminist analyses. Therefore, they work outside the power/victim framework, aiming to investigate the complicated picture of young feminism and to re-theorise gender (see for example Baumgardner and Richards 2000; Harris 2001, 2004; Aapola et al. 2005). As Aapola et al. (2005: 205) described, this wave is 'more individual, complex and "imperfect" than previous waves. It is not as strictly defined or all-encompassing ... especially about personal choices.'

Truly, girls are now having more control over their lives, bodies and sexuality. They may have more freedom when it comes to education, employment and the management of their own finances, but they still face the age-old 'double-standards' of sexual morality. In her latest book *Girl Trouble: Panic and Progress in the History of Young Women*, Dyhouse (2013: 3) argues that it seems that women expressing their sexuality as freely as their male counterpart is still very much

---

[1]Feminist educationalist Weiner (2006) provides an excellent and succinct articulation of 'third-wave feminism.'

taboo. A disproportionate number of girls suffer more from bullying and sexual violence than boys, and face an ostensibly more insidious threat; a crushing social pressure to be perfect in every way (Dyhouse 2013: 1). She refers to the literature on how the language of 'empowerment' used in an attempt to mobilise young women today is something of a double-edged sword; liberal discourse that promotes 'girl power' and 'choice' is merely a smoke-screen by which deep-seated inequalities and oppressions can be obscured.

Bringing such a debate into discussion, this chapter aims to provide new perspectives and directions for feminism by exploring the diversity, tolerance for difference and contradiction, and multi-level praxis. I build up my conceptual framework of 'third-wave feminism' on the basis of Western feminist studies and theorising of young women's activism in current times. By revisiting these studies, I attempt to portray new images of young women as the victors in late modern, globalised economies. In particular, I focus on the following four aspects to examine young women's life experiences:

(a) young women's experience of the female body expression and sexuality;
(b) young women's experience in education and labour market;
(c) young women's position and power negotiation in their parental families;
(d) young women's political engagement and citizenship awareness.

The purposes here are twofold: Firstly, rather than simply reproducing the generational split that has characterised much of the framing of the feminist debate, I would like to call the issue of 'young women' into question whilst I explore it critically. I suggest that we should expand the concept of feminism: 'feminism' ought not to be seen only as legitimate when it takes the form of recognised activism; rather, it can have an important place in the 'micropolitics' of contemporary young women's everyday lives. Secondly, by reviewing how girls and young women in many Western societies get involved with the contemporary feminism, I structure an analytical framework for comparatively understanding the ways in which how young Chinese women construct their meanings of young womanhood and how they engage in feminist activism. I do not intend to draw a shape dichotomy between China and the West, but what I would like to emphasise and to suggest here is that we should provide very careful and sophisticated analysis of the meaning of culture and religion in order not to deny difference with fixed notion of privilege and discrimination.

Bodily Practice and Sexuality

In feminist debates, sexuality and embodiment are one of the most contested spheres in young women's lives. On the one hand, traditional discourses of female chastity and sexual vulnerability, even danger, are still very powerful in discussions of young women's sexuality. On the other hand, there are new and conflicting discourses in circulation. These new discourses emphasise the centrality and positivity of sexuality and a range of possible ways in which sexuality might be expressed for both (young) women and men. In psychological and sociological terms, the process of young people achieving sexual, physical and emotional maturity is deeply gendered. Therefore, for girls and young women, they attempt to delineate these gendered experiences in order to establish normative understandings of what it means to be a girl. If a young woman cannot meet, or reject these norms, she will often be excluded from prevailing definitions of femininity on the basis of their race, class, ethnicity, ability and sexuality (Aapola et al. 2005). Often these norms set up binaries to set young women apart, such as good/bad, virgin/slut, straight/gay and popular/nerd. The widespread anxiety and stress focused on girls' body images has reinforced the coercion of these norms and therefore affecting the lives of girls and young women.

Since the 1960s, Western feminist discourses have emphasised the rights of women to have control over issues that are related to female embodiment, such as sexual relationships, including those that are non-heterosexual, as well as contraception, abortion, pregnancy and childbirth (see Oakley 1981). Some Western feminists strongly criticise the way in which women's bodies are objectified, commodified and sexualised in the media and advertisements. For example, Lloyd (1996) argues that popular media always tends to reify dominant cultural standards of feminine beauty, rather than supporting the diversification of images of femininity when they circulate the images of women. Thin, perfect female bodies are repeatedly emphasised by media as the ideal images of young women. This has already resulted in young women's problems with self-esteem, severe psychological problems and eating disorders. Therefore, female embodiment produced by young women, in fact, has been distorted (Bordo 1993; Frost 2001).

For those slim and beautiful young women, they can always reap the economic and other benefits of the ever-increasing demand of the visual media for appealing images. Accordingly, they become more anxious of the passing age, facing growing pressures to modify their appearance in order to fulfill ever-changing feminine beauty ideals, which are practically impossible to attain. These ideas could be highly problematic in terms of reproducing Eurocentric, imperialist notions of beauty. As Mirza (1992) argued, the predominant belief that only white women are attractive will marginalise girls and women of colour to the place of 'the other' in the process of defining hegemonic notions of female beauty.

Studies have also shown that girls and young women in many developed First World societies are facing more choices of expressing their individualities through their bodies (i.e., Turner 1999; Frost 2001). This can be seen as a very positive site of self-expression, identity-creation and enjoyment. For example, Turner (1999) argues that today's Western culture is preoccupied with the body: its health, fitness, appearance and many other aspects. Yet, it is the questions of how to get it 'right' in relation to the female body that are often contradictory. On the one hand, young women are encouraged to overindulge themselves; on the other hand, they are expected to restrict themselves. They are told to diet as well as to enjoy consumption; to stop smoking as well as to try to drink alcohol; to feel good about one's body as it is, as well as to try to modify it through exercise and so on. It has become increasingly confusing regarding how to maintain a balance of one's body since some young women's bodies are changing so rapidly.

According to Ganetz (1995: 78), the body is one of the most accessible sites for the experimentation to discover what feels best for oneself. For girls and young women, body is essential to the new cultural forms of expression. Yong women will spend considerable energy on different types of 'beauty projects' that require various forms of body modification and adornment. While for many young women the careful application of cosmetic products such as make-up and hair colours, as well as conscious choices regarding clothing and hairstyles are an essential part of their style experimentation; for some, there are even more enhanced forms of body modification such as cosmetic surgeries (McRobbie 2000).

While girls' bodies may still often be objects of the gaze of others, they are also an increasingly important source of their own pleasure. For example, Ganetz (1995: 78) argues that girls and young women find 'personal enjoyment in their own embodied skills and strength.' They try to negotiate ways to express their sexuality, in which they do not need to compromise their independence and agency. They look for ways in which to enjoy their bodies regardless of the beauty norms surrounding them. Frost (2001) further provides a fuller claim, arguing that while maintaining their agency as individuals and citizens, girls and young women also constantly struggle to express their feminine sexuality in socially accepted ways.

Moreover, Western feminists argue that the freedom of expressing female sexuality is also associated with women's equal rights to enjoy sexual pleasure. By studying female sexual pleasure, McClelland and Fine (2008) argue that young women's expression of sexuality always exists at the very line of excess. Female sexuality has historically been linked with excess and fears of what lurks over the border of what is required, necessary and sufficient. Because young women are fundamentally and inherently sexually active, their sexuality always flaunts itself as 'much larger than is needed,' goes way 'beyond sufficient or permitted limits' and therefore is consistently cast as overindulgent. This has captured wider cultural attention and aroused feminist anxieties. Geronimus (1997) has offered an important critique of young women's free pursuit of sexual pleasure by arguing that although the sex young women want and the sex they have are typically intended to be decoupled from reproduction, they are considered too young to reproduce; too young to know enough about their bodies and their capacity; and too young to be sexually pleasured and pleasurable.

In fact, as early as the nineteenth century, fear of excessive female sexuality had accelerated into a moral panic when large segments of the medical community believed that masturbation and sexual excess caused insanity and disease (Whorton 2001). However, the claim of the excessive sexuality in women has also been considered suspect because of its potential to undermine patriarchy—it reveals that women do not depend on men for sexual release and that procreative possibilities are not the only outcome of sexual activity (McClelland and Fine 2008).

Generally speaking, rescuing pursuits of pleasure has occupied Western feminist scholars for the much of the last thirty years (i.e., Hite 1987; Willis 1992). This has meant consistently decoupling female pleasure from reproductive capacities and staking out women's rights to orgasms, contraception, reproductive choice, and relations with other women. Issues of pleasure have also, to a large degree, been supplanted in political organising by issues of sexual freedom—freedom from violence, coercion, homophobia, sterilisation, abuse and so on. Presently, feminists and reproductive rights activists have come to understand that women's sexuality and reproductive freedom must be fundamentally integrated into human rights campaigns. For example, Willis (1992) argues that women's access to abortion, contraception, condoms, childcare, employment and freedom from violence are increasingly recognised (if not enacted) as foundational to global social welfare.

The Education-Work Dilemma

In current times, globalisation, information technology, and a shift to a casual, flexible labour force have fundamentally changed employment practices and opportunities. These conditions have had particular effects on young people living in the West across the socioeconomic scale.

On the one hand, de-industralisation and deregulation have brought massive, global youth unemployment and underemployment. For example, Furlong and Cartmel (1997: 16–17) argue that 'changing labour market structures have not simply provided positive incentives for young people to improve their qualifications; the sharp decline in opportunities for minimum-aged school-leavers in many areas has produced an army of reluctant conscripts to post-compulsory education.' Many Western countries have added other incentives, such as cutting unemployment benefits and other welfare measures for those under eighteen, to enable their young people to stay in school or join a training programme. They have also expanded tertiary education as another kind of post-secondary training (Furlong and Cartmel 1997).

However, more and more of young people who go on to tertiary education or professional training are encountering circumstances where no amount of credentialing seems enough. Along with the rising number of university graduate students, many of these young people are finding that such emphasis on credentials and lifelong learning of transferable and flexible skills does not actually translate into security of employment. For example, based on many East and West European contexts, British youth researchers Wallace and Kovatcheva (1999: 88) argue that 'the outcome of education and training [has become] uncertain, unemployment is a risk and the proliferation of routes and opportunities through education and training has resulted in a very complex and rather open-ended situation for young people.' This is a finding also consistent throughout the United States, Australia and Canada (see Dwyer and Wyn 2001).

On the other hand, middle-class youth who may have always got the opportunity to go to university are perceived as the real beneficiaries of the new economy. Among the middle-class youth, young women have been seen as being more capable of seizing their opportunities when compared with young men.

Unsurprisingly, middle-class youth can rely on their families for a home, financial support, career modeling, professional contacts and advice, and even investments in their businesses. They can also draw on their status as well as their social circles for cultural capital, self-esteem and support. Yet, for those youth without these kinds of resources, flexibility is more difficult to operationalise. As the European Group for Integrated Social Research (2001) reported,

'In terms of the heterogeneity of the phenomenon of young adults according to social origin, educational level and employment situation, we…might distinguish between young people following 'choice biographies' … and those who are marginali[s]ed through education and labour market processes and have no prospect of achieving an autonomous life-project.' (European Group for Integrated Social Research 2001: 105)

For young women in general, they are experiencing both the best and the worst of these conditions. In other words, they are to be found on the fringes of the formal economy, in part-time, casual, insecure, and unprotected labour; however, they are also found among the highest levels of the new professions, enjoying the very flexibility that limits many other of their generation. For example, labour sociologists Probert and Macdonald (1999: 22) have studied the impact of the changing labour market on the loss of full-time job for both young women and young men, finding that new education and employment opportunities have, in fact, grown enormously for young women than young men. With few remaining formal barriers in their way, young women are free to pursue a wide variety of education, training and work possibilities under the labour market dynamics. Rattansi and Phoenix (1997: 139) also suggest that the possibilities of the changed labour market have created greater self-confidence and independence in young women. The success of young women in outperforming young men in school and attaining high positions in the workplace has often been noted as evidence that these young women are the real winners in a changed economic world.

Dwyer and Wyn (2001) also find that young women are better able to incorporate change and redirection into their life plans. They are seen as more psychologically robust and able to both adapt and 'grow up' more quickly. Young women tend to leave home earlier and are less likely to return once they have made this break. They are sometimes perceived to be more ambitious than young men, and also more optimistic about their futures generally and about their employment prospects in particular (Jones 1995; Helve 1997; Rudd and Evans 1998; Miles 2000).

A large-scale Australian research project carried out in 1998 involved 14,804 young women, found that 75 % of those surveyed aspired to more educational qualifications (with only 7 % stating they definitely would not want this), and 91 % wanted children by the time they were thirty-five with 60 % desiring full-time paid work at the same time, and only 4 % desiring no paid work outside the home at the same time (Wicks and Mishra 1998). In an Australian Women's Studies Association conference, feminist theorist Bulbeck (2001) has reflected some of these results in her important comparative research looking at how young Australian women in 1970 and today imagined their future lives. She found that nowadays the majority of young women imagine entering higher education and then having a lifetime of paid work. They are fairly optimistic about combining work and motherhood. Yet, in 1970 the majority of young women did no mention having a job or progressing to higher education when discussing their aspirations.

Canadian sociologists Looker and Magee (2000) have also carried out a large-scale project with a diversity of respondents, finding that young Canadian women have somewhat higher expectations than young men by stating more frequently that they realistically expect to enter fairly high-status positions. The vast majorities expect to go into professional, semiprofessional, or managerial jobs; 21 % anticipate a service or sales job; very few expect to end up in unskilled or low-status jobs.

While the Australian study asked what work the respondents would like, the Canadian research inquired about what they 'realistically expect.' Interestingly, these studies show a similarity in their response rates, which suggest that young women do expect to get what they hope for. Hughes-Bond's (1998) qualitative research with working-class, rural, Canadian young women rounds out this picture. She argues that '[young women] want jobs which they enjoy, and which offer them the opportunity for creativity, skill development, financial autonomy and stability, and an expanding degree of responsibility and power' (Hughes-Bond 1998: 289).

In other contexts, education researcher Basit (1996: 231) studies working-class, British-Asian, Muslim young women, offering some insights into the specific nature of a preferred career. She describes the participants in her research as 'aspired to a wide range of lucrative careers with high status. Some mentioned the jobs of doctors, lawyers, accountants and pharmacists ... A few girls wanted to start their own businesses, and one girl wished to be a pilot.'

Apparently, class, ethnicity, and rurality do not cut across these aspirations in straightforward ways. As Walkerdine et al. (2001: 78) noted, while more privileged young women may have access to knowledge about the requirements of professional work, and expectations of higher rewards, structural disadvantage does not mean one 'could not hope for a secure and interesting job.' So while family migration experiences might strengthen aspirational resolve (Basit 1996; Wicks and Mishra 1998), or geographical isolation might make prospects more traditional (Warner-Smith and Lee 2001), it seems that a diverse group of young women in a range of locations imagine themselves to have better work options than previous generations, and they take employment seriously as part of their identity work.

Therefore, there is a need for a critical ideological shift to accompany these massive changes to youth education and employment. This ideology seeks to construct a new subject for these circumstances. Traditional ways of being a worker, being young, or being a student are no longer relevant. De-industrialisation, globalisation, and widespread labour force insecurity require new ways of speaking, thinking and acting for youth. Most importantly, the current market demands young people who are not only highly skilled, but are also flexible. Those most able to succeed in this climate are young people who can turn tremendous insecurity into freedom and autonomy. These are youth who are qualified, skilled, and well-supported enough to secure highly paid work (or create their own business) in new, risky industries, survive company collapses, and reinvent themselves as markets and industries shift.

Being Daughter and Being Wife

The changing patterns of schooling and the protraction of the education to work transitions which have been discussed so far have led to an extension of the period during which young people remain dependent on their families or on the state. As financial independence through employment provides young people with the resources to leave the parental home and establish more autonomous patterns of residence, extended school to work transitions and fragmented patterns of involvement in the labour market also have an impact on patterns of young people's dependency on their parental families.

In many Western societies, adult status tends not to be conferred solely on the basis of successful completion of the school to work transition, but can be linked to the completion of a series of linked transitions. For example, Coles (1995) suggests that there are three inter-related transitions made by young people, some of which must be achieved before being accepted into adult society. Aside from the transition from school to work, young people may make a 'domestic transition,' involving a move from the family of origin to the family of destination, and a 'housing transition' involving a move to residence away from the parental (or surrogate parental) home. These three transitions are inter-related in young people's life experiences. One dimension impacts on other life events: for example, an education to work transition which is interrupted by unemployment is likely to affect the stage at which young people make domestic and housing transition. The extension of transitions, together with changes in typical sequences of events has implications for the establishment of identity and for processes of individualisation and risk (Coles 1995).

For example, recent social changes, which have led to an enforced increase in the period of youth dependency, have resulted in a situation in which the future is often seen as filled with risk and uncertainty: in such circumstances, it can be difficult for young people to maintain a stable identity (Furlong and Cartmel 2007). Changes in family structures in some developed Western countries together with the introduction of social policies that reduce young people's access to housing support, have represented a new set of hazards to be negotiated by today's youth. While those with access to the appropriate social and economic resources remain less vulnerable to the consequences of failure, others who lack family support can face extreme difficulty. In this context, it can be seen that young people's ability to make successful transitions to adulthood is still powerfully conditioned by 'traditional' inequalities such as class and gender (Furlong and Cartmel 2007).

Thus, studying young people's family models and their relation with their families will be helpful in understanding young person's (especially young girl's) subjectivities and their changing positions in society.

Firstly, the provision of the material, cultural and social resources within a particular family environment will have a strong impact on a young person's access to choices. Without such resources, it will be very difficult for young people, even those ambitious ones, to negotiate their way towards adulthood. Any changes in the family sphere might change the current cultural understandings and formulations of youth (Thomson et al. 2003).

Secondly, the composition of family relationships has been central in defining young people's development. According to traditional psychological theories on adolescent development (i.e., Erikson 1968), girls have been seen as more dependent on other people, particularly their families, than boys. It is also commonly believed that it is necessary for a young person to 'rebel' against adult authorities, such as his/her parents, in order to demonstrate a sufficient level of independence.

Yet, these presuppositions about the necessity of rebellion for reaching a successful adulthood are highly problematic. Feminist critiques claim that there are serious problems within traditional developmental theories since they actually refer mainly to white, male, middle-class young people. Girls, young women and working-class youth have been shown as curious exceptions in the male-centered model, and cultural differences have not usually been taken into account (Aapola et al. 2005). For example, ethnic background will make a difference in young women's attitudes towards their own autonomy. Woollett and Marshall's (1996) study in the British context finds that girls from Asian backgrounds would take their whole family community more into consideration when making decisions, rather than only emphasising their own individualistic goals. Jordan et al. (1991) argue that girls could indicate a high score on levels of independence, but they also emphasise the importance and warmth of their relationships with their families, particularly with their mothers. Their independence has not been gained by rebelling against their parents. Their study also suggested that girls tend to internalise their control, and try to take into account the feelings of others in estimating the consequences of their actions (Jordan et al. 1991).

Certainly, families play a particularly important role in the construction of young womanhood. Being of primary importance in determining the futures of their children, family has historically interacted with other social institutions in the process of shaping youth transitions of girls and young women (Wyn and White 1997). During the past few decades, when family patterns in many Western societies have experienced considerable changes, these changes would inevitably influence young women's exercise of power. For example, social change theorists have summarised that the percentage of full-time homemakers has decreased considerably (Gerson 1991); divorce rates have multiplied compared to the first part of the twentieth century (Beck and Beck-Gernsheim 1995); many young people are postponing marriage (Gordon 1994); the proportion of single people has increased considerably, particularly within urban areas; and there are also more single parents, and many of them are young women (Gordon 1994). All these changes indicate that there has no longer been a single culturally dominant family model, and the diversification of family models is re-positioning young women in the societies under the social changes.

Furthermore, marriage and parenthood is another important factor in young women's identity construction and youth-adulthood transition. Although marriage and parenthood has traditionally been regarded as the 'definitive step to adulthood' (Kiernan 2001: 11), in recent years there has been a greater separation of housing and domestic transitions. Wyn and White (1997) argue that domestic transitions remain a particularly significant step in the attainment of full adult status due to an underlying shift in responsibilities: the young adult is no longer the responsibility of their parents and comes to assume responsibility for others. It has also been suggested that the idea of a clear shift from dependence to independence is an over-simplification. A pattern of reciprocity is often established before young adults leave home and is continued after the marriage (Wyn and White 1997).

For most young people living in the West, marriage can serve as a principle reason for leaving home. During the 1960s and 1970s, it was even 'almost unheard of for young people to leave home prior to marriage' in many working class communities (Leonard 1998: 61). However, in recent years, increased number of young married couple began to live with their parents, and the link between leaving the parental home and marriage, as well as between marriage and their own parenthood, has weakened (Jones and Bell 2000; Heath and Cleaver 2003).

In the UK, for example, Haskey (2005) argues that around three in ten 16- to 59-year-olds (about 4 million people) can be described as people who are living apart together (LAT), with about half of these being in the 16–24 age group. Around six in ten LAT couples say that they are happy to maintain these arrangements permanently (Heath and Cleaver 2003). Heath and Cleaver (2003) also show that in the UK, rates of cohabitation doubled between 1980 and 2000 so that the majority of young people experience cohabitation during their 20s. They refer this as a key change over the last few decades, especially in northern Europe, North America and Australia.

Cohabitation can be temporary, experimental relationships, or may be the first stage in a long-term relationship leading to marriage or may signal a rejection of marriage as an institution (One plus One 2004). To take the case of Britain (which is fairly typical of the northern European countries), of those living with partners for the first time, around seven in ten will be cohabiting for an average of two years with such relationship as experimental (Ermisch and Francesconi 2000). Cohabitation (often a second or third cohabitation) is often a prelude to marriage: in the late 1990s around 80 % of married women had cohabited with their spouse prior to marriage (Haskey 2001).

Protracted transitions and the increased popularity of cohabitation have resulted in a delay in the age of marriage and led to a reduction in rates of marriage. In the European Union between 1971 and 2002, the average age of first marriage rose from 26 to 30 for men and from 23 to 28 for women. While women have tended to marry at an earlier age than men, those whose parents have divorced and those who live with step-parents tend to marry early (Kiernan 2004) and class-based differences in the average age of marriage have been observed in a wide range of countries, partly due to the tendency of the middle classes to remain in education for longer periods of time.

Similar differentials exist in terms of childbearing with the longer transitions to work, which are more characteristic of the middle classes, tending to result in delays in family formation. On average, in Europe there is a gap of three to seven years between a female entering their first full-time job and having their first child (Nicoletti and Tanturri 2005), although overall fertility rates have fallen and significant variations still exist between countries. For example, in Italy and Greece, late labour market entry significantly delays family formation while in the UK, Denmark and Finland the impact is relatively small, partly due to a greater tendency for childbirth to precede marriage (Iacovou and Berthoud 2001).

Across all social classes, the average period of time between marriage and birth of the first child has increased. Among women in Europe, just 5 % of 20-year-olds have children, rising to 28 % of 25-year-olds (Iacovou and Berthoud 2001). There are strong variations between countries with around one in four 21- to 25-year-olds having children in the UK, Sweden, Greece and Austria, compared to little more than one in ten in Italy, Netherlands and Spain (Iacovou and Berthoud 2001). Along with all-age fertility rates, the numbers of teenage mothers has declined in all advanced societies, although the USA, some Eastern European countries and the UK still have levels of teenage pregnancy that are far higher than countries that are similar in other respects (Selman 2003). In all those Western countries, those from lower social classes and those without advanced educational qualifications are more likely to have children at an early age (Nicoletti and Tanturri 2005). For example, in the UK, the average age at birth of the first child was 23.7 among those from semi-and unskilled backgrounds, compared to 27.9 among those from professional and managerial families. Rates of teenage pregnancy were ten times higher in the lowest social class as compared to the highest (Social Exclusion Unit 1999).

Political Engagement, Young Citizens and Feminist Agenda

In many Western countries, it has been observed that young people has shown relatively low levels of interest in party politics with the evidence that they tend to be less likely than adults to register a vote and have a weaker commitment to any political party (see Buckingham 2000).

For example, in Australia, where registration and voting is compulsory with non-compliance leading to an automatic fine, young people are still less likely than adults to register or vote. In 2004, 82 % of 17- to 25-year-olds were registered to vote compared to 95 % of the overall adult population. In a survey of senior school students, Print et al. (2004) asked respondents if they intended to vote in Federal elections when they reached the age of 18, 87 % said that they would definitely or probably vote, with females being more inclined to vote than males. Asked if they would vote if it were not compulsory, one in two said that they were not.

In the UK, of those eligible to vote, just 36 % said that they were 'absolutely certain' to vote in the next General Election (Haste 2005). According to the UK Electoral Commission (MORI 2005), 31 % of 18- to 24-year-olds said that they never or rarely vote in General Elections compared to 9 % of the voting age population. Bynner et al. (2003) research has indicated a similar finding of young people's disinterest in politics, showing that while levels of voting tend to be similar among males and females, rates of participation are higher among mid-aged non-manual employees compared to manual workers and lowest among the younger ones who had never had a job. In particular, levels of voting in the UK are very low among 18- to 24-year-old African Caribbeans and members of ethnic minority groups swayed by politicians' willingness to address minority issues (Sagger 2000).

In Canada, around seven in ten 18- to 24-year-olds typically voted in the 1970s; however, turnout was down to around four in ten by the mid-1980s (Gauthier 2003). Gauthier continues that such decline has reflected the end of a political era in Canada, where there had long been a relatively weak government and a strong opposition of calling for lively and responsive party politics. The 1984 election of the Progressive Conservatives signaled the emergence of neoliberalism, a preoccupation with the economy and a shift away from concerns with social justice. With young people being attracted by issues of equality and alienated by fiscal matters, these changes were directly responsible for a reduction in the youth vote.

In terms of participation in the formal political process, young people's professed lack of interest in politics is reflected in levels of party membership and their voting behaviour. Taking the UK as an example, statistics on the membership of its main political parties show that young people's impression that party politics is largely the preserve of the middle aged is correct. In 2004, less than 8 % of UK members of Parliament were under the age of 40 with the median age having remained fairly stable since 1951. In Australia and some Eastern European countries, the age profile of elected representatives is more balanced, although there is no direct evidence of a link between the ages of elected representatives and young people's interest in politics.

By observing young people's increasing disinterest in politics in the West, Furlong and Cartmel (2007) express their concerns that low levels of participation in elections among younger members of the electorate may reflect a lack of knowledge about contemporary political issues for Western youth. As they argued, '[i]n many respects, the biggest incentive to vote comes from a belief in the ability to influence a political agenda: it is the main opportunity for citizens to have their voices heard and to affect policy. Yet, young people were often cynical about the chances of their having an impact on national agendas.' (Furlong and Cartmel 2007: 130) Findings of young people's voting behaviour in these Western contexts seem to suggest that it has been witnessed the ending of a political era in contemporary Western countries. The evidence also suggests that changes in the current political agenda in the West could re-mobilise young people in general.

Among contemporary Western youth, young women nowadays are also facing radical changes in their opportunities for livelihood, community affiliations and political engagements from those that existed a generation ago. These opportunities are central to the meanings and practices of citizenship.

Thomas Marshall (1950) is considered to be the foundational thinker in the area of citizenship studies in the West. He argues that citizenship encompasses three kinds of rights that are conferred on individuals in society in exchange for their responsibility to that society. These include civil rights, such as freedom of thought and religion, social rights such as economic security and political rights, such as voting and standing for office. Marshall expects that the state would be central in guaranteeing people's social rights, and from this strong state support would develop a responsible citizenry engaged fully in their communities. Although civil rights and political rights are also safeguarded by the state, social rights is seen to be a more strong grounding. The traditional theorising of citizenship also emphasises on the balance between rights and responsibilities. Implicit in the contract between citizen and state is mutual obligation.

However, the traditional conceptualisation of citizenship has been fundamentally challenged by both Western feminists and youth theorists. Both of them point out that the citizen imagined by this framework is an adult male of privilege who is recognised as a rational actor in the public sphere (i.e., Lister 2003; Richardson 1998). Young women are often concerned that opportunities for assertiveness and the political impact of a new emphasis on girls' power have become reduced to empty marketing slogan (Harris 2001). Arguing that both women and youth have been excluded from the public sphere, feminists draw their critique to this conceptualisation of citizenship, suggesting that it is required to assess gendered power within family, marriage and sexuality in order to provide an alternative to the public/private split (Lees 2000).

In her book *The Sexual Contract,* British feminist and political theorist Pateman (1988) powerfully analyses how the social contract, on which democratic governance rests, is premised on the sexual control of women by men. She traces the development of relationships which are based upon equality—the *social* contract—and discusses the distinction between social contracts that are typical of labour relations and sexual contracts that are typical of marriage relationships. She also attempts to demonstrate how sexual contracts are based upon relationships which have been grounded in female subordination and slavery. By critically analysing New Right educational reforms in many Western industrialised nations (especially in the UK, Australia and the US), Western feminist scholars have expressed their concerns about the role of education in the construction of national identity (see for example, Arnot and Dillabourgh 2000). They argue that these reform initiatives should serve to reconstitute the professional teacher as the moral authority on issues of 'nationhood' and national identity. Yet, questions of gender, race, class, and/or sexuality and disability and the kinds of national identities s/he is expected to shape are not addressed in the context of the 'standards/competent' teachers and therefore women's roles remain to be the margins in many national curriculum agendas.

In this sense, what feminists interested are not only in women's citizenship in relation to men's, but also in relation to women's affiliation to dominant or subordinate groups, their ethnicity, origin, urban or rural residence, global and transnational positioning. They will always trace the discursive shifts in the meanings of the concepts, rights, needs, justice, dependency, entitlements and responsibility to expose the relations of power which configure the terms of inclusion and exclusion in the polity (see Kenway and Langmead 2000).

If young people are to be regarded as a vanguard of social change (Fine and Mechling 1991), then the evidence of their political engagement in many Western socio-cultural contexts suggests that the future is essentially conservative. The family remains central to processes of political socialisation and to a large extent young people come to share the political concerns of their parents (Haerpfer and Wallace 2002). At the same time, with a wakening of the link between class and voting (which has been encouraged by the main political parties who appreciate the need to secure the votes of the 'centre') young people often want to know what issues they are supporting and may be reluctant to buy into packages of policies. However, although there is some evidence that the younger generation has a weaker commitment to traditional party politics, existing evidence does not necessarily support the conclusion that political orientations among the young have become individualised. Young people still express collective concerns, although they frequently seek personal solutions to problems which are largely a consequence of their socio-economic positions and expect politicians to act in accord with their interests and values.

An associated matter is the feminist label. In recent days, young women living in many societies have also indicated some similar characteristics in their engagement with feminism. For example, Gemzoe (2003) studies young women in Sweden, pointing out that young Swedish women believe that they are equal when they are still in education, but will only start to see the need of feminism when they get older and enter the job market and/or start family. They may espouse feminist ideals, such as equal pay for work, but they are reluctant to use the term 'feminist' to describe themselves.

Based on the context of Australia, O'Brien (1999) argues that young Australian women will separate themselves from the 'feminist' label, but in the meantime, they are engaged in developing support, solidarity and a cultural space for young women, as well as constructing a feminist critique of gender inequality. Also, these young women distance themselves from the stereotypes of feminists as 'man-haters,' lesbians, and masculine-looking women with hairy armpits and big boots. In the words of O'Brien (1999: 102), 'they simply engaged in local feminist practice without using the title in order to avoid being perceived in a negative and one-dimensional manner.'

In these contexts, young women find the label of 'feminist' problematic, but this does not mean that they are not engaged in feminist practice. They are still drawing on feminist resources and strategies, shaping its agenda and grappling with its unfinished business. The principles and aims espoused by young women are feminist in nature, and their identities and worldviews are deeply shaped by feminist frameworks (Baumgardner and Richards 2000). Griffin (2001: 184) comments that when it comes to the feminist discussion of young people's lives, second wave feminist scholars will always rest on a distinction between 'us' (adult women and 'feminism') and 'them' (young women). On the one hand, adult women want to acknowledge the feminist practices which they feel young women are engaging in, but on the other hand, they feel they have to be critical of their new kinds of approaches.

In the second wave feminists' eyes, being a feminist must mean being part of a pre-defined political movement; yet, these young self-proclaimed feminists some-times want the kudos, or the benefits, without the collective work. For example, Summers (1994) criticises young women for being 'ungrateful,' in that they claim feminism as something that is owned by the previous generation and can only be passed on to appropriate heirs. Garner (1995: 99) also argues that their special ways of feminist work (for example, when young women enact feminism by pressing the charge of sexual harassment) actually represents the 'creation of a political position based on the virtue of helplessness.' The development of a feminist identity among young women is actually 'problematic' because it is based on 'priggishness,' 'a fear of sexuality' and 'disempowerment' (Garner 1995: 99). Garner (1995) further argues that this kind of activism is in fact a misunderstanding of the politics of feminism laid out by the second wave.

By observing young women in these neo-liberal Western societies, many scholars have all noticed that 'feminist' labels have no longer referred to 'power and pleasure,' but brought constraints among young women. Thus, some pioneer scholars pointed out that contemporary young women may face problems as they attempt to put second wave gains into action (such as 'going to the cops' and using new laws and policies), or they may confront with obstacles that are less structural but just as real, such as ideological barriers. As Harris (2004) argued, young women think they have already been empowered, or so deeply in crisis that they struggle to come up with even personal solutions to their problems. In fact, on the one hand, the rejection of the label amongst young women bespeaks a conservative or perhaps reactionary fear of the radical-lesbian-man-hating-militant stigma, as in, 'I'm not a feminist, but I support women's right to social, political and economic equality.' However, on the other hand, the rejection of the label 'feminist' is often code for a rejection of an elitist practice perpetuated by some of feminism's middle-class, heterosexual, white female founders (and their daughters). Here the refusal of the label is a politicised gesture critiquing a feminism that restricts itself to the dis-cussion of a singular idea of oppression derived from the perception of sexual difference as its primary cause.

Conclusion: Feminism Becomes Young

Nowadays, parenting ideologies have changed dramatically in terms of their family education towards their children, particularly towards girls. More parents are likely to negotiate with their children over decisions that affect them, rather than dictating unequivocally what they can or cannot do. The changing parental attitudes have meant that generational positions within families have been redefined. Individuals are required to make continuous decisions about various aspects of their lives even at a relatively young age. Viewing their children as autonomous subjects, many parents are willing to encourage their children's individual agency, letting them construct their own lives in an increasingly confusing web of choices. Therefore, it seems to be good for girls since the traditional patriarchal family model and the monolithic family ideology as disadvantageous for daughters have been challenged.

Yet, the process of developing a more egalitarian family model is still slow. And gender-related power also exists in the public sphere. For example, young mothers, even when they have full-time jobs outside of the home, have to continue to bear the brunt of domestic responsibilities. Meanwhile, most fathers, however, only 'help out' with the household chores. Thus, for feminists, this unequal gender division of housework and the invisibility of domestic violence against women and its dire consequence still need to be criticised.

As what I have reviewed above, this chapter has sketched the 'third wave' feminist agenda on the basis of girls and young women in many affluent First World societies. By outlining young women's expression of body and sexuality, their experience of education and work, their changing positions within parental families and their expectations of their future families as well as their increasing engagement with political affairs and citizenship development within these contexts, I argue that today's girls and young women have regarded feminism as a plain fact of their daily life.

Compared with older generations of women, contemporary young women reject what they deem the 'victim feminism' of their elders (see Baumgardner and Richards 2000; Budgeon 2001; Rich 2005) but feel confident enough to measure feminist positions against their lived experiences. While claiming natural entitlement to freedom from sexual and racial violence, they are also shifting themselves from traditional feminist activism to something more diffuse and less organised. In this sense, feminism is increasingly demanded to be endorsed as a source of personal identity than a tool for political activism at once. And this indicates that the birth of 'young feminism' discourse is becoming more and more closely relates to young women's cultural and political actions providing them with differentiation and emancipation.

Chapter 3
Feminist Epistemology and Approach

There must be more empirical and cross-cultural investigations of the life experiences of women. In other words, we cannot speak of a psychology or sociology or anthropology of women, if the frameworks of these perspectives are applicable to White, middle-class, or professional women only. (Scott 1996: 68)

To try to define oneself intellectually and politically as a Third World feminist is not an easy task. It is an unsettled and unsettling identity … There is nothing inherently wrong about the project of giving an account of oneself—of one's specific location as speaker and thinker, of the complex experiences and perceptions and sense of life that fuel one's concerns, of the reasons, feelings and anxieties that texture one's position on an issue, of the values that inform one's considered judgement of things. (Narayan 2008: 376)

I open this part with two quotations which best presented the values and difficulties of this research project. I give my emphasis on the feminist epistemology and wish to speak as a Chinese feminist living outside Western cultures for the following three important reasons:

Firstly, having lived my life in the capital of People's Republic of China, and having come of age politically in such a context, a significant part of my sensibilities and political horizons were indelibly shaped by non-Western World realities. Secondly, having explicated the ways in which the concerns and analyses of indigenous Chinese feminists are rooted in and responsive to the problems Chinese women face within their cultures in previous chapters, I acknowledge that I might be criticised to be a simple-minded emulation of Western feminist political concerns. However, before justifying this research, I need to speak 'as an insider' to make my point, even as I attempt to complicate the sense of what it is to inhabit a culture. Finally, although associating myself with a Third World feminist was subject to qualification and mediation, it was no more so than many labels one might attach to oneself—no more than calling myself a Chinese, a woman, or a feminist for that matter, because all these identities were not simple givens, but open to complex ways of being inhabited, and did not guarantee many specific experiences or concerns, even as they can shape one's life in powerful ways.

With such acknowledgment, this chapter discusses how I came up with this research design. It starts with an introduction of different types of qualitative inquiry which I had considered. Yet, through the process of reviewing various types of qualitative inquiry respectively, I find that each of these types appear to be consistent with my research goals and planned mode of enquiry in one way or another. Thus, I decide to take some elements from each type and connect them with my research objectives. I suggest that qualitative research methodology should be more open to adaptation in terms of flexible design, mixed paradigms and varied use of tools and methods. Then I review two epistemological theories which I considered to be useful—interpretive interactionism and critical inquiry—to guide this research.

Qualitative Inquiry

In terms of what is qualitative inquiry and how qualitative research could be applied in educational studies, social research methodologist Merriam (1998) provided a detailed and comprehensive illustration in her book *Qualitative Research and Case Study Applications in Education*. She explained that qualitative research is a method of inquiry employed in many different academic disciplines, traditionally in the social sciences, but also in market research and further contexts. Qualitative researchers aim to gather an in-depth understanding of human behaviour and the reasons that govern such behaviour. Thus, qualitative research was well suited to delineate the process (rather than the outcome or product) of meaning-making, and to describe how people interpreted what they experienced. Patton (1985: 1) explained the process of carrying out qualitative research more specifically:

> [Qualitative research] is an effort to understand situations in their uniqueness as part of a particular context and the interactions there. This understanding is an end in itself, so that it is not attempting to predict what may happen in the future necessarily, but to understand the nature of that setting – what it means for participants to be in that setting, what their lives are like, what's going on for them, what their meanings are, what the world looks like in that particular setting – and in the analysis to be able to communicate that faithfully to others who are interested in that setting … The analysis strives for depth of understanding.

In my view, 'qualitative research' or 'qualitative inquiry' was an umbrella term. Authors of qualitative texts organised a diversity of its forms in various ways. For example, Creswell (2007, 2012) presented five 'approaches'—narrative research, phenomenology, grounded theory, ethnography, and case study. Denzin and Lincoln (2011) identified six research strategies of case study, ethnography, grounded theory, life and narrative approaches, participatory research and clinical research.

Initially, I came to believe that justifying this research as an *ethnography* would be more suitable since ethnography can help researchers go beyond an immediate culture and scene and turn to multi-layered and interrelated natural social settings (see Fetterman 1989). Since I attempt to understand how young Chinese women construct meanings of womanhood, I need to build up and develop relations with my participants to study the beliefs, values, and attitudes which structure their behaviour patterns. Ethnography seems to be a holistic approach to investigate young Chinese women's real life worlds. Subsequently, I began to consider that *'critical ethnography,'* which 'strives to unmask hegemony and address oppressive forces' (Crotty 2003: 12) or *'feminist ethnography'* (see Jacobs 2003), which focuses on women's lives with the aim to address oppression owing to the differences of sex might fit into this design.

However, I finally concluded that my intention to provide 'insider's accounts' was not enough for me to categorise this research as ethnography for three reasons. Firstly, ethnography demanded that the researcher lives in the setting, acted as a participant observer (Harvey 1990) and became a member of the cultural setting in order to achieve a deep understanding of reality through participants' perceptions (Jordan and Yeomans 1995). 'The result of ethnographic inquiry is cultural description. It is... a description of the sort that can emerge only from a lengthy period of intimate study and residence in a given social setting. It calls for the language spoken in that setting, first-hand participation in some of the activities that take place there, and, most critically, a deep reliance on intensive work with a few informants drawn from the setting' (Van Maanen 1982: 103–104). Yet, in this research my interaction with respondents was limited to a conventional interview or group discussion format, and was more limited in time. Also, most of my research period took place outside the participants' own environment.

Secondly, although this research aimed to give voices to the life experience of non-English speaking women, my focus on young urban-dwelling educated Chinese women and my purpose to illuminate some concerns about the new production of feminism in the context of China did not match the goal of a feminist ethnography (see Jacobs 2003).The overall purpose of this project and the choice of participants in my fieldwork clearly did not strictly follow the framework of feminist ethnography. As Jacobs (2003) further explained, in a feminist ethnographic research, feminist ethnographers are required to have a dual responsibility to their subjects, recording their lives as they were remembered and interpreting this memory for those who can no longer speak for themselves.

After clarifying this research was not an ethnography, I found that my passion for the topic, my focus on women, my being influenced by critical theorists (particularly feminist standpoint theorists and post-colonial theorists), and the potential to change and to empower women might categorise this research as a type of *critical research*, especially a *participatory action research*. As Patton (2002: 131) commented, critical research 'seeks not just to study and understand society but to critique and challenge society.' Truly, my questions in this research were asked about who had power, how it was negotiated, how social institutions reinforced the current distribution of power in contemporary Chinese society, which were all related to a critical research.

However, with the acknowledgment of the challenges faced by the critical research (Kinchelo and McLaren 2000), I decided not to be fully involved in this research activity nor expected any direct action as the outcome of this research. I believed that any researcher's claim of being involved in the research in order to 'promote change' was required to further clarify their ethical considerations. In my view, the term 'to change' might imply a hierarchical relationship between an expert (who knows what was best) and others (who lacked this sense). Even some critical theorists themselves started to question the arrogance that accompanied efforts to 'change' others (see more on Kinchelo and McLaren 2000). Having said this, I acknowledged, and agreed, that researchers did need to know how to reach people in an open dialogue by encouraging them to reflect upon their reality in order to enable *them* to make their own choices about their actions or change. As noted above, the main goals of my research were to explore the impact of the current social transformation of China on the changing young Chinese femininity and to illuminate some interesting concerns about a new form of feminism which might be developing in such a context. Although I did hope that the outcome of my research would produce effective actions on emancipation and wider consciousness-raising amongst the younger generations of women in China, I thought it seemed unrealistic to seek immediate change or empowerment within the limited time-scale during my doctorate.

Thus, it seemed safer to claim that I incorporated a critical stance toward social justice in this research on women and power. I used such critical perspective to question social institutions with an aim to reveal power dynamics within this particular context.

Then, I found continuities between my research approach and a *phenomeno-logical* approach because I would reveal the ways in which those urban-dwelling university-educated young Chinese women valued and interpreted their gendered experience through encouraging them to be reflective and to tell their stories. As Merriam (2009) explained, the philosophy of *phenomenology* focused on the experience itself and how experiencing something was transformed into consciousness. Phenomenological research was concerned with the modalities of consciousness by which a thing was comprehended. In a phenomenological research, 'the perceived object is neither the object, nor the act of perceiving it... It is the intentional object, or the phenomenal object, which is the way in which the transcendent object is specifically grasped by consciousness' (Giorgi 1995: 35). In other words, a phenomenological approach was particularly well suited to study emotional, affective, and often intense human's conscious experience of their everyday life and social action.

Yet, while believing that phenomenology as a philosophy had exerted impacts on all of qualitative research, I also acknowledged that phenomenology could be seen as a particular *type* of qualitative research with its own focus and methodological strategies. For example, the task of the phenomenologists was to depict the essence or basic structure of experience (see Patton 2002: 106). Thus, it was required that phenomenologists temporarily put aside, or bracketed, their prior beliefs about a phenomenon of interest in order not to interfere with seeing or intuiting the elements or structure of the phenomenon. However, in this research my early engagement with the research field, my own assumptions and my personality found it difficult for me to strictly follow what phenomenology demanded of researchers.

Furthermore, I was also inspired by the *narrative approach* (see for example, Andrews et al. 2008) when I conducted in-depth interviews to collect data. For example, I asked my participants to share with me their life stories, including what they had known about the lives of their parents' generation, in order to encourage them to think more and talk more about the contemporary social change in China. This approach tended to be in line with Denzin's (1989) biographical approach, which emphasised the importance and influence of gender and race, family of origin, life events and turning point experiences, and other persons in the participant's life. It also tended to make use of a psychological approach (see Rossiter 1999), which concentrated more on the personal basis, such as thoughts and motivations. Also, the presentation of the research findings in this thesis seemed to share many similarities with narrative research, in which the common factor was that the researched world cannot be reproduced but had to be represented by some form of narrative analysis.[1] The database was usually formed by the 'text' of the story for what was to be analysed; the philosophy of hermeneutics, which was the study of these written texts, was often cited as informing narrative analysis (Patton 2002).

However, whilst recognising the value of this method in giving voice to human feelings and experiences, I believed that stories were told about stories and narratives thus became a form of social interaction. In other words, much narrative analysis was unclear about its epistemological influences. An analysis of narratives could *not* reveal what someone 'really' thought or felt because any truth was simply a construction, and narratives were skilfully woven to bring into being versions of the self that served specific purposes.

Therefore, I came to the conclusion that I should focus my research on the qualitative component where I could use both deductive and inductive logic in accessing the field. This meant that I had my assumptions about contemporary university-educated young Chinese women's attitudes and values about their gender roles in the family and in the wider society; but this did not mean that I wanted to find the empirical evidence to fit a specific theory. Rather, I would choose qualitative tools to generate substantive theory about the development of young Chinese feminism in a rapidly changing context, and to give my tentative explanations of this new phenomenon.

Eventually, I found that the approach of *grounded theory* (Glaser and Strauss 1967) was an essential part of my research design. Grounded theory did not require that researchers should access the field without previous knowledge or theories; rather, the theory was likely to offer insight, enhance understanding, and provide a meaningful guide to action (Charmaz 2003). In the words of Strauss and Corbin (1998: 12), 'grounded theory is a theory derived from data, systematically gathered and analysed through the research process. In this method, data collection, analysis, and eventual theory stand in close relationship to one another.' The end result of this type of qualitative study was a theory that emerges from, or was 'grounded' in

---

[1]Mishler (1991), Kleinman (1988), Reissman (1993) and Coles (1989) shared a commitment to the value of the narrative method, but they disagreed on the purpose and method of narrative analysis and the form of the analysis often appeared to be a largely intuitive process.

the data. Rich description was important but was *not* the primary focus of this type of study (Merriam 2009). The type of theory developed was usually 'substantive' rather than formal or 'grand' theory. Substantive theory had its referent specific, everyday-world situations. It had specificity and hence was useful to practice often lacking in theories that covered more global concerns. As Strauss and Corbin (1998) confirmed, grounded theory was particularly useful for addressing questions about process, which was, how something changed over time.

Owing to these reasons, when designing this research project, I decided to adopt a qualitative research methodology, using myself as instrumental to understand how the emerging middle-class educated urban young Chinese women constructed meanings of womanhood and how they got involved with contemporary feminism in a Chinese context. I acknowledged that in qualitative research the researchers' understandings were often based on the values, culture, training, and experiences that they brought to the research situations, and that these might be quite different from those of their respondents. Nevertheless, I believed that this did not necessarily mean that qualitative researchers cannot simultaneously be 'objective' in the research itself. On this point, I agreed with Strauss and Corbin (1998: 43) that 'objectivity, in qualitative research does not mean controlling variables. Rather, it means openness, willingness to listen and to "give voice" to respondents.' In fact, during the data collection process in my fieldwork I was open to different views, and tried my best to avoid imposing my ideas and thoughts on my participants. After hearing what my participants said, and seeing what they did without intervention, I represented this evidence as accurately as possible.

Although I was aware that the human instrument had shortcomings and biases that might have an impact on the study, I believed that a good social science research did not mean that researchers should 'eliminate' these biases or 'subjectivities.' As Peshkin (1988: 18) argued, one's subjectivities 'can be seen as virtuous, for it is the basis of researchers making a distinctive contribution, one that results from the unique configuration of their personal qualities joined to the data they have collected.' In this sense, I believed that it was important for qualitative researchers to identify these shortcomings and monitor them as to how they may be shaping the collection and interpretation of data. These issues, such as validity, reliability and ethics, as well as my own subjectivity as the researcher in this study would be further discussed below.

In summary, I took some elements from different qualitative research methodologies and connected them with my research objectives. I agreed with Denzin and Lincoln's (2003: 7) metaphor that: '[t]he qualitative researcher who uses montage is like a "quilt maker" or a "jazz improviser." The quilter stitches, edits, and puts slices of reality together. This process creates and brings psychological and emotional unity to an interpretive experience.' I explored new models of truth, method, and representation in this research design in order to enable this research project to be more open to adaptation in terms of flexible design, mixed paradigms, and varied use of tools and methods. I described my role as a qualitative researcher to be as a 'bricoleur' (Straus and Corbin 1998), 'chronograph' (Janesick 2000), 'jazz improviser' or 'quilt maker' (Denzin and Lincoln 2003) since all my emphasis was on the creative process of putting slices of reality together. In the meantime, I also paid attention that this open selection of choice did not mean that qualitative research lacked a rational justification for each choice (Maxwell 1998). I bore two main theoretical perspectives in mind to guide this research.

Feminist Concerns

According to a notable British anthropologist and social scientist Bateson (1972: 320), all qualitative researchers are philosophers in that 'universal sense in which all human beings … are guided by highly abstract principles.' These abstract principles are what we have called 'theories,' which provide a way of seeing, or an interpretation aimed at understanding a phenomenon in the human world. Fetterman (1989: 15) identifies the function of theory in qualitative research as follows: 'theory is a guide to practice; no study, whether ethnography or not, can be conducted without an underlying theory or model. Whether it is an explicit anthropological theory or an implicit personal model about how things work, the researcher's theoretical approach helps define the problem and how to tackle it.' In this research, I used two main qualitative methodological theories, namely interpretive interactionism (Denzin 2001) and critical inquiry (Crotty 2003) to guide my fieldwork.

I first explained what the theory of interpretive interactionism is and how interpretive interactionism was used in my research. According to Guba and Lincoln (1994: 119), interpretivism emerged in contradistinction to positivism in its attempt to look for culturally derived and historical interpretations of the social world. It holds the view that while the goal of natural sciences is scientific explanation, the goal of mental sciences or cultural sciences is grasping or understanding the 'meaning' of social phenomena. In other words, social or human action is inherently meaningful and to understand a particular social action, researchers must grasp the meanings that constitute that action (Schwandt 2000).

There are three issues that every qualitative inquirer must come to terms with using the resources or any philosophies:

(a) How to define what 'understanding' actually means and how to justify claims 'to understand;'
(b) How to frame the interpretive project, broadly conceived; and
(c) How to envision and occupy the ethical space where researchers and researched relate to one another on the socio-temporal occasion or event that is 'researched,' and, consequently, how to determine the role, status, responsibility, and obligations the researcher has in and to the society he or she researches.' (Schwandt 2000: 200)

In this research on gender and power dynamics, an interpretative perspective assumes that all knowledge, and therefore all meaningful reality, is contingent upon human practices. Truth is constructed in and out of *interaction* between human beings and their worlds, and developed and transmitted within an essentially hieratical social context. I see 'reality' or at least social reality as a complex entity, and regard many aspects of social action as value-laden. Values give meaning to actions and to the life-world, and social 'reality' as such should therefore be viewed in its entirety.

For social realities in particular, it is impossible to encompass all their intricacies and open-mindedness into 'general' laws that govern individual and social actions. It is believed that social actors from their identity and their perception of the world through interacting with their environment and with other social actors; at the same time and subsequently, they effect change or continuity in their surroundings and in the groups and individuals around them (Guba and Lincoln 1994).

The dialectic relationship between structure and agency not only requires social researchers to enquire about actors' perceptions and experiences but also encourages deeper understanding of the structural constraints and resources that also shape their outlook, assessments of what may be possible or impossible courses of action for them individually, and so on.

Therefore, it is important for me to recognise the researched young women's feelings and perceptions of themselves and of the world, as well as the contexts in which their values and rules are *learnt*, in accounting for their choices and behaviours. To relate this to my fieldwork, it means that I have to acknowledge that the participants' own logic and reflection upon their actions will never totally detach from the larger social context and an individual context in order to understand how these young Chinese women construct and negotiate their meanings of womanhood. In the larger social context, expectations of society will uphold certain concepts, within which individuals are expected to act according to specific norms and traditions in order to receive society's support and acceptance. At the same time, individuals contribute to the social context and their contributions become an integral part for guiding social norms and traditions. As Peshkin (1990: 39) claimed,

> Because social interaction is constructed by the people engaged in it, one should try to see it from their point of view and appreciate how they interpret the indications given to them by others, the meaning they assign to them, and how they construct their own action.

However, several questions have been raised while thinking of how I should interpret the meanings construction of these young Chinese women. For example, how far does their expectation about their future roles reflect their individual beliefs, or the expectations from their family or the cultural norms and traditions in the wider society? How far should I go beyond to discover what these norms and traditions are and where they originate? Should I present what seems to be 'taken for granted' or critique the roots of it? Could I draw the link between their practice and their *gendered* consciousness?

Raising these questions, in fact, indicated that I also embraced a critical perspective (see Daniels et al. 2011) both during the process of data collection and analysis and throughout the process of presenting this thesis. In Harvey's (1990: 3 my emphasis) words, 'it is not the difference between the presence and absence of critique, but in which "critique" is an *integral* part of the process and those in which it is peripheral.'

During the process of data collection in my fieldwork, a critical perspective requires me to ask thought-provoking questions to my participants with two purposes: firstly, I would gain information to examine how and to what extent different factors and powers in the institution and social-political context are influencing young Chinese women's ways of thinking and actions; secondly, I would encourage them to reflect upon their existing knowledge of gender and power. As Crotty (2003: 112) claimed, 'in critical inquiry there is a difference between a research that seeks merely to understand and a research that challenges…between a research that reads it in terms of interaction and community and a research that reads it in terms of conflict and oppression.'

Throughout the process of finally presenting this thesis, a critical perspective could remind me to categorise the type of roles young Chinese women perceive for themselves (such as traditional, progressive or revolutionary), and to conclude how their types of gender consciousness are indicating a new production of feminism in a Chinese context. In Gibson's (1986: 5 my emphasis) words, 'critical theory attempts to *reveal* these factors which prevent groups and individuals taking control of, or even influencing, those decisions which crucially affect their lives.'

Therefore, these theoretical perspectives allow me to collect and to interpret data on the basis of my participants' own thinking and reasons, and to understand how my participants' gendered consciousness is affected by these different factors and powers in the wider social and cultural context. In the meantime, I shall also give space to my own critical interpretation of such types of thinking and reasons.

To sum, discussions about methodology in the social sciences rest on the quest for the holy grail of the perfect method—a scientific method that will produce incorruptible data, uncontaminated by the research process itself. Yet, my point of departure has already opposed this position. I maintain that no matter how many methodological guarantees I try to put in place in an attempt to produce objectivity in research, the subjectivity always intrudes. I assert that unconscious defence mechanisms such as projection, introjections and transference are all *relational* and *dynamic*. Despite violating the requirements of neutral observation, they inevitably arise in the research interview, just as powerfully as in any other interaction (see also Kvale 1989). Put simply, in order to examine other people's unconscious processes a researcher must be willing and able to engage with his/her own.

Moreover, when considering knowledge produced in this feminist research, I strongly agreed with the postcolonial theorist Spivak[2] (1988: 285) when she made a claim of representing all 'Third World' others by challenging Western intellectuals. She often focuses on the cultural texts of those who are marginalised by dominant Western culture, including the new immigrant, the working class, women and other

---

[2]Gayatri Spivak (born February 24, 1942) is an Indian literary critic and theorist. She is best known for her translation of *Jacques Derrida's Of Grammatology and the monograph Can the Subaltern Speak?*, which is considered a founding text of postcolonialism. She described herself as a 'practical Marxist-feminist-deconstructionist.' (see also Spivak 2010).

'postcolonial subjects' (Spivak 2010). Like her, I also put my emphasis on the cultural text—in this case, which is the young educated Chinese women dwelling in urban Shanghai. I believed that the knowledge produced from this cross-cultural perspective could contribute to the paucity of feminist work, and to the dearth of scholarship that truly escapes ethnocentrism. By claiming this, I acknowledged that it is also important to not limit a discussion of cross-cultural feminist research to criticisms. Rather, 'we should examine what feminists who do this type of research confront, so that we can build on their experience. This, in turn, can be done only if feminists engaged in cross-cultural research write reflexive analyses of their work.' (Narayan 2008: 380) More discussion of the reflection and evaluation of this research will be presented in the next chapter.

Research Approach

This research was qualitative in nature. I used a multiple-case approach (Yin 1994) to collect data and to report findings. Hesse-Biber and Leavy (2006) argued that qualitative researchers usually had the freedom to make a choice of the number of participants according to the research circumstances and objectives. This open possibility of defining the characteristics of the research sample, in my view, depended on the research goal. Since the main purpose of this research was to illuminate some concerns about the new production of feminism in Chinese context, my research goal was to explore the life experience of a group of young women with similar background and to understand their perceptions on the gender-related issue in contemporary China. Thus, a small-N multiple-case study would be suitable for its strength to gain an in-depth understanding of the on-going women's emancipation and the potential social movement led by the growing number of young urban Chinese women.[3] As Stake (1995) argued, case-study data gives attention to the subtlety and complexity of the case in its own right and therefore it is 'strong in reality.' By carefully attending to social situations, the small-N qualitative case study can display something of the discrepancies or conflicts between the viewpoints held by participants (Stake 1995), and hereafter 'is most often at the forefront of theoretical development' (Ragin 1992: 225). Throughout the research, twenty young women were involved in my fieldwork basing on the following criteria for sampling:

---

[3]When N's are large, there are few opportunities for revising a casing—that is, the delimitation of a case. At the start of the analysis, cases are decomposed into variables, and almost the entire dialogue of ideas and evidence occurs through variables. One implication of this discussion is that to the extent that large-N research can be sensitised to the diversity and potential heterogeneity of the cases included in an analysis (Ragin 1992). Here, detailing each case's particular social circumstances could provide readers with rich information of the way in which the young femininity has been transformed in a rapidly marketised developing country, as well as the extent to which of young urban Chinese women get involved with the global feminism.

- young women aged from 18 to 26;
- unmarried;
- university-educated;
- born and grew up in middle-class family.[4]

Young women were chosen on the basis of their willingness to participate in this research project. I gave priority to those individuals who felt comfortable with being questioned and who could articulate their conscious experiences in order to collect 'information-rich' data (see Shkedi 2005). Also, since this research concerned some sensitive topics by the Chinese standard, such as attitudes towards Chinese politics and women's sexual relationship with men, I asked my potential participants whether they felt comfortable to talk about these issues in my recruitment process.

In short, I categorised my sample in this research project as a cohort of intelligent and middle-class young women owing to their current educational opportunities and family backgrounds. They could be seen as 'promising' by the Chinese standard. Yet, these promising young Chinese women might not be seen as 'high achiever or elite' by First World standards. In China, there were a small number of high officials, high-level employees in foreign-invested companies, and owners of extremely successful Chinese companies, who had incomes that would be high even by First World standards (commonly categorised as 'Wealthy' and 'Very Wealthy' in China), but none of these Chinese people's female child happened to be included in this research project.

To conduct my fieldwork, I firstly got in touch with a professor in psychology in a University X[5] in Shanghai and was arranged to stay in a female student dormitory there (see Fig. 3.1). Then, I used the network selection strategy (deMarrais and Lapan 2004) and the snowballing scheme (Patton 2002) to recruit my participants. Both of these two strategies emphasised the significance of researchers' social networks in identifying samplings. In Chinese context, personal relationship had

---

[4]See Appendix 3 for the categorisation of class in Chinese context. By saying this, I was not going to make generalisation of the shared interest and experience of young women who grew up in such family background across China. Moreover, in this book, I defined 'urban' as 'the first-tiered Chinese city' on the basis of the consideration that contemporary Chinese society is experiencing rapid urbanisation and marketisation. See Appendix 4 for the tiered city system in China and city geography of Shanghai.

[5]University X is a state-run key university under the 'Project 985'. 'Project 985' is a boosting project to promote the Chinese higher education system under the call of the President Jiang Zemin at the 100th anniversary of Peking University on May 4, 1998. The objective is to develop, in cooperation with local government, several top universities to become world-leading (China Education Centre 2004). At the time when I did my fieldwork, this university is made up of 18 full-time schools and colleges, 2 unconventional colleges and 4 advanced research institutes, with 54 departments offering 67 undergraduate programmes. The total number of students is more than 49,000, with over 14,000 full-time undergraduate students and over 7700 graduate students (including those in a Master's programme), among whom more than 2700 are international students. Students in this university come from diverse social backgrounds and different origins. They have to go through a strict selection system in order to get enrolled.

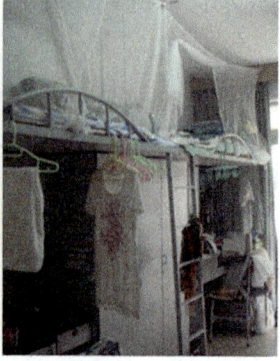

Fig. 3.1 Students' dormitory where I live (the room is shared by 4 female postgraduate students). *Source* Courtesy of University X

always been valued much, and therefore, I decided to obtain my primary partici-pants through word of mouth.[6] Participants included not only students in this university but also their friends or relatives who met the criteria. When I finalised my participants, I obtained their consent for participation (see Appendix 6a, b for Participant Information Sheet and Consent Form).

Since the sample was non-random, it was appropriate for exploring the range of attitudes among contemporary urban-dwelling young Chinese women but not for calculating the proportion that held such attitudes. Although non-random, the sample was highly diverse in age, originality, educational experiences, personality and so on. According to the time and efforts I contributed for establishing rapport with each participant, I used 'high' and 'medium' to describe the degree of trust and closeness between the individual and me (see Appendix 5 for Participant Demographics).

Overall, I followed what Ragin and Byrne (2009) identified as 'positive cases'—that is, cases where a phenomenon (such as revolution) could present. I believed that the choice of a multiple-case approach would enable me to investigate the subculture of these young educated women in-depth and to compare their life experiences through the use of a replication strategy. If all or most of the cases provided similar results, there could be substantial support for the development of a preliminary theory that described the phenomena (Eisenhardt 1989).

---

[6]See Appendix 2 for the report of Cultural Differences Affecting Ethnographic Research Methods in China: A Bicultural Viewpoint Based on the Chinese Model of Thought. Retrieved from its website http://www.kaizor.com/. Elaine Ann, the founder of Kaizor Innovation, a strategic inno-vation consulting company uniquely positioned to help develop appropriate innovation strategies, research and designs for the emerging China market, also pointed out the problems caused by using traditional ethnographic methods in the fieldwork in China. As she noted, 'ethnographic research methods originated from the United States are based on a Western model of thought … this process and method can have problems leading to cross-cultural conflicts and misinterpretation of data when applied to China without considering the fundamental differences in culture… there is reason to believe that ethnographic research methods will require adaptation if conducted in China for results to be accurate and meaningful.'

Next, I collected data from formal and informal interviews and fieldwork observations. This stage lasted three months, during which I had conducted sixty-three interviews (including semi-structured interviews, in-depth interviews and group interviews) altogether along with ethnographic observations (Stocking 1983). Interview questions mainly focused on, but not limited to, four general topics, including fashion and female beauty, career, family, and aspirations and ambitions. I used some printed materials (such as Western and Chinese fashion magazines),and some news topics (such as big international events including the 2008 Olympic Games in Beijing and the 2010 World Expo in Shanghai, and popular national dating show 'You're the One') to elicit data (see Chaps. 4 and 7). In each individual interview, I tried to only cover one or two topics and to encourage my participant to talk more about their ideas (see Appendix 7 for the fieldwork interview probes).

Considering the comfort of participants and the implications for getting quality data (see Grbich 2007), I asked my participants where did they feel comfortable and natural to conduct interviews. Interviews were therefore carried out in both private and public settings of the interviewees' choosing—at home or workplace, in a social venue such as a mall, a restaurant or a cafeteria, and in the classrooms or dining halls of university campus over lunch or dinner. Ethnographic observations and field notes were conducted as well to enable me to better understand and record the context of the discussion. Every interview lasted no more than one hour and a half. Every group interview lasted about 40 min (see Gillham 2005; Robson 2002). Most interviews were audio-recorded; but a few interviews were not since some interviewees expressed discomfort with an MP3. Although I assured them that I would keep confidentiality of all my research records, there was a concern that an audio-record of their comments, particularly on some sensitive issues, was some-how strange. Thus, I did my best to learn to write almost as fast as most of the respondents talked and was able to record most of what was said in these occasions. All interview data were transcribed verbatim into Chinese immediately. Chinese interview transcriptions were translated into English only when they were quoted in this thesis. All transcriptions were reviewed for a second time by listening to the recordings, which were done by the researcher herself in order to keep the data as confidential as possible while the participants still remained in the research setting. Pseudonym was used for each participant.

As noted above, this research aimed to identify the subjective and material implications of a growing focus on new forms of young middle-class femininity in contemporary China. Therefore, I led my interview topics to focus on issues of culture and identity construction by approaching them from several angles, where allowed interviewees to discuss their life experience, as well as their personal problems and concerns. Each interviewee was also encouraged to talk about their vision and imagination of their future and particularly, *where* they viewed that future. These issues were critical, reflecting the immense opportunities amongst these promising young women for not only economic development but also geo-graphic mobility and individual liberation. Therefore, in the final interview, these young women were given opportunity to ask me any questions they wanted to.

During the whole process of discussion, five principles which were suggested by Yin (2009) were born in mind to lead questioning:

(a) I concentrated on asking 'good questions' (see also Denzin and Lincoln 1998; Robson 2002; Janesick 2000) and interpreted the answers. For example, I asked specific questions concerning participants' experience, to which participants had to speak more than one sentence for answering.
(b) I tried to be a good 'listener' and not be trapped by my own ideologies or preconceptions. For example, I encouraged interviewees to give me examples when they conveyed their point.
(c) I tried to be adaptive and flexible, so that newly encountered situations could be seen as opportunities, not threats.
(d) I must have a firm grasp of the main research questions, even if in an exploratory mode. Such a grasp helped to reduce the relevant events and information to be sought to manageable proportions.
(e) I tried to be unbiased by preconceived notions, including those derived from theory, and be sensitive and responsive to contradictory evidence. For example, I explained that power theory could be relevant to contemporary young women's daily experience but did not explain in which way power could be exercised by women.

By conducting these interviews and observations, I had gained a deeper insight into individual's motivations behind her goals, and personal values and attitudes. I had deepened my understandings of troubles and difficulties these young women had experienced, reasons they might confront these problems, and specific strategies they had used, or considered to use in order to solve these problems.

The last stage was fieldwork reflection and data complementation. After intensely emerging myself in Shanghai for four-months, I returned to Beijing for data organisation and analysis. I believed that the geographic distance and emotional detachment from my researched subjects could provide me with a refreshed viewpoint to process the data more objectively. During this stage, I evaluated the quality of my data (saturation and consistency of the accounts), and 'sensed' that I would stop collecting more data (see Merriam 2009).

Dealing with Data

In order to manage data, I created a separated database for each individual. Therefore, in my database, field notes (from observations) and the raw data (transcriptions of semi-structured interviews, in-depth interviews and group discussions) were two broad elements. Field notes documented in different levels were kept separately. For example, there were four types of field notes:

(a) The descriptive type of notes in which I made a record of interviewees' physical characteristics, such as the hairstyles and dressing styles;

(b) Notes on the work with the participants such as the body language and facial expressions during the interviews;
(c) Notes and reflections on my own understanding of the phenomenon, for example, how close I felt to the experience expressed by interviewees and so on;
(d) The reflective type of notes in which I followed the progress of the research, what had been done, how I had accessed the field and individuals, and how I had dealt with problems and so on.

Field notes of type (a), type (b) and type (c) were kept separately along with interview transcriptions in individual's database. Field notes of type (d) were kept in an individual folder.

Data collection and analysis were carried out simultaneously and data were analysed using the constant comparative method (Glaser and Strauss 1967). This data analysis method involved comparing one segment of data with another to determine similarities and differences. The overall object of this analysis was to identify patterns in the data. To be more specific, data were grouped together on a similar dimension. The dimension was tentatively given a name and then it was constructed into a category. The core category was identified when it appeared frequently in the data. Then, I identified the themes that emerged from the core category and search for the meaning (see Merriam 2009).

As mentioned above, when I analysed my data, I first read the interview transcriptions and the set of field notes repeatedly in order to achieve a holistic understanding of the issues. Then I identified units of meaning which became an index to my work (see the Summary Sheet in the beginning of the following chapters). In fact, in my first draft of various following chapters I had on average eight to ten quotations relating to each main coding category; upon deliberation these were reduced to no more than five for succinctness. Although these quotations seem somewhat heavily laden in this thesis, they are actually the most important part of the data as they indicate exactly the participants' experiences and the rationales for their statements.

I was aware that classifying did not mean that all the data (feelings, ideas, comments, personal examples and stories) would be divided into statements without keeping their unity, their meaning and essence, as many researchers had asserted (i.e., Denzin 1998). Thus, I kept individual's account within its own unity and contextualised it accordingly (Maxwell 1998).

For qualitative research, it could be argued that the classification, categorisation and generation of themes in qualitative research were based on the researcher's subjectivity and that other researchers would generate different categories and themes from the same data. I agreed with this argument but I believed that it was therefore very important for qualitative researchers to show a pattern (Boyatzis 1998) or a consistent approach in dealing with statements and ideas which allowed both the researcher and the reader to see clearly the difference between themes and categories and their content.

The data presented in the book came out of 57 formal and informal interviews, 6 group discussions and ethnographic observations conducted over the course of four months of fieldwork in Shanghai. I also included examples from some informal interviews conducted during my fieldwork, field notes, photos and second-hand resources from existing large-scale statistical projects. The aim here was not to make this material homogenous, nor to reach the 'truth' through triangulation, but to hold on to its specificity and richness. As Charmaz (2006) described, this was a 'prism' approach, whereby a range of data could be used to examine central issues by turning different facets to the light.

Also, the issues of validity, reliability and ethics are important for qualitative study. As many authors (e.g. LeCompte et al. 1992; Mason 2002; Silverman 2001) had argued, qualitative research should not be evaluated by the same criteria of validity and reliability developed for quantitative research. According to LeCompte et al. (1992: 343), threats to the validity of qualitative research were 'history and maturation, selection and regression, mortality and spurious conclusions.'

To cope with these threats, I spent another two months to reflect throughout my research on the factors of time, data selection and predicted research results, adopting some ways for participant validity. For example, after transcribing interviews, I gave these female students transcriptions for their comments and correction. I kept clarifying assumptions after re-examining my theoretical position given that there are reflections, predictions, and even hypotheses involved in this research. In addition, LeCompte et al. (1993: 337) claim that the idea of internal reliability deals with the probability that 'within a single study, multiple observers would agree what happened.' Since I went through the process of collecting data in practice mainly by myself, what I could do is to combine multiple research methods, and go back and forth to check with my research subjects in order to ensure that my understanding was correct. Although some qualitative researchers (i.e., Maxwell 1998; Ely et al. 1997) suggest that the use of different tools, such as video, might help ensure the reliability of the data, I finally decided not to use it since it might be an indicator of the lack of trust in me as a researcher. Yet, I believe that through polishing my questioning skills and conducting interviews to the same person for several times could assure better quality of data.

Issues of external reliability cover the 'researcher's position, informant choices, social situations and conditions, analytic constructs and premises, methods of data collection and analysis' (see LeCompte et al. 1992: 343). Regarding these issues, 'informant choices' (sampling), 'methods of data collection and analysis' (research tools) and 'analytic constructs and premises' (data treatment) had been discussed respectively above. 'Social situations and conditions' (including the research site, individual demographics, and contextual knowledge of categorising) had also been provided in the Appendix.

Moreover, guarding against misrepresentation on the part of participants was a significant concern in judging qualitative research. I was aware of the possibility that some might have been misrepresented or distorted certain matter—though as the interviews continued this seemed increasingly unlikely, as many participants said similar things and explained themselves in a similar logic. However, it remained possible that several might have answered certain questions in ways they saw as political correct within the institution or in relation to wider concerns about surveillance and so on. Also, it was possible that their feelings towards their campus life might have led them to speak more favourably of this university than they really felt. These possibilities cannot be completely ruled out, but I did check and compare their responses with relevant existing surveys and report of young people in present-day China more generally, and found out that most of young women did in fact say things that were politically correct but also things that could be seen as politically 'deviant' or 'liberal,' which as shown in later chapters, I took their accounts to be largely truthful.

Despite the arguments I had made on the consistency and coherence of theories and methodology, the whole research would not be reliable and valid without considering my own positions within it. Punch (1994: 94) points out that 'where you stand will doubtless help to determine not only what you will research but also how you will research it'. Particularly for qualitative research, reflexivity or engaging in reflection about the research process is necessary. In fact, my position in this research is one of the most challenging issues because my decision on the research topic, focus, theoretical approach, samplings, and so on, is closely related to my identity as a middle-class urban young Chinese woman student.

On the one hand, it put me in an advantageous position to carry out this research. When I began my PhD study I was 26 years old. The similar age with my research participants enabled me to approach them and establish rapport with them more easily. Such trust was an essential element of my research because it made my participants feel more comfortable in telling me their life stories and true feelings.[7] More importantly, owing to my life experience of living in China for more than twenty years, it was easier for me to capture my participants' natural responses and indications as well as acknowledge the cultural differences in conducting qualitative research in China.

On the other hand, I acknowledged that the closeness with the participants may also bring the ethical issue—how intimate or detached the researcher should be in his/her relationship with the subjects? For instance, as my participants becoming more familiar with me, they began to take their initiative to approach me and share their stories with me. Some students also asked me about my experience in the UK. Under such circumstance, I was cautious about not revealing my personal feelings, attitudes and affections of my overseas experience too much in order not to reduce my influence on their perspectives in relation to the issue of identity. Rather, I provided my participants support, encouragement and respect and let them talk more by changing the topic of my UK experience into questions, such as 'What is

---

[7]I was born in a middle-class family in Beijing, China. Both of my parents worked in the state-owned work unit. My father used to work as an Architecture Engineer in the Infrastructure Department of an esteem hospital and my mother as a Warehouse Keeper in the Supply Department there. Owing to the Cultural Revolution in China, both of my parents did not have the opportunity to go to the university.

your understanding of the UK?'. 'If you have opportunities, whether do you want to go to the UK for education?' or 'Which Western country do you prefer to go, and why?'. Here, I closely followed BERA's ethical guidelines by ensuring informed consent to participate, providing them with detailed descriptions of the research activity, ensuring their understanding of the research process and how the data would be used, as well as reminding my participants of their right to withdraw (BERA 2004).

Truly, this research design is not perfect as there are also many limitations, especially in relation to my data collected from a small number of young Chinese women. This limits this study to achieve any 'statistical generalisations.' Indeed, the issue of generalisability may loom larger in a qualitative case study. Even some experienced qualitative case study researchers (i.e., Hamel 1993: 23) claim that 'the case study has basically been faulted for its lack of representativeness … and its lack of rigor in the collection, construction, and analysis of the empirical materials that give rise to the study. This lack of rigor is linked to the problems of bias … introduced by the subjectivity of the researcher and others involved in the case.' However, I assume that different types of research methodology and method to collect data have their own merits. In my research, for example, it can achieve 'analytic generalisation' (see Yin 1994), such as 'fashionable woman,' 'independent career woman' and 'patriotic lady' in my analysis of these fourteen urban-dwelling middle-class young Chinese women.

Conclusion: Doing Feminist Research in China

In previous chapters, I have demonstrated how the relationships between the changing social structures and the processes (and outcomes) of knowledge production mask the interests of a ruling ideology in Chinese context. In the beginning of this chapter, I further argue that the immense body of knowledge that enabled decades of investigation of gender relations is providing the opportunity to research the possibilities of knowledge. In many ways, there is the need for passionate pursuit of a reflexivity that may enable other forms of knowledge and the possibilities of other ways of thinking and being in the world to be generated. Thus, a feminist approach enables this study to explore the 'other' form of knowledge. Thereafter, I lay out the design of this study by describing the process of sampling, fieldwork conducting, and data collection. I further illustrated the ways in which I managed data and the issue of validity, reliability, ethical issues and limitations of this research. I gave a particular emphasis on my fieldwork experience in China and reflections on this qualitative research.

When I gave my personal accounts of how this fieldwork actually was undertaken, I also offered reflections on how my experiences were linked up with more general questions around social research methodologies and fieldwork findings. The fact that I concentrated exclusively on qualitative research fieldwork in China did not mean that I regarded these problems as being unique to the PRC. On the contrary, many of them might be common across countries. My point of departure was that although fieldwork in China was always subject to many political restrictions, the fundamental issues were universal. Thus, compromises had to be made between methodological rules and the actual reality in the field. At the same time, in order for the discussion of fieldwork methods to be more meaningful it should focus on concrete examples. From my fieldwork experience in this research, what I saw as the most fruitful approach was to stay open to unexpected emerging data *both* within *and* outside the fieldwork and to allow for a re-polishment of the project.

I quite agreed with Thogersen and Heimer (2006) that qualitative researchers ought to employ as many different sorts of research material and data as one can in undertaking their fieldwork particularly in Chinese context. As they noted when they did fieldwork in China:

> Doing fieldwork inside the People's Republic of China is an eye-opening but sometimes also deeply frustrating experience... there are few detailed descriptions in the China literature of how people actually do their fieldwork, and of the problems they encounter. (Thogersen and Heimer 2006: 1)

Therefore, statistical data from yearbooks and specialised volumes, as well as that found in survey research by others reported in Chinese journals, official documents, internal journals, daily newspapers from China in both Chinese and English, whether official, semi-official, or the product of 'reportage literature,' and Western media reports, and research reports would all be included in this study in addition to primary data collected in the defined context.

Particularly, I saw the beginning stage of this study as a very important stage in conducting qualitative research in China since these components were an essential part of the research, offering me a holistic view of contemporary young women's lives inside and outside the university education. I became familiar with the spaces of consumption and leisure that upwardly mobile Chinese occupy, and I came to understand younger Chinese people's—especially younger women's—spending patterns and personal priorities. Thus, my analysis in the rest parts of the book was deeply informed by my grounding in the spaces and practices of contemporary Chinese people in general.

To conclude, as what I had mentioned above, researcher's positionalities during the fieldwork were often simplified into the mutually excluding categories of insiders and outsiders. When I discussed this research design and my fieldwork experiences in China, this simplification was in addition conflated with a Chinese-Western dichotomy that left little room for the sophistication and ambiguity we had come to expect from the methodological literature of other fields of the social sciences. Certainly, these twin dichotomies allowed little room for most researchers of flesh and blood since few if any fit the racial and cultural stereotypes that came together with them. In reality, any researcher was supposed to keep, or to be kept at, a certain distance in the field, whether working in what one considers to be one's own society or in a foreign. On the other hand, it was usually as impossible to be an outsider in fieldwork as it was to be an insider.

Chapter 4
Chinese Beauty and Femininity

Beauty is always objective, not subjective. Thus, the opinions of individuals could hardly count. Beauty reflects the spirit of the times... Real beauty lies in the beauty of aspiration, of morality, of painstaking study, and of the spirit of inquiry, which surpasses the beauty of adornment, of the body, and of the happy life of one's own small family. ('Fragmental Thoughts Regarding Beauty' in *Women of China*[1] 6, 1980: 32)

Feeling good about yourself, this is a kind of confidence. Apparently, the purpose of adornment is to sell oneself to the world in a visual sense, but more importantly is that it pleases you. As long as you like it and think it is good and appropriate you should wear it. (*Shanghai Fashion Times*, June 1, 1992)

In Chap. 2, I have conceptualised 'feminism' in relation to young women's negotiation with power through their bodily practice in many Western contexts. In literally every society, women always strive to make themselves beautiful in order to live up to the beauty standard in their imagination and to gain power. Although the standards may differ from time to time, and from culture to culture, one fact which will never change is that women's temperament, aura, mindset, thinking and action will all shine through their appearance. Thus, analysing the making of women's beauty can give us a taste of the spirit of the time and its aesthetic ability. For example, women's clothing, performing a major role in the social construction of identity, provides an excellent field for studying how women interpret a specific form of culture for their own purposes. It is also one of the most visible markers of social status and gender and therefore is useful in maintaining or subverting symbolic boundaries.

In the context of China, one of the traditional double standards for men and women is that a man is mainly assessed by his talent and ability whereas a woman is

---

[1]*Women of China* is a monthly English-language magazine sponsored and administrated by the All-China Women's Federation (ACWF) and published by the Women's Foreign Language Publications of China since the early 1950 s. It is the authoritative English voice on Chinese women. The magazine strives to communicate the reality of Chinese women's lives, their experiences and ideas through in-depth reports on women's issues, concerns and viewpoints, and the development of Chinese women. Its content encompasses China's nationalities, traditional cultures and customs, and the latest news on exchanges between women of China and other countries (see http://www.womenofchina.com.cn/about_us/).

© Foreign Language Teaching and Research Publishing Co., Ltd
and Springer Science+Business Media Singapore 2016
J. Zheng, *New Feminism in China*, DOI 10.1007/978-981-10-0777-4_4

purely judged by her appearance, as shown in the Chinese idiom *Langcai Nvmao* (see Stockard 2002). I found that such mentality still deeply influences the gender ideology of contemporary young Chinese people. For example, amongst these fourteen middle-class young Chinese women who participated in this research project, many of them still paid considerable amount of attention to their weight and appearance, relating the external beauty of a woman to success. Yet, I also noticed that most of young women of this cohort began to relate their body images, including hairstyle and clothing, to aspirations, hopes, desires and passions. In our discussions of women's body and 'self-consciousness,' they described their 'hearts' (*xinli, xintai*) and 'feelings' (*ganjue*), speaking of their need to embrace wide-ranging 'desires,' from consumption to work to sex. They explicitly contrasted what they viewed as their own life-enhancing practices with the self-sacrifices they interpreted as having dominated lives of their parents' generation.

This chapter draws interview data collected from young urban Chinese women, aiming to find out how do young women respond to fashion and beauty culture in

Table 4.1 Summary of interviewees' attitudes towards hairstyle, clothes and lifestyles

Name	Current hairstyle	Preferred dressing code	Shopping philosophy	Lifestyle attitudes	Self-evaluation
Qian	Naturally straight shoulder-length and tied	Smart	Never buy anything unaffordable	Price oriented	Traditional and economical
Ivy	Dyed and curled	Creative, casual	Stylish comes first	Brand oriented	Luxurious
Rain	Straightened long hair and relaxed	Smart	Neat and tidy make perfection	Price conscious	Rational
Nancy	Straightened long hair and relaxed	Business casual	Price does not make everything	Quality oriented	Rational and presentable
Lily	Curled short hair	Casual	Resist blind shopping	Comfort oriented	Rational
Jane	Naturally straight and relaxed	Casual	Inner beauty is important	Comfort oriented	Individualistic
Fay	Naturally straight and tied	Semi-formal	Women deserve treating themselves well	Brand oriented	Presentable
Julie	Curled and died long hair	Creative	Always short of clothes	Brands oriented	Luxurious
Pearl	Naturally straight short	Casual, sporty	Tomboy is cool	Comfort oriented	Individualistic
Ning	Naturally straight and tied	Smart	Conservative would make no fault	Quality oriented	Traditional
Zoe	Short hair	Formal	Well-dressed women are confident	Brands oriented	Individualistic and presentable

the age of the flourishing global consumerism. Based on my observation, I also provide a critical analysis of how contemporary social change in China transforms young women's view on the body, fashion and power. Data emerged from interviews could be categorised as: hairstyle expressions, branded clothes to represent class and luxury consumption. To facilitate readers, I summarise participants' attitudes towards fashion and their individual strategies in negotiating power through their body and fashion tastes in Table 4.1. Whilst I reveal the accommodation and resistance buried in these young Chinese women's everyday practice, I also explain the uniqueness of girls and young women in China when they use resistance strategies to negotiate power and status boundaries in the local context.

Straight-Black-Hair-Ness

The body is an important site for power struggles between men and women. For millennia, women's subordinate position has been justified by an ideology that labelled their bodies and brains as inferior (Weitz 1998) and has been reinforced by a unique set of disciplinary practices aimed at creating a submissive and 'feminine' body (Bartky 1988). In turn, the centrality of the body to women's subordination has put the body at the centre of explicitly political struggles to improve women's social status, such as the battles to gain reproductive rights and to end violence against women. According to some theorists who study how women's body reflects their subjectivities (i.e., Firth 1973; Synott 1987), hairstyles serve as an important cultural artifact in the examination since they are simultaneously public (visible to everyone), personal (biologically linked to the body), and highly malleable to suit cultural and personal preferences (see Banks 2000). In my fieldwork, I also found that young women used their hairstyles as a symbolism to negotiate with traditional social norms of gender and beauty in Chinese context. In particular, straight black hair has been related to a representative of Chinese beauty.

'Why you choose this hairstyle?' 'Which hairstyle do you think is a 'good' hairstyle for you?' After posing these questions to my participants, we discussed the social, cultural and personal reasons of why hair might matter to Chinese women and how hair could be associated with power in any way. Their thoughts demonstrate the importance of racial and gender ideologies in constructing beauty culture across time. That is, their comments detail that women's constructions of beauty intersect along the lines of racial differences. For example, in Chinese context, traditional standards of beauty used to be associated with purity, simplicity and a painstaking spirit, which all surpass the meanings of the adornment of the female body. As many of my participants claimed, straight black hair has been seen as a good condition of hair since it could best represent female beauty in the Chinese context. While some young women relate 'good hair' to the natural colour and texture of straight black hair, some straighten their hair to look beautiful.

Naturally straight black hair is beautiful for Chinese women. You see, the female images in the whole mythology all wear naturally black long hair. Chinese poets in Tang Dynasty used 'silk hair' to describe the 'good hair,' which is the soft and naturally black long hair. (Qian, 20100420)

Straight and long hair makes women more feminine. I straighten my hair because I think it can make me look softer. (Nancy, 20100423)

Girls will look much more feminine and much more alluring if her long hair is straight and relaxed. It seems that the longer and straighter a girl's hair is, the more feminine and pure she is… It may leave others a very good first impression. (Rain, 20100425)

From these interviews, we can see that although Nancy and Rain choose to straighten their hair and Qian retain the natural texture and colour of her hair, all of them associate Chinese beauty with 'straight black hair.' Their discussions of hairstyles could be framed within a broader context, which is that hairstyle shapes women's idea about race, gender and beauty.

In fact, decades' ago, anthropologists began to study women's hair in order to theorise the symbolism of hairstyle. In *Hair: Sex, Society, and Symbolism*, Wendy Cooper (1971: 7) has discussed both biological and social issues surrounding hair. She contends that hair is an 'easily controlled variable that can denote status, set fashion, or serve as a badge.' As a result, hair has emerged as socially and culturally significant. Cooper (1971) further argues that along with skin, hair is another most important physical attribute for racial classification since hair not only varies in terms of type and texture among different races but also within race categories. Australian gender researcher Maynard (2004: 104) points out that East Asian cultures have traditionally seen long, unkempt hair in a woman as a sign of sexual intent or a recent sexual encounter, as usually their hair is tied up in styles such as the ponytail, plait or any bun. Although for the majority of contemporary urban girls and young women in China, they usually do not tie up their hair in styles of plait and bun any more, it is still true that long hair has some indications of physical attractiveness to the other sex (see Fig. 4.1).

Yet, these traditional ideas about Chinese beauty have gone through a modernisation process, in which some young Chinese women also begin to use

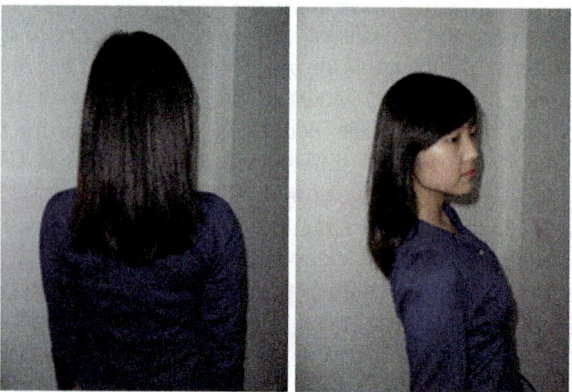

Fig. 4.1 Straight long black hair used to be seen as the most beautiful hairstyle in traditional Chinese standard. *Source* Courtesy of Yueye

individualist and expressive hairstyles as a means to present their female beauty. For example, while Ivy believes that a dyed hairstyle could make her fashionable and unique, Wendy argues that a shortened hairstyle is the latest fashion.

> Black straight hair is dull. I like dark reddish brown. It is fashionable and unique. I always read fashion magazines, and watch TV shows to learn how to deal with one's hair in order to make you her "in." You can see many Hollywood stars' hair is curly. It's so elegant. Many of my friends said it is stylish and they followed my hairstyle, which make me feel really good. (Ivy, 20100422)

> Short hair is my style. It makes me look special. Short hair will make you stand out from the crowds immediately... It's also neat. (Zoe, 20100422)

For both Ivy and Zoe, a groomed hairstyle (either by dying, curling or shortening) could not only symbolise female beauty but also empower the individual by making the person feels 'really good.' By engaging the pervasiveness of the historical fascination with hair as a gauge of female attractiveness, Bordon (1989) also argues that the power embedded in doing femininity well (such as through doing a nice haircut) is power for women even though hairstyle practices may seem like a very limited form of power compared to, for example, winning an election to a government office. Nevertheless, with a minimum investment of money and time, this woman could obtain a desired goal and influence behaviour and emotions of another person.

Moreover, these conversations have also revealed the valuation/devaluation of hair in its natural colour and texture amongst contemporary young Chinese women. This provides an insight into the change of attitudes towards women's beauty in contemporary Chinese society. For example, while Ivy and Rain feel more comfortable to express themselves through trying out individualist and pleasure-driven hair-grooming practices, Qian relates her choice of a natural hairstyle to her traditional value and Chinese beauty standard which sees a natural hair condition as 'appropriate' for Chinese women.

Traditionally, Chinese people relate 'natural hair' to ideas about purity as well as being an act or state that is 'normal,' taking a plain and natural look as beautiful and positive. For example, for the generation of Chinese women born in 1950s and 1960s, they went through the disastrous thee-year famine (1959–1961) in their childhood. In their teens, many of the urban population were relocated to the countryside as part of Mao's policy of 'learning from the peasants.' During the period between 1950 and 1976, the most famous female image was Xing Yanzi,[2] an urban Chinese girl shown on political propaganda paintings (see Fig. 4.2).

---

[2]Xing Yanzi was born in 1940. Her father was a prosperous factory manager, but when Xing graduated from high school she decided to return to the countryside to try to improve the lives of peasants. She organised the 'Xing Yanzi Pioneer Team' to plough the land collectively with her neighbours, and made great achievements. In 1960 a story entitled 'Xing Yanzi strives to achieve her agricultural blue' appeared in the widely-read national newspaper *People's Daily*. Since then, Xing became a national celebrity among young people and Chairman Mao singled her out for praise. In 1964, Xing Yanzi took part in the 9th Congress of the Communist Youth League of China and was elected as a deputy to the National People's Congress.

Fig. 4.2 Xing Yanzi's image in the cover page of China's *Remin Huabao. Source China Pictorial*

   In those paintings, women were dressed in Lenin coats, Mao jackets, and Chinese
tunic suits. They wore naturally straight short hair or occasionally ponytails, and
were without make-up. Also, they showed their expressions of being either warm
and passionate spring-day-like smiles towards comrades, or ruthless, hateful faces
with their fists threatening enemies in order to represent the image of pioneer girls.
Every ordinary woman in China was encouraged to dress in the same way as those
pioneer women. In this sense, although Chinese women of that time had participated
in society, their appearance and dressing style just kept pushing the limit of plain
coarseness. As Chinese feminist Li Yinhe (2005: 35 my translation) explained later:

> When the Chinese leaders shouted out the slogan "time is different, men and women are
> equal," the result was disastrous: men and women all dressed the same, looked the same and
> worked the same… Neutralisation and de-sexualisation were the only two choices for women.

   Therefore, although my participants have offered their different opinions on what
they think to be 'good hair,' their choices of hairstyle have undoubtedly reflected
their constructions of young Chinese femininities in a changing time. Bordo (1993:
254–255, my emphasis) makes a similar point by arguing that:

> When we look at the pursuit of beauty as a normali[s]ing discipline, it becomes clear that
> *not* all body transformations are the same. The general tyranny of fashion – perpetual,
> elusive, and instructing the female body in a pedagogy of personal inadequacy and lack – is
> a powerful discipline for the normali[s]ation of *all* women in this culture. But even as we
> are all normali[s]ed to the requirements of appropriate feminine insecurity and preoccu-
> pation with appearance, more specific requirements emerge in different cultural and his-
> torical contexts, and for different groups.

Try Something New

Compared with the traditional Chinese beauty taste of straight black hair, some women express that they would like to try something new for an individualist view of fashion and beauty. Also, although most young women I interviewed reach an agreement that the alteration of hairstyles has an associated meaning of self-acceptance or self-esteem, they disagree about the effects of external factors, such as their parents' or boyfriends' opinions and pressure, on their decisions about changing hairstyles. On the one hand, they agree with each other that the change of hairstyle could enable them to have the best image of themselves all the time. On the other hand, they explain different factors and reasons which may influence their decisions on choosing a certain hairstyle. For example, when we discussed the reasons for changing one's hairstyles in a group discussion, both Lily and Fay mentioned that they related hairstyle alteration to the effect of boosting their egos respectively.

Interviewer: How often do you change your hairstyle and why?
Fay (20100427): Quite often. Different hairstyles have different feelings and moods. For example, a short haircut is associated with professionalism and shrewdness. I will cut my hair short if I want to look serious and powerful.
Interviewer: How often do you change your hairstyle and why?
Lily (20100427): I change my hairstyles for reasons, such as getting bored of the status quo and fancying a new image or a new style for a change. But the ultimate goal is to look good and feel good. I cut my hair short as a way to make a change and to cheer myself up!

For both Fay and Lily, they believe that hair management and hairstyle alteration is a way for women to negotiate with power and social classifications. For example, Fay associates a short haircut to 'professionalism' and 'shrewdness.' She believes that a short hair could make her look serious and powerful. Lily mentions that she uses the practice of cutting her hair short as a strategy to 'boost ego to do something new.' Their theories of hairstyles have indicated the subconscious effect of hair alteration on their awareness of being as a woman.

After the formal interview, Lily turned to me and told me a deeper reason for her to get her short hair curled. According to her, hairstyle practice is also a way to socialise and to be accepted by her peer group.

> Most female students in Media Studies get their hair curled, no matter their hair is long or short. It seems that Media students should be like that. It's a fashion. I also do the same. It makes me feel that I'm a part of the group. (Lily, 20100427)

Lily's comments illustrate the cultural and social contexts of hair that go beyond its physical nature. The reason why Lily curls her hair is that she wants to be like her fellow students. She realises that hair is a physical manifestation of a certain group loaded with social and cultural meanings—such as the public image of professional Media workers in her understanding. In this sense, hair reflects different perceptions, social identities and different levels of a person's self-esteem, from which we can extract various meanings (see de Certeau 1984; Bordo 1993; Butler 1993; Roberts 1997).

From another perspective, Ning explains her theory of hairstyle alteration during her education-to-employment transition (Fig. 4.3).

> I used to wear short hair when I was a university student, because it's easier to manage. But now I wear longer hair and I change my hairstyles everyday. This could make me feel fresh and confident everyday. A good image in the workplace is very important because this relates to self-representation and professionalism. A professional look means that you have already been a reliable adult. (Ning, 20100427)

These conversations suggest that a sociological understanding of hair and its manipulation as a part of everyday life could focus on the ways in which the body and its functions must be negotiated according to the social situation. As Hiltebeitel and Miller (1998) argued, the growing and cutting of hair has also been related to control in Asian societies, where long hair stands for social regulation, obedience and disciplined religious or cultural conformity, and short or covered hair is a sign of social freedom or defiance.

In other interviews, while some young Chinese women relate their choice of hairstyles and hair management to an expression of their individuality, some express that they prefer to choose a 'safer' hairstyle to avoid the exposure of their individuality. For example, in another group discussion, Julie, her younger sister Pearl, and Julie's classmate Jane shared their opinions on the importance of hair management and hairstyle alteration in their daily practices.

Interviewer: For what reasons do you think you will change your hairstyle?

Julie (20100420): Whether I will change my hairstyle or not really depends on my mood and the situation I am in. Different hairstyles create different images. A neat short haircut seems to be more effective and it's suitable in the workplace. Long hair looks quite relaxed. It's more suitable for dates and holidays because it can make you very feminine.

Pearl: If my stylist suggests that a certain hairstyle might suit me, I will try that.

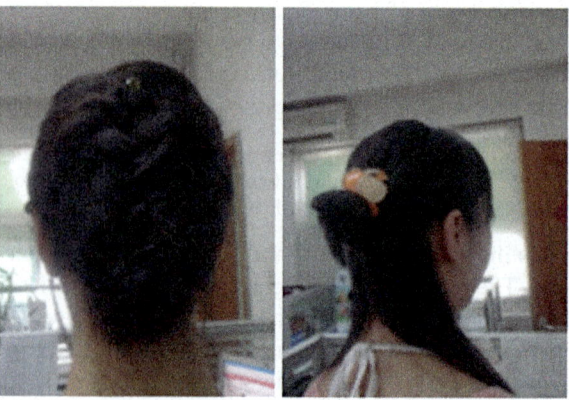

Fig. 4.3 Hairstyle alteration and hair management in the workplace. *Source* Courtesy of Ning

Interviewer: Do you mean that you would like to rely on others' opinions to decide your hairstyles?

Pearl You can say like this. Anyway, stylists are experts. Sometime I also ask my boyfriend's opinion on my hairstyle.

Julie: I would rather rely on myself regarding hairstyles. My mum and my friends could have a say, but I'm the person who makes decision.

Jane: I think you exaggerate the effect of hairstyles. I never think too much about my hair. Neither do I compromise with anybody for changing my hairstyles. As long as you're happy with your hair, that's fine. It also depends on whether you're busy or not... Hairstyle is not my only concern.

For Julie, Pearl and Jane, their exchange of ideas has demonstrated the value of conducting group interviews among friends as a way to gain an understanding about how much hair matters to these individuals. Although their comments on hair management and hairstyle alteration are not without contradiction, it is clear that all these young Chinese women define their hair-groom practices as an empowering act. For example, Julie's comments explicitly define women's hair management as versatile and meaningful. Pearl emphasises that she would like to actively seek advice from fashion experts and people she values regarding her hairstyle practices. Jane's statements, however, relay a stronger sense of empowerment. Unlike Julie and Pearl, she perceives hairstyling to manageability and her own desires rather than to the consequence of such a gendered practice. In this sense, we must remember that individual preference is often shaped by broader social and cultural forces, which always require women to develop their own strategies in order to negotiate their marginal position in a sexist society (see Weitz 2001).

Later, Julie further explained to me in which moods she would cut her hair short.

Julie (20100420): In bad moods. For example, if I break up with boyfriend, I will have the impulsion to cut my hair short. I want a new start. I don't want to keep anything which could remind me of him.

Pearl: That's interesting. You're punishing yourself. (When you cut your hair short) people will be suspicious that you may just break up with your boyfriend. So, why change yourself? if I were in that situation, I would retain my old hairstyle and try something cool—such as getting a new boyfriend! Haha!

When studying the complex role the body plays in sustaining and challenging women's subordinate position, Weitz (2001) argues that using the body (such as women's hair) could be the most common way women use to seek power. Subconsciously or not, women will apply strategies such as de-emphasising resistance to and instead emphasising accommodation to mainstream ideas about attractiveness. Once a woman adopts this strategy, she can use her understanding of cultural ideologies surrounding women's hair to increase its effectiveness. For example, in some Western cultures, women who dye their hair blonde are well aware of cultural ideas that link blondeness to sexuality and beauty. From the conversations presented above, it seems that in Chinese context, long straight hair could serve as a symbol of attractiveness and any other changes of hairstyle related to innovation and individuality.

In a word, understanding fashioning and display of young women's hair is pivotal to the presentation and representation of social identity since its styles, grooming and altering practices have embodied wider historical political and social changes. In Entwistle's (2000: 7) words, hair can be situated as a fundamental part of 'the means by which bodies are made and given meaning and identity.' Like hair grooming practices, clothes and fashion has also been used by my participants as an important strategy to negotiate power in the Chinese context.

Brand, Power and Urban New Class

'What do you think of Western brand clothes and Chinese brand clothes?' 'Are clothes associated with power in any way?' After posing these questions to my interviewees, I explained power could be viewed from the girls' and women's own perspective. Thus, the responses were more insightful than if I had given them only one definition of power, or only one way of approaching the question. In other words, my interviewees could address the question on their own terms. Data collected from interviews suggest topics including Western brand clothes as empowerment, Chinese fashion to support images and perceptions, and top brands as a higher social class.

For example, some young Chinese women in this research project relate Western brand clothes to empowerment. According to them, wearing Western brand clothes can make them feel more privileged among their fellow students.

> The styles of Western brand clothes are generally more feminine and fashionable than the local Chinese ones. Wearing Western brand clothes can make you look more classy and tasteful. That's why I prefer to buy Western brand clothes even though they cost more. (Ivy, 20100422)

> To me, brand is quite important. I don't like Chinese brand clothes because most of them are not stylish. You can say that I'm brand-oriented, but if a branded dress can make you look special, why not? (Julie, 20100420)

> Style is more important than brands. My style is sporty one, and I like NIKE and PUMA. It looks cool. But as for Chinese sport brands, they are not well recognised. (Pearl, 20100420)

Clearly, while Ivy associates Western brand clothes to meanings of 'feminine,' 'fashionable,' 'classy' and 'tasteful,' Julie and Pearl believe that Western brands are usually 'special' and 'well recognised.' In these conversations, Western brands are welcome because they are powerful.

Another young woman associates Western brands to the meaning of 'international.' For example, in an individual interview, Zoe uses her terminology 'better-off femininity' to explain her reason for choosing Western brand clothes (Fig. 4.4).

Fig. 4.4 Fashionable dressing style of young Chinese women. *Source* Courtesy of Zoe

> Western brand clothes associate with a 'better-off femininity' (*gufu xiang*). Because they are always more expensive, not everyone can afford it. I would feel more privileged and more international by wearing a Western brand coat. (Zoe, 20100422)

However, some young Chinese women claim that they feel more comfortable with Chinese brand clothes for different reasons. For example, Qian explain that they choose Chinese brand for financial reasons. Other girls, such as Nancy, Rain and Jane also mention the texture of clothes to explain their theory of clothes and fashion.

> I like to buy local brands clothes because the price is more reasonable. Although Western brands clothes are always very trendy and sexy, you can't wear them to attend class. So, why spend a lot of money on clothes which you can't get opportunities to wear? (Qian, 20100420)

> I don't buy clothes purely for the brand or the price. As long as it's in good quality and I think it's nice and suitable for me, I would buy it. I think Western brands are generally more stylish, but these brands, of course, are more expensive. I can't afford to buy a lot now. (Nancy, 20100423)

> I don't care brands that much. Reasonable price is one concern, and the texture of the clothes is also quite important. I prefer satin, silk and cotton clothes, I have many Chinese brands' dresses which are made of silk or pure cotton. (Rain, 20100425)

> Comfort would be the first criteria for me to choose a dress. No matter which brand is, as long as it fits you well and can present you best, it'll be a good dress. For me, I would rather lead the fashion than being led by fashion. (Jane, 20100420)

As presented above, although these comments are tied to different individual's sense of fashion and ability to exercise control over their desire of craving for more expensive Western branded clothes, these young Chinese women's comments also indicate that fashion is also closely related to race and class.

From another perspective, Ning argues that Chinese femininity is more associated with Chinese brands. She believes that empowerment related to the individual's ability to present oneself appropriately.

Chinese brand clothes are sometimes more suitable for Chinese women. It is because the body structures of Chinese women and Western women are different. Most Chinese women are small and flat, compared with taller and more curvaceous Western women. Many Western brand clothes are designed for a Western body. So, if a woman is short, even if she wears an expensive Western branded long dress, she won't look great. A good image depends on the suitability of the dress to the individual, rather than the brand. (Ning, 20100427)

Clearly, for Ning, Chinese branded clothes might support images and perceptions of Chinese beauty and femininity. Ning further elaborated her point by mentioning the image of white women on television shows, in magazines, and in romance movies. She told me that in her mind, the understanding of a sexy body was associated with the image of blonde Western women who had big breasts and slender waist. The differences of physical features between Chinese and Western women also formed her understanding of fashion, beauty and power.

In broader terms, my participants' comments have also indicated the increasingly important role played by social media in contemporary young Chinese people's daily lives. Presently, the rapid urbanisation and internationalisation in China has fundamentally changed the relationship between consumers and brands by forcing both domestic and global brands to become more flexible, more engaging and increasingly personal. For example, Trendwatching.com, one of the world's leading trend firms, estimates that the continued economic growth of developing countries such as China will lead to more international brands targeting products specifically towards Chinese consumers by altering their products to accommodate Chinese physical features, traditions and lifestyles (The Independent 2011).

Also, interviews with these fourteen young Chinese women have revealed that the popularisation of certain fashions and ways of dressing blurs class and gender boundaries during contemporary socio-cultural transformation in China. For example, for both lower-middle and upper-middle-class young Chinese women coming from diverse Chinese regions, they are trying hard to use fashion to obtain a more internationalised urban middle-class identity. For example, some young Chinese women explain their changing tastes in relation to their identity construction.

My taste in fashion has changed a lot. I was born and grew up in a small town in Hunan. When I was young I was a very plain and thrifty girl. Only after I moved to Shanghai, did I cultivate some consciousness of fashion, and get to know some international brands. Especially when I had a summer internship in a foreign-invested company, I began to like Western brand clothes. It was a dream that someday I could buy a top Western brand evening dress, such as LOUIS VUITTON... I save very hard in order to buy a VERSUS coat, which is cheaper than a LV evening dress. It felt so good when I paid for it. But it cost me three months' hard work...' (Nancy, 20100423)

In Nancy's conversation, it is clear that she understands the symbolic meaning of fashion. She critically reflects how she starts to be conscious of brand names and how she changes her desires of top international brand clothes. According to Nancy, after moving to the most modern and cosmopolitan city in China, she began to dream about having a LV evening dress, even though she was not from an urban well-off family. The sign values of the top Western brand could help her construct an urban middle-class identity. Yet, when she eventually affords a VERSUS coat, she feels that her urban middle-class identity has been reinforced and therefore she would like to return to her ordinary lifestyle. In the case of Nancy, we can see that the discourses which surround one's identity construction do not remain identical throughout time, nor are they passively accepted by all subjects in society; instead they are resisted, changed and reformed, as suggested in Skeggs' (1997) work.

Echoing upon Nancy, Ning and Fay also talked about their changing attitudes towards dressing styles, especially towards Western brands clothes by sharing their life stories of personal development.

> I didn't care about the brands at all when I was an undergraduate student. But when I became a postgraduate student, I began to learn some brands because I think branded clothes can make me look professional. But I can only afford some ordinary Western brands now, so not top ones. (Fay, 20100427)

> I think "brand" is just something which can make you think that you would look good in a branded outfit, but it has nothing to do with the real *you*. When I was a student, I never bought expensive brand clothes. Only after I began to work in a foreign company did I change my dressing style. I like smart dress because it represents a professional image. (Ning, 20100427)

In other interviews, Nancy and Jane expressed their understandings of fashion in relation to class and identity construction. Although both of them were born and grew up in lower-middle-class families in Hunan Province, Nancy and Jane held different views on the relationship between Western brand clothes, fashion and middle-class identity.

Interviewer: What do you think of the relationship between fashion and class? For example, do you think Western brand clothes can represent a higher class?
Nancy (20100423): Definitely. Fashion is marked by class. For example, GAP, H&M and Zara are Western brand, rich brand. KAGENA, AMINTA and 1 % are Korean and Japanese style, middle-class brand. That's what I learn from my roommate.

While Nancy emphasised the uniqueness of individuals to define fashion, Jane gave her emphasis on the communality of young women in the same major to define fashion and class.

> Girls studying foreign languages, business, media and arts usually dress more fashionable than those studying scientific subjects. You may tell the difference of girls' major from their clothes and dressing style. (Jane, 20100420)

Both of their views on fashion and its relation to class reflected the complexity of gender reconstruction and new middle-class formation under contemporary social change in the context of China. Throughout China's Mao era, the push to recast society into a proletarian paradise in which all were equal also recast the impulses of Chinese women—conformity was not only enforced from above, it was also the natural outgrowth of an ideology that valued the communal over the individual. Thus, the desire to express one's individuality was constrained to a large extent at

Fig. 4.5 A wedding photo of a thirty-something Chinese couple dressing in *Zhongshan* suit and *Qipao*. *Source* Courtesy of Mr. Wu

that time. For Chinese men, the Mao suit or *Zhongshan* suit (see Fig. 4.5), a form of national dress, became widely worn by not only government leaders but also Chinese male majorities as a symbol of proletarian unity and an Eastern counterpart to the Western business suit. For Chinese women, Western brands clothes had been seen as a 'disgraceful fashion' because they were largely associated with a luxurious capitalist lifestyle (Wu 2009).

During the reform era China unofficially abandoned communism and this was accompanied by the discarding of the looks, styles, and aesthetics of communism. The separation of fashion from morality and political ideology also legitimised the expression of individuality—in opposition to both communist collectivism and traditional conformist values. Under such social change, the biggest benefactor is the younger generation of Chinese women born in the largest and riches cities in the Post-reform era. In fact, as the 1990s began, women gained more freedom to express their femininity, individuality, and modernity through their dressing styles (see Fig. 4.6 for a comparison of the wedding dress of young Chinese couples born before the Economic Reform and after the Economic Reform).

Wu's (2009) pioneering research on modern Chinese fashion has systematically studied how the opening-up policy in the late 1970s impacts on a wider acceptance of Western fashion brands by the Chinese people. For example, she recalled that

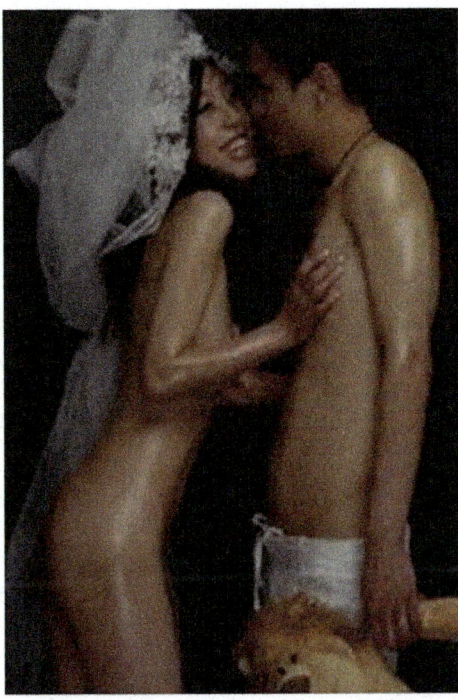

Fig. 4.6 A wedding photo of a twenty-something Chinese couple dressing in almost nothing. *Source* Courtesy of Ms. Xiao

when Pierre Cardin, the first haute couture designer to enter the Chinese market, held fashion shows in Beijing and Shanghai in 1979, Chinese authorities were concerned about the fear of Western 'spiritual pollution.' At that time, only artists and professionals were permitted to attend the shows. Western fashion had been seen as a perfect manifestation of the capitalist lifestyle and therefore been treated as a taboo subject. Although there still has been an apparent disconnection between avant-garde designs and the mass of Chinese people nowadays, it is true that Western fashion and Western brand clothes have a strong appeal to contemporary young Chinese women.

Elsewhere, in discussing fashion as a way of thinking about the everyday tension between social control and personal agency, Western feminist scholar Annamarie Jagose stated at the beginning of the chapter 'Fashion' in *Interpreting Everyday Culture* (Martin 2003: 140) that

> Like many of the forms of everyday life, fashion seems too trivial to warrant serious consideration ... Like other commodities, clothes offer a dynamic field for studying the interface between culturally available commodity forms and the construction of a sense of self. This is because clothes are not simply material objects of practical use, but also acquire meanings and values that transfer to the consumer within a fashion system.

Urban Lifestyles and Luxury Consumption

Since the early years of the new millennium, when Chinese people began to become obsessed with Western brand names, the hype surrounding Western brands has involved not only the clothing and accessory industries but also luxury consumption and exotic lifestyles. For example, young Chinese women in this research program state their desire for 'imported' products, ranging from food, cell phones, cars, home furnishings and lifestyles. For them, Western fast-food and coffee chains, such as McDonald's, Kentucky Fried Chicken, Pizza Hut, and Starbucks, have turned into fashionable and affordable places to socialise with friends.

When we talked about their perceptions of the contemporary social change in China, all my participants agreed that contemporary young Chinese people were leading modern urban lifestyles characterised by fast pace and fierce competition.

> In fact, I don't quite like the lifestyle in Shanghai. The life pace is so fast. Everything is expensive. For me, I'd rather lead a peaceful and plain lifestyle. I never buy anything unaffordable. That's vain and wasteful. So, I always ponder whether I really want to settle down here or not. (Qian, 20100420)

> I like Shanghai for the rich cultural life. You can experience lots of new things. I always dream for a fashionable lifestyle. I hope that I could get a good job when I graduate so that I can stay in Shanghai. (Rain, 20100425)

> Shanghai is definitely the best place to "do business." But clearly, it's not a good place to live if you are not very rich. I think the lifestyle here is not healthy at all. Working people have too much stress. Sleep becomes a luxurious thing. I'd rather slow down the pace a little bit. (Nancy, 20100423)

Lily and Jane, however, emphasised the rationality of lifestyle choices when we discussed the contemporary social change in China and young people's changing consuming habits. While Lily put her emphasis on rational shopping as a way of a fashionable lifestyle, Jane offered a different perspective of attaching more importance on investment as a colourful and healthy urban lifestyle.

> I want to lead a fashionable lifestyle, but I also support rational shopping. I think it's wiser to look around first, and then think for a while when you spend money. Young people are too luxurious nowadays. (Lily, 20100427)

> To me, a colourful and healthy lifestyle is what I'm looking for. I think investment more on travelling, further education and cultural events could make my life richer and healthier. (Jane, 20100420)

In the group discussion, Ivy and Julie mentioned luxury goods, such as luxury handbag and expensive global brand beauty products to explain their opinions on luxury consumption. They argued that as long as the family condition permits, spending parents' money on expensive products could keep their fighting spirit and encourage them to achieve their personal success in the future.

Interviewer: How do you think buying luxuries in your age?

Ivy (20100422): I like luxuries. Some people may think it's vain, but I don't agree with the idea that buying luxury goods in our age must be vain. As long as your family condition permits, it's totally reasonable to buy some luxury goods.

Interviewer: How do you think buying luxuries in your age?

Julie (20100420): Buying luxury goods is more like a kind of encouragement, or a treat, to oneself for hard-work and achievements. My parents would ask me what I want to have when I make some achievements. In such a case, even if I asked for some expensive international brands, they wouldn't refuse me as long as my request was reasonable.

Clearly, for both Ivy and Julie, they rejected the idea of linking luxury consumption and women's vanity in a simple way, but related luxuries to an encouragement or an award for their achievements. This reflected a growing sense of self among the younger generation of Chinese women.

In another interview, Ning defined her understanding of luxury consumption and further explained that buying luxuries reflected her changing lifestyles.

> For me, expensive makeup, top brand clothes and international travel are all luxury consumption. I think although these are expensive, they represent a higher social status. If I can get promotion next year, I will buy myself an ARMANI coat as an award for my hard work. When I save enough money, I will travel widely so that I can see the world. (Ning, 20100427)

Their comments also indicated the unique situation of the luxury market in China. Although these three young women still live with and are financially supported by their parents, some of them have already had the opportunity to possess luxury goods. In fact, due to China's one-child policy (see Chap. 6), most contemporary girls and young women in urban China are the only children in the family who have been pampered since birth. Their consuming habit is different from their parents'. They like VERSACE jeans and NIKE shoes while their parents may still cling to their own habits of frugality born of hardship. For many of contemporary Chinese young people, luxury goods and international brands are associated with a Western lifestyle, which is something to be longed for.

In fact, during the past three decades, China has become one of the fastest-growing markets in the world for international brands, and by 2008 nearly every global label had a presence in Mainland China. With sales exceeding $6 billion, China was the third largest luxury goods consumer in the world in 2004, accounting for 12 % of the world's total. At present, it has been seen that international luxury brands have entirely dominated the luxury market in major Chinese cities (Wu 2009). According to *China Daily* (2005), China is projected to consume roughly 29 % of the world's luxury goods (including fashion, wine and cars) in 2015, supplanting Japan as the largest luxury brands consumer.

Moreover, some of the young women also believe that there are other reasons, such as the Chinese herd mentality and external pressure from their international colleagues in the workplace, that have resulted in young people's desire of luxuries. For example, some women explain the role of luxury consumption in contemporary

Chinese women's lives by touching upon a deeper meaning of the 'face-saving' Chinese culture.

> I buy luxurious brands not only to make myself feel good but also to make my parents feel 'have face.' Luxury yesterday may become necessity today. If all other people around you have a branded something but you don't have one, it's a very 'face-losing' thing. (Fay, 20100427)

> I always update my high-techs. There are always new ones coming out, such as iPod, iPhone and iPad. My fellow students always get the latest one. If I still use the old one, it's quite embarrassing. (Ivy, 20100422)

Fay also told me that she needs to buy a top international brand suit for a coming interview. 'The first impression is crucial, especially if you want to work with people of other nationalities in international companies.' According to her, famed global brands could make her feel more presentable and confident in the workplace.

Like Fay, for this young generation of Chinese women who were born after China's economic reform, they have learnt English since their primary education. This enables them to be also more mobile and 'international' than previous generations in their career choice. The direct contact with the outside world has also resulted in their rising desire of consuming international brands or even luxuries. Thus, when global jobs put contemporary young Chinese women at the same table with international competitors, buying Western branded clothes and luxury goods have become a strong excuse for these young Chinese high achievers.

In other interviews, some young Chinese women described their dream of travelling around the world when we discussed luxury consumption and lifestyles. For example, Julie, Pearl and Zoe mentioned that travelling was a luxurious lifestyle for them.

Interviewer: Which kind of lifestyle are you dreaming for?
Julie (20100420): I hope that I can lead a life, which allows me to travel widely so that I could enjoy different types of delicious food, and shop around the world. That is a really luxurious fantasy for me.
Pearl: I want to go travelling as well. Paris is the first place I'd like to go. In my mind, Paris is a romantic city. You can see lots of sexy ladies and handsome guys on the street. My parents promise me that they will take me to Paris if I can go to a good university. That's all my motivation to work hard now.
Interviewer: Which kind of lifestyle are you dreaming for?
Zoe (20100422): I quite like travelling. So I hope that I can have a lot of money and sufficient time to experience different lifestyles. If I can get a job which allows me to travel a lot, I'll be so happy about that.

The comments presented above have further indicated that the emerging urban middle-class in China has now become an important market for the global luxury industries. Presently, doing well materially is probably the number one concern for the Chinese middle-class. Born during the reform era in the 1980s and 1990s, the Chinese young people in these families grew up in a less frugal environment than the generations of their parents and grandparents. They have adjusted to a new lifestyle characterised by the regular consumption of imported foreign brands and even luxuries, even though hard working and plain lifestyles have been revered as virtues by the Chinese people for generations. These teenagers and twenty-somethings like imported brands from iPod to Izod, and their childhood memories are associated with KFC, Coca-Cola, Haagen-Dazs and the internet. They are far more inclined to spend than to save and therefore they tend to be more susceptible to brand-name marketing.

Focusing on the impact of contemporary Chinese youngsters on the global luxury market, business and market researchers have also identified that China has experienced a relentless surge in consumer buying power since the 1990s. For example, from market researchers' perspectives, some leading business consultancies (see more example, KPMG 2007; Deloitte 2009; McKinsey 2009) have analysed the current phenomenon of the rapid growth in demand for imported foreign-brand or even luxury goods amongst the younger generations of Chinese, pointing out that Chinese consumers have now become wealthier and more accepting of Western retail formats—with international supermarket chains, department stores and mass retailers. These have paved the way for luxury retailers to invest in their expansion in the Chinese market. In fact, Luxury brand companies, such as LOUIS VUITTON, BALLY, GUCCI and FERRAGAMO, opened their outlets in major Chinese cities more than ten years ago, initiating the first wave of luxury retailers' expansion in China (Wu 2009). When a considerable portion of the urban population in China begins to view luxury products as an affordable necessity nowadays, the drive to conform will further spur the rich as well as the middle-class to become luxury consumers. According to China Daily (2005), as Chinese consumers turn toward luxury goods as a means of rewarding themselves for their success or as a token advertising their wealth, analysts believe that growth in the world's most populous country could boost Asia's share of world luxury sales to 60 %.

However, China may prove to be quite unlike any other developing market. Running counter to the growing habit of consumption in China is the traditional propensity to save. While the emerging middle-class will spend increasing amounts of money in enjoying life, they will continue to save heavily. Therefore, although luxury consumption in China is growing, for most people the dominant social idea is still prudent consumption and undertaking no more than you can perform. The majority of Chinese urban residents continue to live on a modest amount of wage income. This indicates that the Chinese mainland luxury market is still in its formative stages (see also McKinsey 2009).

Today, even casual observers would take notice that many Chinese urbanites have begun to enjoy a far-better material life decorated by fashionable clothes, imported cars, luxury mansions, and regular transnational vacations even in their young age. The new affluence reflects the rise of an urban middle-class of entrepreneurs, professionals and technical workers benefiting from the transformative economy during the period of the economic reform. By observing the change in lifestyles and consuming behaviour of this emerging Chinese middle-class, The Guardian (2011) vividly described Red China in the twenty-first century in the following way: 'David Beckham is an icon. Louis Vuitton handbags are a "must have" … and sales of the latest Volkswagen Golf GTi are buoyant… football, cars and fashion are what intrigue the Chinese most about Europe. Next up is perfume, historical sites, music, film, nature, technology and beer.'

Conclusion: Local or Global?

This chapter discusses how fashion relates to class and power for urban-dwelling middle-class young Chinese women. As shown above, young Chinese women are dreaming about a fashionable and Westernised lifestyle. In fact, as capitalism comes to China packaged with Western consumer culture, Western fashions, and Western aesthetics, both Chinese first-tiered and second-tiered cities are experiencing a rapid expansion of global fashion chain stores. For example, in order to increase their Chinese share, the international branded fashion stores begin to re-shape their business strategies with a specific focus on contemporary Chinese brand-conscious and price-sensitive urban youngsters. As Wu (2009) also noted, high fashion industries, luxury goods and exotic lifestyles which were once seen as a taboo subject in China have become more and more popular among the emerging Chinese middle-class urbanities. The possibility and availability of material enjoyment might contribute to one of the most apparent changes experienced by young women in contemporary Chinese society.

From the data, it is not hard to find that young Chinese women used some interesting and unique strategies, such as buying Western brand clothes to acquire a First World's identity when they attempted to seek power and to negotiate gender and class in a traditionally male-dominated Chinese society.

For instance, the conversations presented above have shown how these educationally and economically advanced young women see luxury consumption and luxurious lifestyles as part of their identity construction. Changes in young women's consuming habits have also mirrored the structural and ideological changes that are taking place in China—while the post-Mao era has witnessed the birth of the Chinese market economy and the reawakening of Chinese fashion, the post-reform era has further experienced the re-construction of young Chinese femininity and the rejuvenation of the appetite for luxury goods and lifestyles for contemporary Chinese people.

Certainly, the export of Western culture (especially American culture) through media outlets like television, radio, sales, movies, DVDs and CDs has been extraordinary in almost every modern society in current times. However, while the distribution of information has become increasingly concentrated and controlled by the lens of the dominant hegemonic culture of the capitalist West, there has been a need to draw feminist concerns over the widespread dissemination of sexualised images of women.

In the rapidly modernising Chinese society, for example, when a growing number of urban young Chinese people begin to become capable of leading a

Western lifestyle regarding enjoying money, fashion, style and pleasure, we should also bear in mind that: what the aggregate data on per capita income growth fails to reveal is an increasingly severe income inequality between the urban and the rural, and even between city-dwellers. For urban Chinese girls and young women in particular, when the aura of youth and beauty is gradually touching the product and turning any plain object into a commodity, question could be asked: to what extent could Chinese femininity retain its original flavour? Or, alternatively, as what Doctoroff has written:

> While beauty in the West is often transformational and edgy with consumers less afraid to stand out from the crowd, Chinese women seek a more accessible, inclusive form of beauty. Features that stick out are not generally perceived as attainable or attractive. As such, in advertising, Chinese prefer to see Chinese faces, although a truly iconic foreign celebrity will also work because Chinese admire expertise, power and status. (Doctoroff, 2007: 48)

In the meantime, while the cultural flow of commodities, capital and information through advances in communications technology enable contemporary young Chinese women to move beyond government censorship of local media and to have more freedom in expressing their femininity, it deserves to be noted that women's advancement in the areas of employment and opportunity, health and well-being, political empowerment are still limited. In other words, compared with the impressive change in women's labour force participation, the kinds of occupations in which women have been employed have changed relatively little.

At the time when I did my fieldwork in Shanghai, hundreds of young Chinese university women students are expected to graduate and enter the labour market quite soon. In my causal talk with these young Chinese women students, many of them told me that they were interested in working for service sectors or seeking government employment which was linked to health, education or welfare. Some women further explained that it was because they believed that these jobs were more suitable for women and could provide social stability and protection. However, whether flocking to these traditionally feminised sectors will protect women or worsen the situation of sex segregation in employment?

Chapter 5
The Work-Marriage Dilemma

Women's employment must be linked with women's liberation. Economics is the foundation. Without participation in social production, women would have no economic status. This would in turn undermine the equality between men and women in politics, society and family.

—Friedrich Von Engels

In Chap. 2, I have discussed the change of education-to-employment transition in relation to contemporary young women's lives in many Western contexts. To some extent, there are good reasons for optimism about women's employment nowadays since continuous feminist campaigns have created a new and beneficial social and economic situation for their women. In this sense, it seems that women in these so-called post-feminist societies are having the best of both worlds nowadays— taking jobs when they like, on an equal basis with men, but retreating to the sanctuary of the home to revert to their other role as homemaker and mother whenever they please. However, as what I have argued previously, when compared with men, women are still placed in a disadvantageous position in the workplace.

This chapter focuses on young women's experiences of education, employment and their future marriage in Chinese context. By drawing upon the qualitative data in the research, I aim to provide an insight into the following questions: What expectations do the young Chinese women have for their career? And how do they envisage their marriage and plan for their motherhood in the future? Throughout this chapter, the terms 'work' and 'employment' are used interchangeably for stylistic variation and simplicity. Strictly speaking, work covers a broader range of activities than employment. In Table 5.1, I have summarised my interviewees' perceptions on work as well as their expectations and concerns of their future marriage. In general, data collected from interviews and group discussions around the topic of 'present-day urban young women in employment' has revealed both progress and problems regarding to the gender equality issue during China's societal transformation. Two themes have emerged from data, which are 'different understandings of "good jobs" and "ideal jobs" for women' and 'different strategies to gain opportunities for career development.'

© Foreign Language Teaching and Research Publishing Co., Ltd
and Springer Science+Business Media Singapore 2016
J. Zheng, *New Feminism in China*, DOI 10.1007/978-981-10-0777-4_5

Table **5.1** Summary of interviewees' perceptions on work and marriage

Name	Career expectation	Criteria of career choice	Short-term plan	Pre-marriage sex	Ideal age for marriage	Self-evaluation
Qian	Intellectual	Flexible, less competitive	Job hunting	Disagree	25–26	Traditional, conservative
Ivy	Manager	Challenging and well-paid	Studying abroad	Agree	Not sure	Open
Rain	Not sure	Self-improving	Job hunting	Disagree	27	Principled
Lily	Media person	Competitive	Studying abroad	Depends on the situation	Not sure	Modern, open and principled
Jane	Free-lancer	Self-improving and flexible	Postgraduate studies	Depends on the situation	26–27	Open but principled
Helen	School teacher	Reputed and respectable	Doctorate studies	Disagree	26–28	Traditional
Fay	Engineer	Well-paid	Work	Disagree	Not sure	Traditional, conservative
Julie	Entrepreneur	Interesting and well-paid	Studying abroad	Depends on the situation	Before 30	Modern
Ning	Office lady	Stable and self-improving	Staff training programme	Disagree	28–30	Traditional, conservative
Sue	Free-lancer	Interesting and flexible	Getting married	Agree	25	Modern, open
Irene	White-collar	Interesting and self-improving	Postgraduate studies	Disagree	28	Traditional
Momo	Government official	Powerful	Studying abroad	Depends on the situation	26	Modern
Beth	Entrepreneur	Challenging	Work	Depends on the situation	Before 30	Modern
Emily	Manager or director	Interesting and well-paid	Studying abroad	Depends on the situation	30	Modern

Cowgirl in Work

Firstly, the majority of young women who participated in this research project have confirmed that young Chinese women nowadays are enjoying more freedom in choosing their career than their mothers' generation. For example, Ivy and Emily have shown a great degree of confidence and determination in their career development, believing that women could take any career as they want and could be as successful as men as long as they work hard.

> I want to be a manager in Fortune 500 companies in the future. I believe that as long as I work hard I can succeed. I don't think there is any difference between women and men in the employment. Women can be as successful as men in any career if they want to. (Ivy, 20100510)

> I like interesting jobs. If it's well-paid, it'll be the best. I once had a summer internship in my dad's company and I learn a lot from this working experience. My line manager is a woman. She is efficient, capable and very clever. I hope that I could be like her in the future. (Emily, 20100510)

While both Ivy and Emily seem to argue that they see interesting and well-paid jobs as an ideal job, some young Chinese women express that they hold traditional views on women in the labour market, arguing that some external factors, such as social attitudes of gender roles, may influence their decision to choose a 'female's job' rather than an interesting but challenging job.

> I prefer to work in the university because I want to work in a relatively less stressful environment and have more freedom to manage my own time. I think teaching is more flexible and less competitive. That's my concern. (Qian, 20100512)

> Both of my parents want me to be a teacher in the future since it's reputed and respectable. My mom said public service unit is the second choice. For me, it's good to have two holidays each year and also I can have more flexible time for the family. But if I want to work in the university, I have to work hard to get a doctorate. (Helen, 20100512)

Clearly, for both Qian and Helen, they associate 'a good job' with some traditionally feminised job such as teaching. Their comments have not only revealed the continuity of gender role stereotypes in traditional Chinese values but also have reflected the unique characteristics of women's employment in contemporary China. For example, Helen mentions 'public service unit' or 'work unit' (*danwei*)—a common form of employment in the People's Republic of China prior to Deng Xiaoping's economic reform in the late 1970s—to define her ideal job. For Helen, an 'ideal job' equals to a stable job. Previously, 'work unit' acts as the main Chinese employment form, serving as the first step in a multi-tiered hierarchy linking each individual employer with the central Communist Party infrastructure. It is not only a production unit but also an all-encompassing welfare institution that covers employees' health care, accident insurance and maternity leave. In these ways, the 'work unit' system has been associated with job security and good benefits in the context of China (see Li and Wang 1996).

For Chinese women who were born and grew up in the 1950s and 1960s, Chinese women's employment policy was framed within the Engelsian concept of women's liberation and gender equality. Employment was taken for granted as an important component of a woman's life, even though far from all women experienced a sense of liberation by participating in social production. As shown in the conversation, 'teaching' and 'public service unit' are always associated with 'more stable' and 'well reputed,' and therefore Helen's mother expects Helen to get this type of secured job in her future.

A similar point of getting a stable job as the 'ideal job' for women has also been emphasised by other participants. In two individual interviews, Rain and Jane express their uncertainty of women's career development in a rapidly capitalising economy in general and the difficulties for current Chinese female university students in particular.

> I'm not sure what exactly I'm going to do. My major is Education. It used to be a good major, but now lots of graduates in Educational Studies cannot get a job. So, I may try some business and management related jobs to enrich my experience. It becomes harder and harder nowadays for women in social science subjects to get an ideal job. (Rain, 20100425)

> I feel I have no specific career goal. Maybe a free-lancer suits me. The most important thing is that you should always learn something. People have their own "ideal job." A well-paid job which is seen ideal for A may be not ideal for B because it is too busy and stressed; meanwhile, an 'ideal job' with flexibility and freedom for B may seem to be low-paid for A. So you can't really say whether a certain job is ideal or not unless you have experienced it. We have too less opportunity to have working experience as a student. (Jane, 20100420)

As these accounts suggested, looking for 'an ideal job' has also undergone rapid change during China's economic development and social transformation. In the socialist, planned economy, the state used to guarantee urban employment while prohibit labour influx from rural areas. Thus, local governments would assign each resident a permanent job either in a state or collectively owned enterprise. Once assigned, mobility was largely restricted to promotion within the 'work unit.' At that time, some large state-run work units may offer housing and childcare as well. Although employee benefits may vary in different industries, within the same work unit, men and women, old and young, generally can receive comparable benefits (Li and Wang 1996). Therefore, 'state-run work unit,' such as government offices, non-profit organisations, and educational institutions, has been seen as ideal for women owing to its lifetime security.

Yet, since the economic reform in the late 1970s, marketisation has disturbed previous job assignments, promotion and allocation of resources such as housing provision by the workplace, and therefore has resulted in a disturbance among young Chinese people looking for jobs, particularly among young women, as they feel lost in the contemporary labour market. As some of my participants further pointed out, the phenomenon of gender inequality still widely exist in the labour market, especially when women are seeking promotion and further career development.

> I think the real issue [of gender equality] is whether Chinese women can get top positions or not in the workplace. It's hard for women to get a managerial position in China because the whole society believes that males are more capable than females to make crucial decisions. But as a woman, I think that we should always fight for our equal rights for career promotion. (Lily, 20100515)

My current line manager is a woman. She is always the last person to leave her office. I can imagine that if I want to get promotion, I have to work as hard as she does. (Ning, 20100427)

In these conversations, it is clear that Lily and Ning have their own career ambition. On the one hand, they realise that women always have more obstacles than men to overcome in order to achieve success in employment; on the other hand, they indicate a strong determination to make feminist efforts for their equal rights.

Qian and Fay also talk about their concerns about gender equality in the labour market, but they put an emphasis on the impact of Chinese 'household registration system' (*hukou*) on the gender-related issue.

I don't want to settle down in Shanghai because the competition here is too fierce and unfair. For example, people who are originally registered as a Shanghai household can always have privilege when they apply for jobs. When I went for job interviews after my undergraduate studies, some employers asked me whether I can solve the *hukou* problem myself … In the job market, male Shanghaineses are better than female Shanghaineses. Female non-Shanghaineses are always ranked the last. It's not fair. (Qian, 20100512)

I did experience inequality in the labour market. Last year, my job applications were refused simply because I'm not from Shanghai. The interviewers said they preferred to recruit local people because they were more stable. Maybe they think that I'm just looking for some work experience and won't stay in their company permanently – not "safe" in their words (Fay, 20100515)

Although Qian and Fay have experienced inequality in the employment in different ways, both of them believe that the existence of the *hukou* system in China is the root of such inequality. In fact, during the period of China's social transformation, some structural changes indeed have exerted a negative impact on the gender equality issue in China. As they mentioned, *hukou*, a major source of sociopolitical control and governance in the People's Republic of China, has produced some social tensions and conflicts, such as limiting women's equal opportunity in the labour market nowadays.

By limiting immigrants' working opportunities in urban areas, the *hukou* system not only results in the rural-urban dichotomy (such as the sharp difference between the 1st-tiered city and the 2nd-tiered city) but also enlarges regional gaps even within the same-tiered cities and creates an environment in which rapid but highly uneven economic growth has occurred under the aegis of a strong authoritarian state. Wang (2005) provides an exclusive analysis of China's *hukou* system, arguing that *hukou* has played a key role in directing and allocating resources internally and shaping the socioeconomic landscape since the early days of the PRC. Because it generates countless examples of social injustice and grievances and has become the target of criticisms and reform efforts over the years, reshaping the *hukou* system is essential in order to meet the voracious demand for labour and population mobility in the thriving market economy. Recently, decrees from Beijing and spontaneous actions and reactions by local governments have combined with the protests and pressures from victims of the system to lead to many adaptations and some relaxation of the system. Many young university students, especially female students become campus activists in order to fight for their equality rights in the labour market and begin to develop their individual coping strategies.

Coping Strategies

During my fieldwork, my participants talk about their experience of a variety of part-time jobs, voluntary work and formal employment. In order to fight for their equal rights in the workplace, they adopt different strategies, ranging from pursuing an advanced degree, seeking overseas education, and continuously modifying their career goals and plans, to coming up with creative and impressive ideas to deal with their bosses.

For example, in a group discussion, Julie, Beth and Emily discussed their concerns about gender equality in the labour market, arguing that women should explore their own ways to achieve success.

Interviewer: What do you think is the most important factor for women to succeed in the work place?

Julie (20100510): For me, career development is very important for women's success in the long turn. I may not be picky about my first salary. But, if I can't feel any hope for promotion or further development, I will definitely change a new one.

Beth: Yes, women are always in a disadvantageous position in the labour market compared to men. We have to explore our own way to survive and to succeed. After set up a clear goal, I would make progress step by step. A wrong decision will delay my progress.

Emily: But you have to experience different types of jobs in order to find the most suitable job for you. I don't want to give myself a very specific idea that I must do this or I must do that. I want to get different experiences and improve myself through experience. Only by experience can I understand myself better.

Clearly, these three young women hold different opinions on women's career choice and success. While the right career choice is seen as the most important factor for Beth to make progress and to achieve success in the workplace, Julie and Emily value the process of achieving success in their career more. Their conversation, once again, indicates the impact of changing employment patterns on gender-related understandings of a 'good job' amongst female students in contemporary China. For example, during recent years, the Chinese employment pattern has experienced the change from job assignment by government to a current job market in which different ownership forms coexist and compete. While the change of employment patterns brings freedom of mobility and opportunities, it also results in further discrimination and insecurity. As Beth further argued:

Since most women retire earlier than men, it is better for women to apply for a job which can provide employers with opportunities for development and progress. But the reality is that many jobs prefer male employees, and in terms of development opportunities, if there are any, men are always given priority. Girls are worrying whether they can find their ideal job after they graduate or not even though their scores in the university are the highest. (Beth, 20100510)

Indeed, the structural changes of China's industry and economic development have resulted in a new gender-related inequality in the Chinese labour market. According to Li and Wang (1996), throughout the 1980s, China's high growth economy created millions of jobs annually, with women as well as men sharing in expanded and diversified employment opportunities. Yet, for most jobs, women retire at an earlier age compared to men, being 55 years of age for women for cadres and professionals, comparing to 60 for men; 50 for women workers, comparing to 55 for men workers. In this context, there are disproportionate numbers of elder women in the state sectors who have found themselves in the category of 'surplus labour,' being among those laid off or forced to retire prior to the legal retirement age. For those who are young and are seeking employment, they have to further equip themselves with knowledge and skills in order to succeed in the increasingly competitive labour market.

In another individual interview, Qian complained about the difficulty of Chinese women graduates getting a good job, arguing that the purpose for her to study for a Master degree was to stay in the university longer and to avoid unemployment.

My major is Chinese literature. I don't know what kind of job I could do with a Bachelor Degree of Arts. I sent out more than a hundred CVs but they all had no reply. Although my scores at university are quite high, it's not useful. Companies want to have student from Economics and Finance majors or students with working experience, no matter how bad their academic scores are in reality. Also, males are highly preferred... This is quite unfair. That's why I decide to continue my postgraduate study. It's better to stay in the university than to be unemployed. (Qian, 20100512)

Clearly, for Qian, her superb academic record almost counts for naught. The painful experience strengthens her determination to fight for gender equality in employment. In fact, when facing persistent and pervasive gender discrimination in employment, many young Chinese women have begun to adopt individual strategy, such as acquiring higher degrees or studying abroad in order to compete with men. This might contribute to a major reason for the rapid increase in women's enrolment in postgraduate programmes in China in recent years (see Liu and Wang 2009).

I will go to Hong Kong for my postgraduate studies because I think the quality of education there will be better. Also, a Master degree from Hong Kong might be more valuable than the degree from the Mainland. Many people want to work in media, so the competition is very fierce. I have to put some shining point on my CV in order to get a good job. (Lily, 20100515)

Similarly, in an interview carried out at Julie's home, Julie told me about their plan for going abroad for an education in order to be more competitive in the labour market in the future.

Interviewer: Will your parents worry about you if you study abroad?
Julie (20100510): It's all right. I will talk to my family over skype when I go
abroad. It's so convenient now. Lots of my classmates are also preparing for
studying abroad. Almost all my parents' friends' children are studying abroad. It's
very common now. I feel that if I don't have an overseas degree, I won't get a job in
the future... But I haven't decided which British university is the best choice for my
major so that I could get a good job after graduation.

In the accounts presented above, almost all young Chinese women mention that
a good qualification might help them in their future employment. Although how
successful this strategy will be remains to be seen, the ramifications of a large
proportion of female higher degree and international degree holders in Chinese
society will be significant. At least, the huge gap between young women graduates'
expectations and social reality can be expected to give rise to growing feminist
activism by encouraging this cohort of Chinese women to pose serious challenges
to gender boundaries in the Chinese labour market in the 21st century.

Apart from obtaining an advanced degree and studying abroad, some young
women also try something creative and impressive in order to stand out in job
recruitment.

> Dress well and look smart in job interviews. And try to be interesting and creative. I always
> tell myself that 'you are working in a foreign-invested company. It's not Chinese gov-
> ernment sectors. Thus, you should be unique and special.'... My mum said she will support
> me financially regarding all my investment in job hunting. (Sue, 20100518)

> Leaving your interviewers a good first-impression is very important, particularly when you
> apply for jobs in foreign-invested companies. Before attending a job interview, I bought an
> expensive professional suit. I think if two candidates have the same qualifications men
> probably will have more credits. But if the competition is between two female candidates,
> the more beautiful and good-looking one will definitely have more chances to get that job.
> That's human nature. (Helen, 20100512)

> Now, I begin to invest more on myself to prepare for my career. I want to be a "White
> Collar Beauty" in the future. I think I need to loose more weight. How I wish I could be
> taller! ... For women, you can't ignore the function of your appearance in your career
> success. So, do all your best to look perfect. (Irene, 20100518)

These accounts reflect the dynamics of changing gendered practice in women's
employment in China. Quite interestingly, as early as the 1980s, Chinese feminist
scholars began to criticise Maoist gendered employment policies for impeding
economic growth. However, at that time, Chinese feminist critiques simply pointed
to urban women's high employment rate as a relic of Maoist egalitarianism and a
source of inefficiency in enterprises rather than critiquing the skewed gender
structure in the workplace. At that time, newspapers openly advocated 'women
return home' as urban reform since China confronted severe unemployment
problems compounded by more than ten million 'returned youth' from the countryside (see Wang 2003). Therefore, in order to survive in the workplace, Chinese
women began to develop their coping strategies. A serious challenge to equal
employment had loomed in public discourse.

Yet, two decades of economic reform involving privatisation, commodification and expansion of the service sector have also created many new occupations with a distinctive gender label, which points Chinese feminist critique to a new angle. For example, the new job market is even more highly gendered than its predecessor, with women channelled primarily to the service sector and secretarial jobs while men are recruited for technical and managerial positions. In this context, a group of young women has to achieve upward mobility by drawing on human capital, specifically their youth and beauty. As shown in the three interviews scripts presented above, 'dressing well,' 'buying expensive suit for interview' and 'loosing weight' have been used by contemporary young Chinese women as individual strategies in order to succeed in the increasingly competitive labour market.

Since the 1990s the 'iron rice bow' of job security in urban China has been replaced by the 'rice bowl of youth' (*qingchun fan*) and 'White Collar Beauty' (*bailing liren*). Everywhere attractive young women have been sought to represent the shining image of 'modernity.' Office ladies who dress fashionably have become role models for young women looking for jobs. Booming service, commercial and entertainment industries post numerous age-, gender- and, often, height-specific advertisements seeking women under the age of 25 and above 165 cm in height. Stylish, elegant, or sexy, young 'Misses' (*xiaojie*) are displayed in re-modelled or newly built 'modern' hotels, restaurants, department stores, travel services, night clubs and dance halls. As older state industries lay off women workers over 35, these 'modern' young Misses, many with no particular education or technical skills, are entering the rising industries (mostly in the private sector, some with foreign investment) where their youth and beauty provide a ticket to incomes several times higher than those of their older sisters. It is also such 'shining' images of 'modern' 'White Collar Beauty' that exerts influence on some current urban university students' understandings of women's success in the labour market.

However, another common practice for contemporary young Chinese women, especially those who are competitive and good-looking ones in the fast lane, is that they often 'fire' their bosses in search of rapid upward mobility with their time-limited human capital rather than clinging to a stable job. Since Ning is one of those who have formally experienced employment, I asked her to share more with me about her experience of job hunting and her strategies of getting equal rights in the labour market.

> I changed my previous job because I felt bored and disappointed in my pervious Korean company. I repeated the similar things every day but I can't see any hope for further progress. My Korean boss is bad-tempered and impatient. Many things have put me on the edge. So, eventually I told myself that I have to have a change... I came to Shanghai for a new start. I meet new friends and have new colleagues. This company is nicer than the previous one. I'm taking a staff-training course at the moment. My life is so full now. (Ning, 20100427)

In other interviews, I asked my participants whether they would 'fire' their boss if they did not feel happy about their work. Some give me their confirmed answers by arguing that they cherish opportunities for further development rather than a 'basically-OK' status quo.

I think I will. If you are not enjoying a job, definitely you can't do it well. In that case, I think things will become worse and worse. If so, then why not give yourself a change? (Ivy, 20100510)

If I could get a better job which gives me more room to develop, I would say 'goodbye' to my old boss. For me, a promising future is better than a "basically-OK" status quo. (Fay, 20100515)

From these conversations, we can see that Ning, Ivy and Fay, representing a new cohort of well-educated and strong-willed 'single-child girls' (see Chap. 6), has openly challenged the gender- and race-related inequality in the labour market. Voices from other young Chinese women also suggest that the adoption of the 'one child' policy in the late 1970s also contribute to the major reason for the rise of confident, assertive and competitive young women in contemporary Chinese society.

Clearly, almost all my participants during my fieldwork express their worries about their employability and finance in the future to different extent, but this has no overall effect on their current attainments since the strategies they use to ameliorate worry align with sound educational determination and practice. My findings also show that young women in Chinese context might devise some interesting strategies to cope with worry and stress, such as seeking support from their parental families and choosing an overseas education to avoid the highly competitive local labour market. This might contribute to a unique characteristic of young Chinese women in higher education, compared with their counterparts in many First-World contexts, where women students mainly apply self-helping strategies, such as curtailing their student life and building supportive friendship groups, to consolidate their attainment (see for example Kettley et al. 2008).

In my analysis, I give my emphasis on the uniqueness of current urban employment in contemporary China in order to depict a fuller socio-cultural context for understanding women and employment. For example, during China's rapid capitalisation and marketisation in recent decades, new employment patterns have broad social ramifications entailing realignment of social classes and gender position, which particularly affects urban dwellers' relationships to the state and reshapes their identities.

Chinese feminist pioneer Wang (2003: 160) described the on-going change of employment patterns as 'a gendered process in which urban men and women of diverse social positions engage in contestation at multiple levels.' Such a 'gendered process' can still be interpreted here. From the discourses identified above, we can see that the younger generation of Chinese women do want paid employment, among whom many also begin to long for interesting jobs and well-paid work just as much as their male colleagues. They have the same work orientations, work commitment and ambitions as their male colleagues. Yet, in reality, young women are still confronted with discrimination, overtly and covertly, in the labour market in contemporary China society. While some indicate a strong fighting spirit towards inequality, some show their helplessness and disappointment. For those who are deeply disappointed by the unpleasant experience they have had in job hunting, they begin to pin their hope on getting a good husband as their second career choice (see Fig. 5.1).

Fig. 5.1 A Chinese cartoon: work/marriage dilemma confronted by Chinese female graduates. *Source* Jiaran Zheng

Eve's Passion Fruit

While more and more young women in contemporary China are persistent in their pursuit of independence through education and employment, there has also been increasing depression among them regarding their private life since they are too busy at studies and work to have time for relationships under the rapid societal change. The tension between work and marriage has become increasingly intense particularly among those twenty-something university-educated urban Chinese women.

When it comes to the question of the long-term relationship, in general, all my participants express that they are open to talk about relationship with men. Some argue that it has become increasingly common for contemporary Chinese university students to live together before marriage. Yet, these young women also raise their concerns about sex-related problems such as whether or not university students should cohabitate before marriage and how to get a decent and responsible boyfriend in a relationship. For example, Lily's comments represent the general attitudes towards relationship in this research project.

> I think it's quite common for university students to have boyfriend or girlfriend, and to live together. Some of my previous roommates move out from the campus dormitory and live with their boyfriends. As long as both of the two feel happy about it, it's OK. No one really cares. But I think for girls, they should know how to protect themselves in a relationship. (Lily, 20100515)

In a group discussion, Beth and Emily reached an agreement that they would like to enjoy a relationship, but they also expressed their worries about a relationship, arguing that the decision of cohabitation before marriage should be made carefully.

Interviewer: What do you think cohabitation before marriage? Whether you would consider it in your relationship?

Beth (20100510): Nowadays, it has become more and more common for student lovers to live together before marriage. Even high-school kids have their boyfriend or girlfriend. This shows that the society is more tolerant. But I think it really depends on the situation. For me, relationship in campus will definitely be some sort of distraction. I don't want to be too involved in a relationship. Only if I meet a certain person who I'm pretty sure is THE one, I won't mind.

Emily: Yes, I agree with Beth. It depends on the situation. It's somewhat problematic in terms of the relationship. I think the decision of whether or not you and your boyfriend live together is quite serious.

Since Julie did not express her opinion too much in group discussion, I asked her privately later whether she would like to talk more. Julie explained:

In fact, I do have a boyfriend. But we do not live together. I still need more time to see whether he is the right person for me. I usually don't talk about my relationship openly because I don't want others to gossip. (Julie, 20100510)

Elsewhere, Qian and Ning are two other participants who show their strong disagreement with cohabitation before marriage.

My parents won't allow me to have a too close relationship with a boy. They always told me that a woman should respect herself and love herself well so that she could have a happy marriage in the future. I think they were right. Women should have some "bottom line" in the relationship. (Qian, 20100512)

There is no rush of living together. I think women should be "reserved" and realistic in a relationship. 28 to 30 is a good age for women to get married. You could date with different guys, but just not give him everything before you totally trust him. (Ning, 20100427)

Clearly, for these girls, virginity is seen as an important factor for women to have a happy marriage. Interestingly, during the fieldwork, many students use the adjectives 'conservative' and 'shy' to describe their personal feelings and understanding of relationship in the beginning of our discussion of this topic. This has shown that although sex is a biological function, the expression of sexuality is strongly influenced by psychological, sociological, cultural, and historical factors. For example, in China, sex education has long been neglected in the formal school education. According to a major national newspaper *China Daily* (June, 1998), it is not until 1988 that the first training course in sex education in China was arranged at the People's University in Beijing. After 1990, the situation had been improved, particularly in the more economically and culturally developed major cities. In 1992 about 1000 researchers in China began to work on sex-related matters (China Daily, June, 1992). According to *China Yearbook of Sociology 1979–1989* (1989: 176), in 1992 sex education was offered in just about one-quarter of the colleges in the country, starting much later than many developed countries.

As a consequence, Chinese women regard sexual relations as a 'duty' from which they receive little pleasure (see Liu et al. 1997). Many men and women grown up in the 1960s and 1970s in China were raised to regard sexual intercourse as a necessary, albeit perfunctory, activity. They show disinterest in sexual intercourse and de-emphasise the body as a site of sensual enjoyment. Therefore, for these young women's parents' generation of Chinese people, they are reluctant to talk about sex openly and are 'strict' with their daughters regarding relationships (see Chap. 6).

However, some young women hold a much more open attitude toward relationships. Sue tells me about her experience of having an American boyfriend, explaining that her cross-cultural relationship helps her understand the meaning of sex and woman's sexuality in a different way.

> When we first were together, I was quite shy. I don't feel quite confident about my body. But my boyfriend always praises my body and tells me that I should open myself. So now I feel that I become more and more active. I tell him my feelings every time; and he is very considerate…Because of him, I do think I open up my mind and get to know a new "myself." Although I don't know about our future, I'm still feeling very lucky to have him. That's the fate. (Sue, 20100518)

Apparently, Sue has learnt how to express her sexuality openly through her relationship with an American man. In other words, the cross-cultural communication helps Sue further discover herself and encourage her to reflect her self identity. According to Zizek (2005: 127), sexuality is the 'sign of a certain structural faultiness,' the effect of which is that it can never 'find satisfaction in itself, because it never attains it goal.' The inherent faultiness of any social structure refers to the basic impossibility that any system—whether political, economic, religious, or kinship oriented—can shape order in a fully consistent way. In the case of Sue, her expression of sexuality is built upon the cross-cultural communication. This particular experience exerts a positive effect upon the cultural impasses that define her female subjectivity and points in general to the failure of the existing gender pattern in an established social order of traditional Chinese value.

The 'Goddess' and 'Erotic Capital'

Since many young women mention that they are worried that cohabitation before marriage might be not good for a long-term relationship, I ask them their understandings and expectations of marriage. In fact, I found that the topic of 'how to marry well' is very popular among young university women students in the Chinese context. Many young women who participate in this research project argue that marriage to a woman is as important as career to a man. They believe that a good marriage could help women succeed in both their personal and professional life. Therefore, women should work hard in order to get a good husband as well. For example, in a group interview, Julie, Beth and Emily gave their definitions of a 'good husband' and a 'good marriage' respectively.

Interviewer: Do you think marriage is important for women? What do you think is the most important factor for women to get married well?

Julie (20100510): Definitely, having a good husband is just like getting a good job. Women need to work hard in order to find their true love. Both inner beauty and outer beauty can help a woman marry to a good husband.

Beth: Yes, marriage is important for women. If a man loves a woman more in a marriage, the woman is lucky. The most important thing is to get such a man who loves you more.

Emily: But good men are really rare nowadays. Most men are not single-minded. So, if you can find a man who is considerate, responsible and loyal, you must grab him as soon as possible. Usually beautiful girls have no problems at all to get a man, because all men are visual animals. Good-looking women are always popular in the labour market.

However, Momo holds a different opinion on the role that marriage plays in a woman's life.

> I think although marriage is very important, but it is NOT the only important thing in a woman's life. Friendship, career, there are many other things in life. The most important thing for women is to be independent. I don't think a woman can manage her marriage well if she takes her husband as the centre of her world. A woman needs to be beautiful always to attract men, but she doesn't need to work too hard to go after men. (Momo, 20100513)

Clearly, for Momo, a woman's value is not limited to the private domain. In fact, I was impressed by the fact that Momo has a clear idea and a strong determination that women should gain independence before marriage at her age. Yet, although she sees women's capability and self-reliance as a more important thing than getting married, she also values women's biological attraction in the marriage market, relating a good marriage to women's appearance.

By studying contemporary young women's everyday practice in relation to feminism, some feminists have theorised that young women are usually adopting their gendered strategies in order to negotiate with power dynamics within relationship. For example, quite recently, British sociologist and former social servant Hakim (2011) has presented a new theory of 'erotic capital' to explain contemporary young women's usage of an attractive appearance as their feminist strategy in both domestic and public spheres. She argues that erotic capital, as a fourth personal asset, is an important addition to economic, cultural and social capital, and is not only a major asset in the mating and marriage markets, but can also be important in labour markets, the media, politics, advertising, sports the arts, and in everyday social interaction. According to Hakim (2011), a central feature of patriarchy has been the construction of 'moral' ideologies that inhibit women from exploiting their erotic capital to achieve economic and social benefits. Therefore, for a long time, feminist theory has been unable to extricate itself from this patriarchal perspective and reinforces 'moral' prohibitions on women's sexual, social and economic activities and women's exploitation of their erotic capital (see Hakim 2011).

In another interview, Ivy also expressed her opinion on the relationship between 'how to marry well' and the usage of 'erotic capital' in the marriage market by young women in contemporary Chinese society.

There is nothing wrong with openness in relationship as long as you can be responsible for yourself. Similarly, nothing wrong with good appearance. But how to use it is meaningful. You see the dating show "If You Are the One"? Young and beautiful girls go up to the stage to search for their Mr. Right. But I'm seriously doubt whether they are able to find true love or not in this sort of entertainment show eventually. (Ivy, 20100510)

Ivy gives an example of the Chinese reality dating show 'If You Are the One' (*Fei Cheng Wu Rao*) to explain her position. Her comments suggest that the nation is still captivated by the courtship narrative that relates women's appearance to a successful marriage. The programme of 'If You Are the One' in China is equivalent to the reality dating show 'Take Me Out' in the UK. In each episode of 'If You Are the One,' there are 24 women from different educational backgrounds and occupations being presented with a parade of eligible bachelors. In the beginning, these women evaluate guys one-by-one and turn the spotlight on the man they want to marry. Then, the men are subjected to abrasive questioning and ego-deflating sound effects of rejection. After the women's questioning, each bachelor asks the women questions and makes the final decision who he would like to take from the stage. During one episode, when a 23-year-old beautiful Chinese girl Ma Nuo refused a young man who cannot afford an expensive car, she said 'I'd rather cry in a BMW than laugh on a bicycle.' This saying made Miss Ma famous overnight across the whole country. For viewers tune to this programme, they can see beautiful women, brutal rejections and plenty of money worshiping, as Ivy criticised in the conversation.

Moreover, this 'entertaining' show about women's martial aspirations is also fuelled by an implicit pathologisation of singlehood and is often offered in concert with more serious reminders of how time pressures are biologically enforced, specifically by declining fertility rates for women over the age of thirty. For example, almost all girls being selected by the show are in their early 20s. They are eager to get married before the year 25 because they believe that it will be harder for women in late 20s to get married. This mentality effectively shames Chinese women collectively into believing that if they do not marry and reproduce now it may soon be too late.

As the ratings of the show climbed, its critics became louder and more numerous, calling it a frightening window into the degradation of social values. Central government propaganda officials have also issued a directive calling the shows 'vulgar' and faulting them for promoting materialism, openly discussing sexual matters and hurting the credibility of the media by making up false stories (Yang 2010).

'Leftover Woman'

When discussing the issue of marriage, almost all my participants express their concerns about a successful long-term relationship and have agreed that it has been a hard choice between career and marriage for Chinese women nowadays. While some offer their strategies on how to get married to a decent man, others express their concerns about how to manage their relationships successfully in an increasingly fast-paced and modernised urban life. For example, some women argue that a campus couple may face a harsh reality of getting married after graduation.

> If students couples want to get married after graduation, they have to get a job in the same city. Getting a good job in Shanghai is really hard. If the two have disagreement or they cannot be together, the relationship will be in danger. (Irene, 20100518)

> I think if the campus couple cannot be together later, it'll be very sad. Love is romantic, but reality is cruel. I don't know when I could get married. (Rain, 20100425)

In another interview, Qian made a similar comment on the reality of women's marriage by emphasising on the parental pressure.

> I feel it has become harder and harder to be a woman, especially if you want to succeed in your job. My parents always said that I should focus on my studies and think of relationship after I graduate. So, I don't have a boyfriend in my undergraduate studies. But now, they said women should work well as well as marry well. They urge me to get a boyfriend and get married before 25. How it is possible?! I feel quite stressed when thinking of this. (Qian, 20100512)

However, unlike Irene, Rain and Qian, Fay holds a more critical viewpoint on women's marriage by insisting that she would get married after she enjoys some career success.

> I think financial independence is the most important thing for women. I'd like to get a satisfying job first and then get married. Only if I can earn my own living can I keep my dignity and negotiate with my husband in the relationship. Then, I can decide which kind of man I'd like to marry. After I gain some success in my career, I can choose to go home if I'm too tired. That's my choice. I think in a healthy relationship, men and women share their interests and help each other grow up. I'm quite independent and professional. I have my career goal and want to fly high. I don't want to be tied up with endless house work. (Fay, 20100515)

As a self-proclaimed 'independent and professional' woman, Fay expresses her feminist concerns about a relationship and wifehood. In fact, representations of wives in the public discourses of the Post-Mao period have depicted Chinese women with a very different range of subject positions. Against the collective-spirited, selfless, and androgynous images of the earlier discourse, the 1980s gave new meanings to the notion of wifehood (see Wang 2003). The wife could now be variously represented as the pretty and endlessly available companion to a busy husband, the financially comfortable domestic manager, the busy professional mother, or the diligent educator of a growing child. As Fay argued, women nowadays have the choice to withdraw from employment to identify entirely with domestic concerns, or to become the 'super women' (*nv qiangren*) who enjoy a shining career without having a family. Or, they could manage to combine mothering with success in public life. In this sense, the current growth of the market, private entrepreneurship, and increased consumer capacity indeed can find full expression in a new range of diverse possible identities for young women living in contemporary China.

In another interview, Helen conveyed a similar point of the importance of women's independency. Yet, she also argued that women need to learn the art in order to manage career and marriage well at the same time.

It's an ideal if a woman can both "work well" and "marry well." But it is manageable as long as she has learnt the art. For example, she has to sacrifice – or at least, comprise – a bit between work and marriage. In the relationship, a woman needs to be tender and soft as a good wife. In the workplace, she needs to be strong. Otherwise, a woman cannot be happy in the relationship. Nowadays, there are lots of "leftover women" in urban China. I think these women just cannot manage relationships well. (Helen, 20100512)

Clearly, for Helen, woman who is 'obedient' (*tinghua*) to her husband, considerate of his needs, and 'tender and soft' (*wenrou*) is a virtue even in the new era. Since she believes that men would like to choose a wife who would put her interests after their own, she expects to regulate her own behaviour—such as being 'tender and soft' in her marriage in the future—in order to avoid marital conflict. According to Evans (2002: 350), *hanxu* (reserved and shy) is one of the 'Chinese characteristics' for a female image. 'Soft and gentle' is even a symbol of national difference and dignity when refer to women. Such gender affirmation of masculine authority serves as the root of gender inequality in the Chinese context. Elsewhere, discussions being held in Chinese popular magazines, such as Women's Encyclopaedia,[1] further solicites readers' reviews on the attributes of the 'good wife,' which is fore-grounded on the image of the supportive, caring, and servicing wife.

Moreover, in this conversation, Helen mentioned the term "leftover women" when she expressed her concerns about marriage. As she noted, there are an increasing number of professional women in large Chinese cities nowadays who claim that they prefer to get married until they enjoy some career success, an independent income, and the pleasure of a single life. In so doing, they can accrue sufficient wealth and independence to acquire a stronger negotiating position in courtship and marriage. Focusing on the career development, these Chinese women are usually above the age of 25 and are still staying single. Therefore, the term 'leftover women' ('*Sheng Nv*') has been coined by Chinese media to refer to this growing battalion of Chinese women in their late 20s and 30s who are well-educated, well-paid, career-minded, and single, unlikely to get hitched anytime soon (CNN report 2010). Although '*Sheng Nv*' began to be recognised as a new expression in China in 2007, the phenomenon of 'leftover women' has already been common in more advanced countries such as Japan, Korea and the United States for a long time.

When I discuss the issue of Chinese 'leftover women' with my participants, Momo draws a diagram to further explain the reason of why more and more urban well-educated, well-paid and well-independent women have been left (see Fig. 5.2).

---

[1]Women's Encyclopaedia is a popular and national magazine published by Beijing Women and Children's Press to discuss Chinese women's issues (Women's Encyclopaedia vol. 2, 1991).

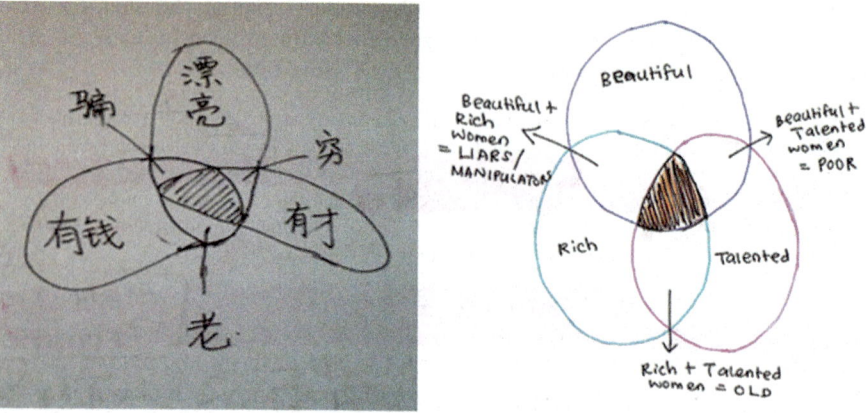

Fig. 5.2 Diagram of 'leftover women'. *Source* Courtesy of Momo

> Men marry women who are beautiful, or rich, or talented; but they avoid the overlaps. Beautiful and rich women are untrustworthy; talented and rich women are too old to bear children; as for women who combine looks and brains, they can be a bit too intimidating, and also, these women are poor. And for women who are all three, they are always too challenging and therefore unattainable. These are the *"Sheng Nv"*. (Momo, 20100513)

As Momo said, women who are both beautiful and intelligent have been seen as 'intimidating' and 'challenging' in contemporary Chinese society. In fact, as a well-performed student studying in this reputed university, Momo herself expresses her uncertainty about her marriage, arguing that she is worried of becoming such a 'leftover woman' in the future.

Indeed, among lonely city dwellers, Chinese *Sheng Nv* shoulder double pressures nowadays—one is from work and the other is from gender. In the work place, *Sheng Nv* are not treated differentially because they are women while in their personal life, they are often advised to remember differences between women and men. Although multitudes of *Sheng Nv* are financially independent, they are still not given the due respect as an individual and they are still expected to perform the inferior role when they are connected to men. In de Beauvoir's (2009: 739) words, '[e]ven the woman who has emancipated herself economically from man is still not in a moral, social or psychological situation identical to his. Her commitment to and focus on her profession depend on the context of her life as a whole.' Indeed, no matter how extraordinary a 'leftover woman' is in her capabilities or career, her socially imposed secondary position in relation to men is still not changed.

Julie also expressed her opinions on 'leftover women'.

Interviewer: How do you think of 'leftover women?' Will you feel worried if you are still single in your 30?

Julie (20100510): Maybe a little. But generally I think it's just a title which people put on women. Women need to have their own career and become independent. I won't be worried about my marriage that much. I know some girls who have never had boyfriends, but get married in a certain age. There is nothing to be worried about. I will get married before I reach 30, which means that I have several years to look for my Mr. Right.

For young Chinese women, it seems that they have to work extremely hard to acquire their individual agency and request a feminist identity by fighting against her own feelings of weakness for being a woman and external cultural surroundings as well. Their accounts have indicated that although most young Chinese women who participate in this research project see themselves as feminists to acquire independency and equality, they also display the same ambivalence when they try to understand themselves as women and search for their identity in a country of shifting values and dislocation. In fact, my research experience of the younger women coincides with my own identity-searching path, which suggests that, cosseted or protected and idealistic or with little preparation for the details of life while very young, they can suddenly be faced with finding their own way in the world which may not be so smooth, caring or forgiving. Young Chinese women are subscribing to both customary and modern attitudes, during which many of them begin to hover between the new and time-tested ways of relating and behaving. They are encouraged both to change and also to conform to older norms, and this has generated some confusion and anxiety. In this sense, although more and more young Chinese women in urban areas now enjoy wider options in employment and marriage, they also feel confused and anxious about their burgeoning lifestyle aspirations.

In sum, I have discussed contemporary young Chinese women's perceptions on love, marriage and sexual relationship with men in order to reveal the change and continuity of power and gender pattern in the domestic sphere. Conversations presented above have clearly indicated that the popular conception of marriage as the most vaunted and desirable institution in women's lives has changed little in contemporary Chinese society. Wealth and power are still the principal sources of status for men, while physical attractiveness is the principal source of status for women in marriage markets. Heterosexual marriage remains the sine qua non of most young Chinese women's lives—relentlessly mythologised as both the greatest achievement and the producer of the greatest happiness. In this sense, male dominance in physique, age, and financial status seems to be a continuing advantage in mate selection, because women want it that way. It is women, not men, who most eagerly seek male dominance in marriage. The new style marital relationship is influenced neither by class nor money, nor does it consist of simple physical attraction. Rather, it is based on unanimity of political consciousness and harmonious sympathy of ideas and emotions. Husband and wife are tender toward each other; they also honour each other and respect each other's rights and domestic position. The new-style martial relationship is also reflected in mutual responsibility to each other and to society. Since husband and wife have joined their lives together, they have the responsibility to help each other and cooperate in ideological matters, studies, and daily life. They should share responsibility for domestic affairs and childcare.

Conclusion: How to Have a Perfect Marriage?

With a particular focus on the experiences from fourteen Chinese girls, this chapter has shed light on how the emerging Chinese middle-class young women make the choice between work and marriage. In some sense, my communication with these young women can benefit interventions which aim at raising their self-consciousness and supporting the development of young feminism in Chinese context.

Through my previous analysis, it can be seen that some of the identified discourses point to a structurally patriarchal context, in which women in China can always meet with resistance and at times even hostility. Meanwhile, my analysis has also revealed that there are always competing discourses, which come along in parallel to resist restrictive constructions of gender and support equitable gender relations either in employment or in marriage.

In fact, becoming and being a feminist has increasingly been seen as a fractal model of identity construction. This process involves four intertwined components: knowing (consciousness), feeling (emotions), belonging (identity) and doing (action), each of which exists not only at the individual, but also at the collective level. In the context of China, a distinctive characteristic of feminism is that while it has proliferated and become increasingly prominent, its integration into the larger culture and society has paradoxically grown stronger too. This is not to say that feminism has become popular in China. The narratives of these young active female students clearly indicate that re-actions to feminism remain largely hostile and dismissive. Nevertheless, my analysis also reveals that despite the ongoing antagonism between feminist positions and mainstream patriarchal culture, the ongoing work of maintaining the boundaries between 'independent women' (*duli nvren*) and 'super women' (*nv qiangren*) reinforces the attachment of feminism to its cultural traditions.

As Hakim (2011) argued, all intelligent, educated women are feminists—but radicalised feminism rejects sex and sensuality. When I explore these young Chinese women's expectations and concerns about marriage during my fieldwork, I found that many of them are actively involved in their individual feminist strategies in order to fight for equality in Chinese context. There might be no difference between the way patriarchy and feminism regard women who make the most of themselves when they are not the most brilliantly intelligent beings in the world. Yet, evidence presented above also shows that women with more 'erotic capital' can always more easily gain temporary success either in their professional field or in the marriage market. In this sense, it seems that women with 'erotic capital' should be envied for having it as part of their armoury, rather than dismissed as mere bimbos. This might contribute to a unique characteristic of young Chinese women's self-realisation and emancipation in the 21st century.

As well-educated and well-trained women gain their own more independent middle-class status so also are they encouraged to repudiate their social inferiors and celebrate their own individualistic success. In contemporary urban China, the education system now looks favourably towards young women and rewards them for their effort. The result is that the younger generations of Chinese women come to be widely understood as potential bearers of educational qualifications, an active and aspirational subject of the education system. Since they have had access to the means of becoming successful and competitive, it seems that more and more of those urban university-educated Chinese girls no longer need the support of each other. For them, the landscape of self-improvement substitutes for the feminist values of solidarity and support and instead embraces and promotes female individualisation and condemnation of those who remain unable to help themselves. The next chapter focuses on the impact of changing family structures upon contemporary young Chinese women's identity construction in the post-reform era.

Chapter 6
A Pampered Daughter

[In China] an important difference since the 1980s is that the power balance has irreversibly shifted to the junior generation, and the next generation of young women is bound to be more self-confident and powerful in pursuing individual interests and initiating changes in family life. (Yan 2009: 151–152)

Parental investment did not just derive from the desire for a comfortable retirement. On the contrary, parents ... were willing to sacrifice their own lives for those of their children. Parents saw no contradiction between the cultural model of parental love and the cultural model of parental investment, which itself depended on the assumption that the love between parents and children would last all their lives. Spending money on a child was simultaneously an expression of unconditional love and an investment in parents' own future. (Fong 2004: 140)

In Chap. 2, I have discussed the power dynamics in relation to the changing position of young women in their parental families in modern societies. In the context of China, family reverence is one of the most basic and defining values of the Chinese people, and filial reverence has been seen as a necessary condition for developing any of the other human qualities of excellence. In Confucian tradition, human morality and the personal realisation which it inspires is grounded in the cultivation of family feelings.

By drawing interview data collected from the life stories of twelve young middle class Chinese women, this chapter attempts to find out young women's understanding of intergenerational power relations nowadays, and the external and social causes which might contribute to the shifting power balance in their private life. In my analysis, I carefully incorporate Western feminist critique of gender hierarchy in the domestic sphere on Chinese situation. For example, I take up the indigenous concept 'Chinese familism,' with particular reference to its characteristics such as the male-dominated 'patriarchal culture' and the value of 'ultimate concern' for the destiny (*guisu*) of the daughter to understand Chinese context. Second, I employ Western feminist theories that relate the development of individual autonomy and consciousness of selfhood to modernisation driven by commodities or market economy. Furthermore, I take a critical stance in understanding how market-driven

© Foreign Language Teaching and Research Publishing Co., Ltd
and Springer Science+Business Media Singapore 2016
J. Zheng, *New Feminism in China*, DOI 10.1007/978-981-10-0777-4_6

Table 6.1 Summary of interviewees' perceptions on parental family

Name	Family type	Decision maker	Family values	Parental expectations	Self-description	Family motto
Qian	Traditional, authoritative	Father	Harmony, filial piety	High expectation of educational success and female cultivation	Obedient, lovely	Always avoid conflict and offence
Ivy	Modern, individual	Self	Happiness	Emphasise individual development	Naughty, cheeky	Sharing is most important
Lily	Supportive	Father	Happiness, filial piety	Free environment, emphasise individual development	Independent, mature	Never ever touch their bottom line
Dan	Modern, equal individual	Mother	Happiness, trust, respect	High expectation of educational success and art cultivation	Trouble-maker, rebellious	We are equal, we are friends
Lucy	Supportive	Parents	Cooperation	Emphasise individual development, musical cultivation	Obedient but independent	Parents are always for your good
Helen	Supportive, traditional	Parents	Harmony, filial piety	High expectation of educational success	Reliable, mature	Filial piety means respect and obey
Pearl	Modern, equal individual	Daughters	Freedom, happiness	Emphasise individual development	Spoilt, cheeky, rebellious	I don't care too much
Wendy	Supportive	Parents	Harmony, filial piety	Emphasise individual development and happiness	Spoilt, cheeky	Doing housework is the best way to please parents
Zoe	Supportive	Self	Healthy, happiness	Emphasise happiness	Independent, mature	I like to make my own decision
Momo	Equal	Mother	Happiness, harmony	Emphasise individual development	Naughty	Family is always my backup
Beth	Supportive, modern	Mother	Cooperation	Emphasise individual development	Independent, mature	My mom is my idol
Emily	Traditional	Father	Responsibility	Emphasise happiness	Mature, helpful	Family is top one

autonomy weakens the value of 'ultimate concern' towards the female child and examine how this may generate the dissolution of traditional gender pattern in contemporary China. Table 6.1 provides a summary of these young Chinese women's parental family and their resistance and negotiation in families.

How to Become a 'Good' Daughter

Although the 1949 Communist Revolution and the post-Mao reforms have massively rearranged Chinese marriage, family and affective life, the patriarchal familial structure and related values in traditional China has been thoroughly entrenched in contemporary Chinese society. Gender hierarchy in the domestic sphere has been presented as locally variable, mediated by other sorts of ties, and at the same time extremely adaptable to the successive environments of revolution and reform in the context of China.

In my fieldwork, I asked my participants some questions such as 'Can you talk more about your family, such as your family relation, the closeness between you and your parents, and who plays a more authoritative role in family matters?' When I ask them to describe their family models, some women describe their families as 'traditional,' which is characterised by Confucian values such as the authority of father and the Chinese virtue of filial piety, others define their families as modern families with characteristics such as equal and democratic relationships which are built upon traditional Chinese values. For example, in individual interviews, Qian, Lily and Emily described their families as traditional Chinese families, and explained that their father made important decisions about major family affairs, playing a more authoritative role in the domestic life.

> My dad has the final say of all major family matters, including big family buying and decisions on important family issues. For example, when I chose my major and universities for my undergraduate studies, my dad helped me gather information and make decisions. He is the boss of the family. (Qian, 20100512)

> My family relation is quite close. But maybe different from others, I feel I'm more attached to my dad. Whenever I came across difficulties, I would first turn to my dad since he can always give me good suggestions. I think he is more authoritative and reliable. (Lily, 20100622)

> My family is quite traditional, in which both of my parents are strict with me. I was especially afraid of my dad when I was a kid because I thought he was always serious with me, either about my studies or my personal growth. Now I'm grown up, I see him as an authoritative advisor and a mentor, to whom I could turn for help when I need insightful and trustful ideas. (Emily, 20100510)

These conversations have reflected the deeply entrenched traditional Confucian values of the family and family structure in which the male plays a more authoritative role in the inter-generational relations. In a Confucian worldview, the family has ontologically defined one's existence, meaning there has been little or no space present for individuality.[1] According to Lucian Pye (1992: 199–200), '[f]rom early childhood Chinese are taught that individualism is evil…and that security can be found only by sticking to the assigned roles in the collective.' Therefore, the family is defined as an economic unit to represent the collective, having traditionally been made up of Chinese people who are related through sanguine ties, marriage and adoption. The involvement in shared common property, as well as shared consumption also delimits the membership of a family. This collective is held together by the patrilineal system, in which males are the thread connecting generations through time, and where a male offspring being absent such a line would be in jeopardy of dying off.

Therefore, ideally, the family under one roof consists of multiple generations with the oldest living male as the head, subsequent son with wives, and beyond that grandsons and perhaps their wives and children. In this structure family is held together lineally through time by the patriliny, and it is this structure that has been the primary contributing factor to the subjugation of women throughout China's long history (Pye 1992).

While Qian, Lily and Emily emphasise the authoritative role played by their father in their families, other young women argue that there has been a more democratic relationship in their families, in which family members lead a harmonious life. For example, in a group discussion, Dan and Lucy mentioned the emotional function played by their parental family and discussed how their parents influenced their attitudes towards family building.

Interviewer: Can you talk more about your parents? You can say anything about them, such as their marriage, their family philosophy, and how you feel about your relation with them?

Dan (20100512): For me, my family is like my emotional back-up, and I will only go home when I feel weak… Although my dad always blamed me for not doing things in the best way, I'd prefer his strictness because I know it's for my own good. Generally speaking, my family relationship is harmonious and supportive. My parents love each other and can always discuss about family issues.

Lucy: I feel the same. I have been away from home for three years, but I still feel quite attached to them. My parents knew each other through match-making and got married in their early thirties. Since they have me in their old ages, they love me quite much and always support me. Because of that, I always hope that I could have a family of my own in the future similar to my parents'.

Similarly, other young Chinese women also talk about their family by mentioning some traditional Chinese values required for the younger generation, such as filial piety

---

[1]The idea and concept of 'individualism' and 'individuality' had previously been devoid in China. At the turn of the century, modern concepts, such as 'subjectivity' and 'individuality,' as well as 'religion' were brought into China by Chinese intellectuals for the particular purpose of national formation and self-strengthening. 'Individualism' was translated from Japanese via Japan and was appropriated by intellectuals through what Liu (1995) has coined as translingual migration.

and obedience. For example, Qian, Helen and Emily further explained their definitions of a 'traditional' family and their understandings of being a daughter in the family.

> Quite often, I would listen to my parents rather than argue with them... For me, obedience means respect. I'm old enough to look after myself and to be a reliable daughter. (Qian, 20100512)

> When I said my dad has more authority, what I mean is that I have more belief in my dad and will always turn to him for advice. My mum is mainly in charge of daily matters. She will also turn to my dad for big decisions... (Helen, 20100526)

> When I was young, I got Lucky Money (*yasui qian*) on every Chinese Lunar New Year day. My parents allowed me to manage the money in my own way. Yet, I have to tell them how I used the money. If they thought it was used in an unreasonable way, they would help me "save" the money. So, in fact, every time when I got the money, I had to ask them what I should buy in order to really get my Lucky Money. (Emily, 20100510)

As presented above, these accounts actually have not only depicted the locally varied positions of being a daughter in contemporary Chinese families but also revealed the changing position of Chinese women in the domestic sphere over generations. In traditional China, the female child always plays a subordinate role in their private life. For example, more than two decades' ago, Wolf (1987: 1) observed that 'the birth of a daughter [in China] was a disappointment; the birth of a second daughter brought grief and perhaps death to the infant; the birth of a third daughter was a tragedy for which the mother was most assuredly blamed.' Thus, women's contributions to their original family are seen as being near to nothing in 'the way of enhancing their [family] state status, increasing their wealth, or providing for their care in old age.' Baker (1979: 24) portrays the crudeness of such a structure by stating that '[t]he family was a residential and economic unit composed of males....forced to import women as brides, and it disposed of females born to it by marrying them off to other families.' Jacka (1997) also states that traditional marriage practices means that women are temporal members of their natal family prior to marriage and after marriage they would become outsiders. Since fertility has always been seen as a woman's primary purpose in traditional Chinese families, daughters are required to listen to the male head in the family and obey their older generations. This directly ties a female child to the patriliny of which she is not a part, but to be expected to give birth to a son who could carry on the lineage. More or less, such a traditional gender hierarchy can still be seen from Qian's, Helen's and Emily's accounts of their family models and their inter-generational relationships respectively.

Unlike these young Chinese women, Lily expresses her understanding of family and her relationship with her parents from another perspective. She emphasises that it is the children's responsibility to look after their parents because filial piety has been seen as a virtue in the domestic sphere.

> My parents spend a lot of money and energy on me, such as paying for my clothes, entertainment, and education. I feel that I owe them quite a lot. When I grow up, I will work hard and earn lots of money to return to them. I would take them to travel and to eat out in expensive restaurants. I have the obligation to make my parents happy when they grow old. (Lily, 20100622)

As Lily suggested, it is the children's 'obligation' to make parents happy and it is such 'obligation' that enables Lily to construct her understandings of being a daughter in the domestic sphere. Within the philosophy of the Chinese world order, the concept of harmony has played a central role in guiding social behaviour. In Confucian thought, 'family' serves as a paradigm of harmony, and an individual's primary moral obligations to other social institutions such as the community and the sate. The principle that ties 'man' together is humaneness (*ren*), the fundamental virtue and highest attainment of moral cultivation in which love, respect, benevolence and loyalty comprise the essential emotions. The younger members in a family should show filial piety to the older in order to maintain a harmonious relation. As Confucius said in the *Shih Shu* or *Four Books* (17–18th century), '[f]ilial piety and fraternal love are the root of humaneness' and '[m]an is a social being; all actions must be in a form of interaction between man and man' (see The Analects 2010).

However, it should also be noted that such humane principles are paternalistic, lacking even a hint of the ideals of individual liberty. For example, a superior member (e.g. a parent) has the duty of showing benevolence and care for a subordinate member (e.g. a child). In return, the subordinate member has the duty of showing obedience.

In a group discussion, Dan and Lucy further conveyed their different viewpoints regarding to the meanings of 'being a good daughter'.

Interviewer: What do you think of being a 'good' daughter? How do you describe yourself in your family?

Dan (20100512): I'm always a trouble-maker. In this sense, I don't think I could call myself a 'good' daughter. You know, my mum wants me to stay in Beijing for my undergraduate studies so that she can look after me. But I want to escape from her control, so I came to Shanghai. She was really angry with me. She always said 'if you are more obedient, the family could be more harmonious'.

Lucy: Well, that doesn't mean that you are NOT good and you are BAD! It means that you have your own opinion. In this case, I would rather insist my decision. Everyone should have their independency—that's not simply 'good' or 'bad'.

Clearly, for Dan, 'good' means 'obedient'. In her family, obedience relates to harmony. The failure to maintain such a social norm would make troubles and therefore is seen as a threat to harmony. For Lucy, such a logic is apparently too simple-minded. In her own words, 'parents are always for your good'; and in the meantime, 'you listen to their advice and then you make your own decision and take responsibility for your choice'. Their difference does not mean who is right or who is wrong. Rather, it indicates a norm which regulates people's performance in the private sphere.

When probing the roots of such a social norm, it is not hard to find that the Confucian construction of women as subjects in society is defined in terms of their relations with men (being mother, sister and wife) and thus cast women as secondary within the collectives of the family and the community in the traditional mind. Within the dynamics of Confucian thinking, freedom entails neither legal rights nor psychological notions of self-expression and personal choice. The person is fundamentally related to a larger whole, thus social order and harmony requires individuals to cultivate themselves to take responsibility for others. In this way, social obedience is absolute; unity in the hierarchical structure is contingent on the maintenance of a relationship of power dominance and on whether the superior members could uphold their duty to be benevolent and caring. As Croll (2000) analysed, in the Confucian view, a man is born into society and cannot prosper alone: the individual depends on the harmony and strength of the group. Such kinship affection could only be achieved when 'men' love and serve first their family, then the country and then the world. In this sense, the interview scripts presented above have indicated that these contemporary young Chinese women's understandings of family are still—at least in many cases—influenced by traditional Confucian values.

Truly, in the context of China, it is traditional Confucianism and feudalism that reinforces the inferior status of women for thousands of years. The constant poverty the mass majority experienced, especially in rural areas, is a vicious cycle. On many occasions, the poorest families have to sell their land to rich landlords on unfair terms, and sometimes even their children and wives, to avoid starvation. Therefore, over generations, female children in Chinese families always face the same destiny of serving for the elders and males. When the status disparity between the rich and the poor becomes greater and greater as time goes by, a few rich landlords largely dominated the ownership of land and tenant peasants are kept in serfdom. As reviewed in the beginning chapters of this thesis, the feudal system eventually paves the way for the Communist revolution, in which Chinese women, especially Chinese daughters are provided with a new destiny.

Modern Chinese Family

Interviews with participants during my fieldwork also indicate that there has been a visible and significant decline of parental authority and power in the domestic sphere in contemporary Chinese society. The decline of parental power and authority is a result of a set of social changes occurring in larger social settings, such as the implementation of the new marriage law and other government policies, the sate-sponsored attack on patrilineal ideology and kinship organisation, and public ownership that disable the family as a unit of production (see Baker 1979). For example, Ivy, Zoe and Momo share a similar view regarding their family model and their self-reliance in the family.

> I don't like being told by others what I'm supposed to do. I think they should support me to grow up in my own way. My mum said that she is so lucky that she only has me. If there are two children in the family, we will definitely drive her crazy. (Ivy, 20100617)

I like to make my own decision. My parents will offer me their suggestions and support. It's good for my personal growth. Because I make my decision and pay for the result, my parents always trust me. (Zoe, 20100517)

Sometimes my mum said that I am self-centred. But I don't think this is a bad thing; at least I feel I'm mature enough to be responsible for my own life. (Momo, 20100522)

The centrality of these conversations is the contribution of individual agency to the shifting power balance across the generational line, especially the role played by young women in contemporary Chinese families after the adoption of the single-child policy in the late 1970s (see Fong 2004). In order to control population growth, China set its birth limits at two or three children for each family with the slogan as 'one is not too few, two is enough, and three is too many' before 1979 (White 2003: 185). By 1979, however, China's Post-Mao leaders had become so concerned about the likely impact of population growth on their new development plans that they took the extreme step of launching a one-child-per-couple policy—the most extensive, aggressive and effective attempt ever made to subject child-bearing to direct state control and regulation. As one of the most momentous policies introduced in the late 1970s, the single-child policy in China brings about far-reaching demographic and social implications, such as the centralised invest-ments to the single-child's education regardless of the child's sex (see Liu 2006) and the possibility of the growing power of the daughter in urban Chinese families.

Among my participants, Julie and her younger sister Pearl are exceptional cases of the single-child urban Chinese family. Therefore, I ask them about their parents' view on bringing up two girls in family.

Interviewer: How do you feel as a second child in family?
Pearl (20100513): My parents told me that they paid a lot for getting permission to have me. So, I think that might be a reason why they always pay careful attention to me.
Interviewer: Do you mean that your parents love you more than your sister?
Peal: I don't think so. They also pay a lot attention to my sister. She always gets what she wants. But I have to have her old clothes and toys before they agree to buy me new ones. My mom said it's lucky for her to have two girls rather than two boys. But how I wish I could be a boy. If that, I can have everything for myself.

In the case of Julie and Pearl, we can also see the dramatic and unique insti-tutional change in modern families in the context of China during the passing decades. As Pearl mentioned, their parents have paid for the permission of having a second child in the family. In fact, in the mid- and late-1980s, some provinces and regions in China relaxed the previous one-child policy, allowing couples to have two children, if properly spaced. Officially, these two-child provisions are usually limited to peasants living in poor, remote or mountainous areas, but the relaxation sometimes spills over into more prosperous areas. A tough new wave of enforce-ment in the 1990s tries to rein in those who have exceeded their official birth quotas and re-impose a strict one-son or two-child policy, but stiff enforcement provokes stiff resistance and mounting conflict. Calls for policy reform grew even more widespread in the late-1990s and early-2000s, but fears of a fertility rebound led policy-makers to reject any change to the official national policy. Still, the social context of the 2000s was a world away from that of the 1980s, as China came to face severely skewed sex ratios due to female abortion, a migrant population of more than one hundred million, frequent and widespread confrontations between villagers or workers and local officials, and a new generation coming of age that was itself the product of the one-child policy. What they did support was a modified approach to enforcement that relied more on education and positive incentives than heavy-handed, target-driven enforcement tactics (Fong 2004).

Nevertheless, because of the one-child policy, it is for the first time when Chinese young urban couples are released from the prospect that a secure old age depends on producing male children. Also, a growing proportion of women in modern urban families have to work full-time, only to pull a second shift of housework, cooking and child care at home. For example, many Chinese girls have discussed domestic duties and responsibilities in their parental families during the fieldwork, arguing that another reason for them to enjoy more freedom is that their parents are too busy to look after them when they are very young. The modernised family patterns push them to make decisions for themselves and to be independent at quite a young age.

> Since I'm very young, my dad usually have no time to accompany me and my mom—he is always travelling for work. Sometimes three of us get together once a week or biweekly. My mom always supports me. So, I get used to make big decisions for myself. I see no problem at all for working and living away from home. (Ivy, 20100617)

> My parents know that I'm quite independent and I can deal with my things well. Since I went to junior high school, I lived in the student accommodation. So, they usually don't ask too much about my personal life. As long as I could get myself married and live happily, I'm sure they won't mind whatever I do or wherever I live. (Helen, 20100526)

> They said they will support me for my postgraduate studies in Hong Kong because they expect me to get a well-paid job in Shanghai, or get a rich and nice husband, or both. But I know that I should get what I want by myself, no matter a good job or a big house, not totally relying on them. (Lily, 20100622)

As these accounts suggested, Ivy, Helen and Lily hold a strong belief that they can take charge of their own lives. In particular, Helen and Lily mention their wonders upon their marriage and future livings, arguing that their promising future biographies and marriage perspectiveness have gained themselves more attention and power in their parental families. Interestingly, in contemporary Chinese society, patriliny, patriarchy and patrilocal residence are both structuring and being struc-tured by gender and class. In old times in China, most unions have traditionally involved the transfer of a women to her husband's household, which, at least initially, has often been headed by her husband's father or a senior agnate. This means that a woman usually has to live up with her husband's parental family upon marriage. Although not all newly married couples have lived patrilocally, residence with the husband's family has remained both numerically and symbolically significant. This has been especially the case in rural areas (see Watson 1996). However, along with the rise of house prices in urban areas, such as Beijing, Shanghai and Hangzhou, young married couples cannot afford to buy a house for their marriage, and still need to live with their parents. Young women who were born in local areas usually have been seen as having more power in the marriage market, and this contributes to a new reason that raising a daughter becomes popular in contemporary Chinese families.

Apart from discussing the relationship between private space and self-independency in families, young Chinese women also talk about their role in their parental families regarding food and family chores in other interviews. For example, Qian and Momo talk about their ways to return their parents' love respectively.

> Sharing more housework is my way to be a filial daughter. Since I didn't go home very frequently these years, I think I really need to do something for my parents when I was at home. That's the daughter's responsibility. (Qian, 20100512)

> My mum always sends me lots of local delicacies from my hometown because she knows that I love to eat them. I know they always leave the best things to me. So the only thing I could do is to treat them well back when I grow up. (Momo, 20100522)

Clearly, for both Qian and Momo, they see filial piety as the virtue to be a family member, arguing that it is their responsibility to return love and care to their parents when they grow up. Like Qian and Momo, other young Chinese women also mention that they feel their filial love especially strongly when parental illness force them to stop taking their parents for granted. For example, in a group discussion, Beth and Emily explained the reasons why a girl had become more adorable in contemporary Chinese families.

Interviewer: Tell me more about your relationship with your parents?
Beth (20100510): I'm quite close to my parents. I will only want to go home when I feel really tired. I know that my parents will always be there to support me.
Emily: Yes, I assume that girls may get more emotional support from their parents.
Beth: Parents could also get more emotional support from girls. My mum always said daughters are more useful than sons in the future because daughters are more caring and considerate.

In all these conversations, we can see that almost all my participants express that they have certain power in their parental families. Yet, we can also see from the conversations that they are sometimes limited by certain rules and social values which make them to be unable to fully liberate themselves from their parental families (see Watson 2000 for a comparative discussion of contemporary young Chinese people's family life).

Truly, the understanding of dynamic gender relations for contemporary Chinese girls and young women in their domestic domain can not be achieved apart from an understanding of the traditional Chinese familism. When abstracting the social formation of Chinese society, the pioneer Chinese sociologist Fei (1983: 127) coins the term 'familist' to describe the essence of Chinese society and the mechanism of

Chinese people's interaction. According to Fei, China can be visualised as concentric circles (*tongxin yuan*) of family and social relationships spreading from a centre, which is oneself, to the surrounding society. In this structure, each family takes its position at the centre, and draws a ring around itself. The Chinese scholar Lu Feng describes such mechanism as 'a society with clan character' (*jiazu xing*), which is a resemblance of what Durkheim (1984: 127) called 'segmentary societies based upon clans'.

In the past decades, familism has remained as an important research anchor for scholars from other cultural backgrounds to understand the Chinese way of private life. Along with the implementation of the opening-up policy in the late 1970s, some of the values of the market economy were to a large extent at odds with those of Chinese familism. The rise of individual autonomy begins to counter the values of traditional familism in many ways. Especially in the economically more developed southern provinces in China, many family rituals and activities have been suppressed. However, although it seems that the influence of traditional Chinese familism has been largely weakened in the modern Chinese way of life, familism and its values system still greatly affects the ideology and behaviour of contemporary Chinese people in general and Chinese women in particular. This serves as an important illustration of the tension between tradition and modernity in Chinese context.

Expectations for Daughter's Academic Achievement

In China, strong gender-specific expectations of women and men are traditionally rooted in Confucianism. Gender stereotypes are largely manifested in such notions as 'Men are born superior to women,' 'A woman without talent is a virtuous one,' 'The role of a woman is virtuous wife and nice mother' and so on (see Croll 1995; Guo 2000; Lin 2000). Therefore, for Chinese parents, their 'ultimate concern' for a female child is to expect their daughter to have a perfect destiny—having a good marriage and leading a good life in the future. While these traditional notions and parental expectations still could be seen from narratives of my participants in this research project, these contemporary young Chinese women also express their resistance to parental expectations and begin to describe their biographies based on notions of personal responsibility and self-realisation. Themes emerged from my data in this research project which could be categorised as: parental expectations for daughter's academic achievement, parental expectations for daughter's feminine characteristics, and resistance and negotiation strategies in family.

'Do your parents have some expectations for you?' 'What are their expectations?' When I ask these questions to my participants, most of girls express that they their parents have great expectations for their academic achievements. Many of them describe higher education (and preparation for a career) as a natural progression for them. This is particularly unquestioned and normalised for those participants from upper-middle class and mass affluent families, whose parents hold strong expectations that their daughters should be academically successful.

> Before I entered the university, my parents expect that I can go to a good university. They were quite strict on my studies and always asked me to get high grades in exams, saying that I would have a difficult life in the future if I didn't study hard. Now, they are quite satisfied with me for getting into this university, saying that they don't need to push me to study any more. (Qian, 20100512)

> I think the only expectation of my parents for me is to be a good student and perform well in the school. I'm always wondering whether it's right or not to push children so hard on their scores. I don't know whether I would do the same to my child when I become a mom. (Helen, 20100526)

> Study, always study—that's the only thing my parents care about. Even in the beginning of my undergraduate studies, they have already begun to think about which university and which major I should do for my postgraduate studies. So, I just follow their plan. (Dan, 20100512)

As these young women mentioned, their parents hold great expectations for their success in the educational system. This reveals the traditional Chinese mentality of children's educational performance. In China, performing well in education has been seen as the only way to succeed. The Chinese cultural model of upward mobility through academic achievement has its roots in the imperial civil service exam system, which began under the Han Dynasty (202BC to AD220), became the main path to elite status under the Song Dynasty (960–1279), and lasted until 1905, when it was abolished as part of the Qing Dynasty's last-ditch efforts at reform. Though scholar-officials usually manage to pass their status to their children by providing them with education that is unavailable to the majority of the population, the civil service exam system still produces just enough cases of upward mobility to prevent class boundaries from completely solidifying, defuse tensions between different factions among the elite, and promote a cultural model that promises upward mobility to those who invest heavily in education (see Esherick and Rankin 1990).

To promote de-stratification, the Maoist government (1949–1976) tried to destroy this cultural model by persecuting intellectuals and severely limiting the socioeconomic rewards of academic achievement (Pepper 1996). The post-Mao government revived this cultural model, which fitted in well with the capitalist world system's emphasis on credentialed cultural capital. Yet, this revived cultural model is not identical to the one associated with the imperial civil service exam system, which has been salient primarily for the male members of a relatively small number of scholar-official, merchant, and landed gentry families who are already at or close to the top of their society. Rather, a combination of the pre-revolutionary valorisation of education, the employment of women, the socioeconomic democratisation of the Communist revolution, and the meritocratic ideologies of the capitalist world system produce a much more powerful and widespread cultural model that promise upward mobility for all youth, regardless of their gender or socioeconomic backgrounds.

Moreover, interviews with young women also contain narratives of how some have revised their educational and occupational aspirations under the influence of their parents. Quite interestingly, most commonly these represent changes from goals that fit with a more traditionally feminised role or do not require strong educational qualifications that they probably could not realise to masculinised or professional occupations. For example, in a group discussion, Beth and Emily discussed their 'mind shift' of women's employability.

Interviewer: What's your aspiration of going abroad for your studies, Emily?
Emily (20100510): To be quite frank, I'm not very looking forward to it. It's my dad who highly recommends me to go abroad. I know he is right, but life may be easier here. To have good life in the future or to have good life in old days, that's the question.
Interviewer: How about you Beth? What do you want to do in the future?
Beth: I want to have my own business in the future. So I will go to work to have more experience when I graduate. My mom is my idol. I hope that I could be as successful as her.

Similarly, in an individual interview, Wendy also expressed the parental expectation and influence on her academic achievement. Yet, Wendy also emphasises that her parents expect she could develop her future career in her own way.

Wendy (20100522): My parents expect me to have higher grades. But they seem to put more emphasis on my own interests. They said that they want me to follow my own way to grow up. They never made any decision for me.
Interviewer: Do you mean that they will support you in *anything* you decide to do?
Wendy: In some way, yes. They always said that they want me to be happy. For them, individual happiness is the most important thing. They encourage me to do what I really want to do and what I'm good at. As long as I can go step by step, I could have my own success. Their support makes me very motivated. I'm quite lucky since I know some of my friends' parents are very pushy. I don't like that.

These conversations have revealed the uniqueness of gender construction in the domestic sphere in Chinese context. As mentioned previously, in terms of the gender equality in the employment, women may face a 'glass ceiling' produced by their extra burden of domestic responsibility, by cultural models that favour men in elite professions, and by inequalities between elite husbands and their less elite, hypergamous wives. But it is also true that women also enjoy the protection of a 'glass floor' created by the hypergamous marriage system, by cultural models that favour women in the educational system, and by the rapidly expanding market for feminine jobs in the service and light industry sectors. Particularly in the Chinese context, young women enjoy the strong support from their parental family who not only hold great expectations for their academic achievements but also make valuable and meaningful input to help their daughters to gain educational success. In this way, this 'glass floor' has prevented these young women from sinking to the bottom of society, into poverty, crime, and unemployment.

Not only for expecting for a 'good-score' girl, Chinese parents also expect for a gentle and soft daughter. In this sense, it could be concluded that family plays an important part in young Chinese women's construction of femininity. For example, many of my participants told me that their parents believe a girl without a musical education will miss the cultivation that is essential for refined taste and manner, which are crucial components of female charm. As Dan and Lucy discussed in the group interview:

Dan (20100512): I used to have lots of classes, such as piano class, dancing class and painting class during weekends. My mum said they would be good for me in the future.
Lucy: I quit my violin class. That's too hard.
Interviewer: So you don't like to play violin?
Lucy: No, my mum pushed you to learn it. She always said that a girl should be artistic. It makes her look more tender and charming.
Dan: That's also what they told me. But luckily, I do have some interests in painting.

Their conversations have indicated that the gender-related social norm is actually deeply embedded in the Confucian definitions for proper female conduct according to the so-called 'three obedience and four virtues' (*sancong side*) (see Croll 1995; Guo 2000; Lin 2000). One of the four virtues is physical charm which requires that the female person must be clean of person and habits and adorn herself with a view to pleasing the opposite sex. According to these young Chinese women, their parents deem it important that girls should turn out 'feminine,' and it is their responsibility to rectify it if the daughter behaves in the 'wrong' way.

In fact, it is a view shared by most of my participants that they are required to be gentle and soft as a 'typical oriental female person (*dongfang nuxing*) should be,' as they put it.

My parents are very strict about my behaviour. Especially my mum, she always said girls should not be too wild because gentleness and softness are the main characteristics of oriental women. (Qian, 20100512)

My dad requires me to be obedient at home. I can understand him since the people of his generation are quite traditional and conservative. Although I agree with him that the image of a "typical oriental female person" looks desirable, I'd prefer to be myself. (Wendy, 20100522)

I learnt knotting, sewing and painting when I was quite young. Can you imagine that? My mum said these were a must for a girl. (Lucy, 20100512)

As these young Chinese commented, in the Chinese mentality, it is important that a girl should learn something about music, chess, calligraphy and painting (the four classical Chinese fine arts) because these cultivate artistic tastes and graceful demeanor in the girl. Thus, the emphasis of girls' parents is to beautify the child as well as to develop her person in a more all-round way rather than training the girl as a professional artist. Some interviewed young Chinese women also mention that they admire 'Oriental Talented Females' (*Cai Nu*) in Chinese history who are both talented in these fine arts and graceful in demeanor. As Lucy (20100512) followed, 'these classes are graceful and delicate.'

Zoe also mentions that her parents have exerted great impact on her personality and artistic cultivation. She relates the construction of her girlhood to the duty and responsibility of a girl's education in her family.

> I appreciate my mom's previous efforts on my extra-curriculum classes. Because I'm good at piano and guitar, I'm quite popular in the university. I think parents may seem to be too strict and harsh on their children because they have the duty and responsibility for the good of the child. (Zoe, 20100517)

As Zoe said, her parents work very hard to keep her practicing different things in her childhood and at the same time they insist that Zoe should learn the main school subjects well. For Zoe's parents, it seems that this might not be an easy task to achieve, as their daughter sometimes does not really want to do it. However, it is the patience and persistence of Zoe's parents that eventually helps her become a talented person.

In other interviews, some young Chinese women mentioned the impact of their parents' expectations on their personality and their self-awareness of being a young woman.

> One should not take for granted that a woman is supposed be good at art and language. For example, I was asked to learn electronic piano when I was in junior high school since my parents said women have musical talent. Yet, I prove to them that they are wrong. My piano class sucks. Then when I went to senior high school, I gave up the music because I was told that English and mathematics were more important. (Momo, 20100522)

> My parents play a very important role in my personality development. They give me not only a free environment but also their full support. So I have a good personality. I've always had plenty of friends, yet people are surprised by how much of a loner I can be. I think possibly the best way to develop one's personality is to learn how to enjoy being alone and to entertain myself as well. (Lily, 20100622)

Interestingly, in Momo's case, she briefly mentions the possibility of higher education and employment in relation to the cultivation of female characteristics but this is quickly passed over in favour of what she is 'supposed to do' under the influence of their parents. This clash between ambition and material conditions is reminiscent of the aspirations and fantasies expressed by some of the young women in contemporary Western contexts in the research of Walkerdine et al. (2001) which co-exists with contradictory behaviour or circumstances. Clearly, for both Momo and Lily, their parents hold high expectations for their personal success and kept changing their expectations according to the environment.

As these accounts suggested, some aspects of the cultural model of gender actually work to the advantage of young women in the context of China. When Chinese parents expect their daughters to be more feminine and invest in the education of such 'female character' cultivation (such as music, foreign languages and arts), girls who conform to this cultural model of gender are more studious and obedient than boys, and thus more successful in their personal development.

Resistance and Negotiation

'Will you argue with your parents and persuade them to change their decision?' When answering this question, while some young women express the idea that 'arguing with parents is seen as something impolite and disrespectful,' (Qian, 20100512), some argue that they would like negotiation with their parents when their opinions conflict.

Interviewer: Will your parents push you to do something which you don't like to do?

Helen (20100526): Sometimes yes, such as extra-curriculum classes. They will make my whole schedule full on every vacation. But I know that these classes are good for me in the future.

Interviewer: Will your parents push you to do something which you don't like to do?

Wendy (20100522): Yes. But I will always try to argue with them and persuade them to change their minds and listen to me. Last summer, my mum register a GRE course for me. I hate it. I successfully persuaded her to give up the language class by taking a voluntary teaching programme in a poor village in the North Jiangsu Province.

Clearly, both Helen and Wendy are not entirely satisfied with the fact that their parents make decision on their behalf and indicate their resistance to their parents' power. In other interviews, some young women also expressed their inclination to negotiate with their parents instead of passively listen and obey.

> I would say never ever touch upon the bottom line of your parents. Otherwise, you'll be in big trouble. I once cheated on my parents. It's not a nice story in the end. From then on, I never do it to them even though sometimes I have my reason. (Lily, 20100622)

> I don't care too much. This does not mean that I'm selfish. It means a clever strategy between resistance and negotiation. Sometimes negotiation is important when it's better to avoid face-to-face conflict. (Pearl, 20100513)

> Oh, my parents always pay attention to my own interests and ask my opinion before they make a decision. But I should be careful not to irritate them before I wanted to ask something from them. (Ivy, 20100617)

From these accounts, we can see that in spite of the significant difficulties and disadvantages when many of my participants make decision on their own, most of the interviews of my participants in this research also indicate a sense of optimism in negotiating with their parents. Such optimism allows these young Chinese women to imagine a better future in which things could be different. This is consistent with studies of young women's feminist activism in families in many Western contexts, in which Western feminists agree with the neoliberal discourse regarding the assertion that ambitious young women could be rewarded in a meritocratic system through continuingly improve themselves (see for example Baker 2010).

Yet, the interviews also reveal that the one-child generation of young Chinese women has been empowered by the expectation of their parents' dependence.

Particularly for girls, the one-child girls reciprocate their parents' love by showing their great self-confidence of in their future. This contributes to the uniqueness of young women's resistance to the gender hierarchy in the domestic sphere in the Chinese context. For example, in a group interview, Dan and Lucy talked about their experiences of negotiating with parents and self-reliance.

Interviewer: Will you try to argue with your parents and to persuade them to change their minds and listen to you?

Dan (20100512): Always. My mum also said that I'm rebellious. But I think it's something about defending your own position to get what you deserve.

Lucy: This is because you're too ambitious. You don't know that you have already got enough actually. Most times, I think my parents are right, and I don't argue. I just listen to their advice.

Dan: I don't think I'm ambitious. I just don't want to be limited by them. Sometimes I argue with them because I think I can do better and I deserve more.

Lucy: I didn't say being ambitious is a bad thing though...

In this conversation, the idea of wanting something 'enough' is invoked. For these young women, in order to gain success in a world assumed to become much freer of ascribed roles, it is strength of belief and being in control of one's destiny that determines what one can do and who one can be in the future. The unbounded possibility that is associated with new femininity and 'other girls' is assumed to be attainable—even for those women who were subjected to the limitation of external resources. In order to lay claim to this modern, sophisticated young womanhood, complaints must be replaced by ambition and determination.

In another group discussion, Emily and Beth also expressed their strong determination and self-independency when they discussed domestic negotiation with their parents.

Interviewer: How do you describe yourself in family?

Emily (20100513): A mature daughter. A helper who never makes trouble.

Beth: That's cool. I'm trying to be more mature. But sometimes I'm quite rebellious. I may get short-tempered. I know that's pretty bad.

In other individual interviews, some girls mentioned their different attitudes towards marriage when we discussed their experiences of resisting parental pressures.

The most possible thing for me to have an argument about my parents is marriage. Whenever I told them I may come back with a Hong Kong husband, they were always angry, saying that I'm not realistic. A Shanghai husband is what they want. But love is really unpredictable. Also, Hong Kong men might be more wealthy and considerate. On this point, I really can't compromise with them. (Lily, 20100622)

My parents were always annoying, urging me to get married as soon as I graduate. So, whenever they mentioned about my marriage again, I'd rather do some housework to please them in order to avoid their naggings. (Wendy, 20100522)

Around the topic of domestic negotiation with parents, these three participants mention an emerging phenomenon that contemporary urban Chinese women have begun to entertain the possibility of transnational upward mobility through marriage to foreign citizens. Clearly, for Lily, she no longer represent 'traditional' values of support and nurturance to bride-seeking Chinese men. Rather, she hold different attitudes from her parents regarding marriage and argue that overseas Chinese and foreign men may represent the possibility of modernity and wealth (see also Ong 1999).

As these accounts suggested, because most only daughters in contemporary urban Chinese families do not have siblings with whom to interact, contemporary young Chinese women have to learn to be children on their own. Parents and play groups can help, but ultimately children become conditioned to depend on themselves. Although this self-sufficiency can have its benefits, it can also mean that only children in contemporary Chinese families are inherently alone as their personalities develop.

Yet, we can also see that the further development of girl power in the domestic domain still has a major limitation in Chinese context. For example, in many cases, we can see that these young Chinese daughters' power mainly has only reflected their ability to impose individual will on their given choices of educational subjects or extra-curriculum activities. In other areas, such as mate-choice, marriage negotiation, and family division, these young women rarely challenge their parents, which are justified by their family's economic provision and 'good will for themselves.' In other words, although many of my participants here have presented an image which alters the traditional Chinese expectation of virtuous daughters, their exercise of girl power in their parental families has not brought about radical changes in gender equality.

Conclusion: Act Like a Girl

This chapter has presented data of parental expectations for young Chinese women and their negotiation with power in the domestic domain. Discussion of some attitudes regarding parental expectations for daughters' academic achievement, artistic cultivation and familial negotiation of private space, food, chores and social relations that these young Chinese women hold has provided evidence that this single-child generation of young women in Chinese context has been spoiled a lot by their parents. Although not all my participants have these attitudes, they are common enough to cause adults to cite them as distinguishing characteristics of the singleton generation. These attitudes do not seem unusual when I compare them with attitudes prevalent among the First World youth and children I have known or read about, but these contemporary young people seem to be horrifying to adults.

Clearly, data collected from the life stories of these young Chinese women has indicated the change of traditional Chinese family structures and values, and parental expectations for Chinese daughters. When I further excavate into the fundamental structure of Chinese society in order to understand meanings of my participants living in contemporary times, I found that the inter-generational relationship between these young Chinese women and their families is not only embedded in the binding elements of social norms and values, it is also inherent in a patriarchal structure that in many ways appear 'Chinese.' As what has been argued in the previous chapter, these norms and values have deeply influenced Chinese women's career choices and marriage expectations when they envisage their own future families even in contemporary times.

In fact, in the context of China, revolutions and reforms from the final years of the Qing dynasty—the last dynasty in Imperial China—to the present have been both corrosive and preservative of family arrangements, reconstituting gender relations in ways that can be distressingly predictable or intermittently surprising. Across the long twentieth century, key meanings of modernity have been worked out in public discussions—official, intellectual, pop-cultural and overlapping— about family, sexuality and gender difference.

Considering the long history of the patriarchal gender system in China, modern Chinese women have good reason to congratulate themselves for their steady rise up the ladder of prominence in society and for their growing individualism. Yet, it is also true that part of traditional Chinese wisdom, such as the appreciation of father's authority and familial harmony, including harmony between the sexes, still exerts a strong influence on contemporary Chinese society. The interview scripts presented above have clearly shown that many present-day young Chinese women continue to accept the idea that failure to maintain a harmonious relationship in their private lives would result in social disharmony and a breakdown of all the rules of propriety. In the meantime, it has been also delightedly noticed that many young Chinese women who come from the emerging Chinese middle-class and affluent families have begun to realise that the so-called harmony between men and women is superficial if it is based on the absolute dominance of the male and the complete subordination of the female. In this research project, for example, although young Chinese women have expressed their different understandings of parental family and their familial relations here, they have reached a consensus that in the private domain there cannot be real harmony until men and women can live with dignity and respect as equals.

If it is true that traditional Chinese family values have fundamentally oppressed especially Chinese women's and children's rights in the past and present, it is also true that families have been significantly responsible for much of the happiness enjoyed by human beings, and have served to mitigate much human sorrow and grief. In virtually every human culture, family values can be seen as necessary for living full social, moral and religious human lives. The importance of inter-generationality in people's relations and interactions can be appreciated anew. That is, a different way of defining oneself in relation to others can be envisaged; a more robust concept of social justice might replace the narrow definition currently in vogue; and even death and dying may be approached differently. Therefore, rather than drawing a sharp critique of the traditional Chinese values and family structure on the inferior position of the female child, my purpose here is to call for a more in-depth inquiry about the concept of the family in further research and to ask which aspects of the family should be rejected, which elements might be modified, and which should be strengthened. At the least, I hope to invoke a further question of what makes Chinese culture Chinese. More expansively perhaps, it may also invite thinking about the question of what makes human beings human.

Chapter 7
Her China Dreams

As a woman, I have no country. As a woman, I want no country. As a woman, my country is the whole world. (Woolf 1938)

The global citizen is someone who is aware of the ways in which her life is interconnected with those of others across the world. These interconnections can be a cause of poverty and injustice: the consumerist lifestyles of rich Western countries form part of a global pattern of poverty and debt. But the interconnections also give us an opportunity: to challenge these injustices, simply through looking again at the way we live. (Global Citizenship Project 2003: 6)

In Chap. 2, I have also outlined the relationship between contemporary young women's engagement with political activism and a re-conceptualisation of gendered citizen in the West. In so doing, I offer my critiques of traditional understandings of citizenship and inclusiveness.

By critically engaging with empirical data collected from the context of China during the period when China has hosted two grand international events—the 2008 Olympic Games in Beijing and the 2010 World Expo in Shanghai[1]—this chapter explores to what extent are these young Chinese women interested in politics and national/international events and their view of citizen in the 21st century? I present my participants' perceptions on the self in relation to the nation, and explain how Chinese feminist desires and national imaginations in broader terms are reflected upon these promising young Chinese women's subjectivities. My goal is to discover the process of women's political participation and citizenship awareness in the Chinese context. Table 7.1 summarises fourteen young Chinese women's interests in politics and their understandings of citizenship.

---

[1]The 2010 World Expo occurred in Shanghai from May 1 through October 31, 2010. This event is part of the same lineage as London's 1851 Crystal Palace Exhibition and the Columbian Universal Exposition of 1893 which helped put Chicago on the global map. It has also helped China be seen as a country that regularly holds grand spectacles.

© Foreign Language Teaching and Research Publishing Co., Ltd and Springer Science+Business Media Singapore 2016
J. Zheng, *New Feminism in China*, DOI 10.1007/978-981-10-0777-4_7

Table 7.1 Summary of interviewees' views on political issues and citizenship

Name	Interests in politics	National expectations	Describing 'feminist'	Describing 'good citizen'	Self-evaluation and self-expectation
Qian	CCP member	Stronger and wealthier	Economically independent, cool	Educated, legal, hard-working	Kindhearted; being successful
Ivy	Not interested	Less polluted, more polite and educated people	'Iron Lady', democratic and adventurous	City representative, polite, environmental friendly	Ambitious; having my own brands
Lily	Open, liberal	Open access to information	Independent, adventurous, female leader	Open-minded and international	Open, active, self-disciplined; being successful
Dan	Not interested, liberal	More foreigners coming to China	Controller, revolutionist	Legal, responsible	Diligent, kind; travelling a lot
Lucy	CCP member	More made-*by*-China	Female leader	Honest, patriotic	Honest; being kindhearted forever
Jane	Open, liberal	Chinese people travelling broadly	Self-responsible and harmonious	Patriotic, positive, brave	Kind, independent; leading a peaceful life
Helen	Open, liberal	Sustainable development	Economically independent	Sensible, legal, sympathetic	Easy-going, open; being strong
Fay	Open	Food safety, less polluted	Posh word for freedom and independence	Wide horizon, open-minded	Mature, independent; being successful
Wendy	Not interested, liberal	Holding more international events	Peaceful, humanistic	Educated, patriotic, honest, kindhearted	Independent; being strong
Sue	Not interested	Less polluted	Scary, manipulator	International	Independent; having good family
Zoe	Not interested	Open access to information	Economically independent	Legal, educated	Ambitious; having balanced career and life
Momo	Open	Less traffic jam	Female leader	Open-minded, positive	Easy-going; perfection
Beth	Open, liberal	Strong and powerful	Economically independent	Honest, kindhearted, hard-working	Diligent; having good family
Emily	CCP member	Democratic and social justice	Strong and cool	Patriotic, kindhearted, legal	Mature, independent; being successful

Joining Communist Party: Pros and Cons

Generally speaking, my participants in this research project have indicated growing interests in political issues. Many of them are open to express their opinions on Chinese politics in public and actively get involved with social activities and grand national/international events. For example, for those who have joined the CCP, most of them expect to get more opportunities to organise students' events or wish to practice leadership skills. During our discussions of contemporary social changes in China, they share with me about their experience of participating in the 2010 Shanghai World Expo and the 2008 Beijing Olympic Games. Almost all of them express a strong determination to contribute their own efforts on building a more open, democratic and wealthier China in the 21st century and indicate a strong sense of patriotism when talking about the further development of China.

'How do you think of joining the CCP in the university? Tell me the reason why you want to join the CCP.' When I asked those who were CCP members to share with me about their understandings of Chinese politics and Party membership, some mentioned that joining the CCP was an honour in the university and some emphasised the benefits of being a CCP member in the university campus.

> The status of CCP membership can be useful especially if someone wants to work as a civil servant in the future. I joined [the Party] in the second year of my undergraduate studies. It is a symbol of being excellent and active. And also, I love my country. (Qian, 20100613)

> Being a CCP member can help you getting involved with many social activities. Last year, I had an opportunity to organise a summer camp, during which I practiced my leading skills and broadened my network. I also had more opportunities to attend some important meetings as a representative of our department... I think it's a nice experience. (Emily, 20100610)

> I think a good thing of joining the CCP in the university is that you can practice your leadership skill. You need to work hard to be the role model for your fellow students. (Lucy, 20100612)

Clearly, for Qian, Emily and Lucy, joining the party is both a form of 'political capital' and a means of networking which is critical for personal advancement and other benefits. Another girl emphasised that her parents have exerted strong influence on her decision to join the Party.

> My dad is a civil servant. He encourages me to join the CCP in the university. He said a CCP membership might be a bonus point when I apply for a job in a state-run enterprise. Also, if I want to be a leader in the future, it might be useful. So, I'm considering joining the CCP. (Momo, 20100628)

For other young Chinese women, although they express that they have no interest in joining the Party, some give their opinions on being a student CCP member and express their expectations for future changes in China.

> I didn't join the CCP. I think people who want to have a political career might be interested in joining the CCP in the university. I hope that those who are the CCP members could share more responsibilities. (Jane, 20100526)

> Good politicians and governors should make changes and improve Chinese people's lives. The current government is performing quite well. I hope the future ones could do better. Student CCP members are student leaders, so they should work hard and represent the interests of other students. (Dan, 20100615)

Although the passion for high achieving in the university is widely shared among other participants, the majority of young women interviewed seem to hold more liberal attitudes towards Chinese politics. For example, in an individual interview, Lily told me that she was open to any discussion about Chinese politics and her attitude might represent the majority of contemporary Chinese students in campus.

> I'm open to any political issues. I think it's quite normal to talk about politics and make comments on the government in public for university students now. We are supposed to express our dissatisfaction and critiques to anything unfair or morally wrong. (Lily, 20100622)

In fact, during my fieldwork, I was very impressed when I heard these young undergraduate female students discussing the current government in such an open and mature manner. Following their discussion of the current Chinese government, I further asked these young women about their perceptions on China hosting the recent two grand international events—the 2008 Olympic Games in Beijing and the 2010 World Expo in Shanghai and their expectations of China's future (see Fig. 7.1). While some women describe these events as 'fun,' seeing the opportunity of serving as volunteers as 'gaining some new experience' (Helen, 20100628), some express their patriotic feelings through getting involved with these events.

Fig. 7.1 Student volunteers of the World Expo. *Source* Courtesy of Momo

I'm proud of having these International events at my home country. It definitely shows that China now has the ability to organise grand international events. You can't do it if you're a weak country. I think it's a good opportunity for China to further open itself to the world. It is also a good opportunity for other countries to have a better understanding of Chinese culture and Chinese people. And it's our responsibility to present a strong China. (Fay, 20100603)

Although I'm not an Expo volunteer, I feel very excited about this event being held in Shanghai. We can use this opportunity to introduce a new Shanghai to people from other countries. I hope that Shanghai could become an international city as London and New York soon. (Ivy, 20100617)

In these conversations, both Fay and Ivy express their national imagination. Their comments have also reflected how young people's national identity and self-esteem intersected and overlapped in the current period of China's social transformation.

In the group discussion, Beth and Emily also expressed their enthusiasm towards the further development of China in relation to hosting these big events.

Interviewer: What do you think of China hosting the 2008 Beijing Olympic Games?
Beth (20100610): Quite excited. I went to the Bird Nest and the Water Cube. These buildings are outstanding. I think China has become a significant country that other countries cannot ignore nowadays.
Emily: Yes, I went to see the Opening Ceremony. It was grand. I felt so proud of being Chinese.
Beth: You know, the Bird Nest is credited as the world's largest steel structure **and** the most complex stadium ever constructed. Now it becomes another tourist cite in Beijing apart from the Tian'anmen Square and the Forbidden City. I hope that we could host more international events in other Chinese cities in the future.
Interviewer: How about the on-going World Expo in Shanghai?
Emily: Haha, I'm the volunteer!
Beth: Me too. I'm quite looking forward it.

As these accounts suggested, the centrality of these young Chinese women's national identity is economic advancement for China's successful integration into the world. Within the polarised frame of 'we' and 'foreign,' these young Chinese women repeatedly emphasise characteristics of patriotic feelings and nationalist belonging, rarely referencing the opportunity to participate in public life as a way to engage with or challenge the state.

When studying nationalism and national identity in Chinese context, Unger (1996) once argues that Chinese nationalist feelings, which have centred loyalty on the state or an ethnicity or both, have fundamentally implied how China and Chinese people define themselves for centuries. Even now, Chinese nationalism still remains as the one bedrock of political belief shared by most Chinese people living in the Mainland. The very success of the current thrust to make China 'rich and strong' (that once-again-fashionable phrase of late 19th-century Chinese nationalist reformers) through hosting the most recent two grand international events has begun to feed Chinese pride, and even might potentially invite thoughts of Great Power muscle flexing. In this sense, it is hoped that China could play down jingoistic inclinations to ensure its successful opening and integration into the world economy for further modernisation and development.

Dilemma of Chinese Patriotism

While it is true that patriotic propaganda has shaped the views of contemporary young Chinese people, there are complex variations in the way they express their love of country and the degree to which this dovetails with official nationalism. As some of my participants recalled, they take patriotism as granted since they were children.

> When I was young, my parents and school teachers would be very angry if I said anything negative about China. I think everyone wants to show the best aspects of her/his country to others. Especially for Chinese people, they don't want to lose face for themselves or for their country. That's why people don't want to tell the truth to unfamiliar people or foreigners. (Qian, 20100613)

> Since we were in primary school, the teacher had taught us that we should work hard so that we could make a contribution to our country when we grew up. When China was poor and weak, Chinese people were not confident in front of Western people. So China used to be called "the sick man of East Asia" (*dongya bingfu*). But, now everyone can see the rapid development of the Chinese economy in recent years. China needs such recognition internationally. I'm very proud to introduce China and Chinese culture to people from other countries. (Wendy, 20100620)

In these conversations, both Qian and Wendy mention their school experience of patriotic education, commenting that they prefer to say good things about China. However, unlike Qian and Wendy, Sue and Zoe seem to be more objective when they were asked about their opinions on China. They show their deep concerns and sometimes disappointments of social problems in contemporary China.

> Air pollution is a big problem for China. There are so many industries which are emitting over-leveled waste gas everyday. And cars. The environment has been badly polluted. Eventually, we'll get paid of everything. (Sue, 20100620)

> I know it may be not right to criticise my own country since I love my country. But I have to admit that China do have many problems, such as transparency and openness of accessing the information. Facebook blocked. Twitter blocked. Youtube blocked. China needs to be more open to different opinions and information. (Zoe, 20100603)

The conversations presented above shows a urgent concern of China's development, which also reflects a deeply-rooted patriotic education tradition among contemporary university students in China. In fact, it has been an official ideology of promoting patriotism through school education and national media in the Chinese context. For example, in 2008 the Chinese government boycotted French goods after President Sarkozy of France met with the Dalai Lama. Likewise, Chinese media encouraged Chinese people to fill cyberspace with tirades against any Japanese politician who visits the controversial Yasukuni Shrine—a site that honors the souls of all of Japan's war dead, which includes several Class A war criminals responsible for brutal policies toward the populations of China and other Asian countries. The most recent nomination of Liu Xiaobo for the Nobel Peace Prize further stirred anger of the Communist government, who warned that this decision would hurt China's relations with Norway. After these occasions, Chinese schools have even reinforced their patriotic education in the classroom (see Unger 1982 for the discussion of Chinese education under Mao).

In this sense, it seems that patriotic fervor has successfully emancipated the worldview of the contemporary young Chinese students. However, popular nationalism is not a force that the authorities can turn on and off like a tap. It is also overly simplistic to think that the payoff for a patriotic education is a mass of angry youths ready to do the Communist government's bidding whenever it feels like calling on them. In fact, Chinese nationalism remains a double-edged sword, which does at times buttress the regime but can also develop in ways that threaten the political status quo of communist China (Unger 1996). While it is true that patriotic propaganda has shaped the views of young Chinese, there are complex variations in the way they express their love of country and the degree to which this dovetails with official nationalism. Even contemporary China's leaders are well aware that some of the biggest challenges faced by previous Chinese regimes, up to and very much including the Tiananmen Uprising in 1989, have been driven in part by patriotic fervor. As Lily, a final-year undergraduate student in Chinese Media Studies, vigorously responded when I asked her opinions on the openness of current information channels in China:

> Why people can not get access to the information freely?! I think it is because the government doesn't want people to know other perspectives which may be negative for its image. It's a lack of confidence. A mature country should have the confidence to deal with the divergence. (Lily, 20100622)

In a similar manner, two postgraduate students give their critique on some social issues in contemporary Chinese society, arguing that China is still a developing country in which great threats and potential dangers co-exist in an overheated economy.

Interviewer: How do you see the issue of the wealth gap of China?

Beth (20100610): That's problematic of China's economy, as what you have mentioned the wealth gap between the urban and the rural. Also, the current inflation rate is high. The house prices in big cities are crazy. Young university graduates cannot find jobs to make a decent living. All of these are warning signs to the economic bubble in contemporary Chinese society.

Emily: Yes, wealth gap is one of the urgent issues facing China. Because China develops so fast, it brings about many problems, such as imbalanced and risk. To deal with the difficulties, we need to make every try carefully.

While Lily openly draws her criticism regarding the free access to information in China, Beth and Helen give their critical thinking of the social issues in contemporary Chinese society. Around the topic of social issues, other young women also offer their defense and different opinions on China's problems.

Although I'm well aware of many social problems in China, I'm not very happy for people from other countries talking about these problems and blaming China. My American boyfriend always said bad things about Chinese politicians and the government. I'm not happy with that. He is not Chinese anyway. None of his business. I can talk about China's human rights and the global warming issues, but he cannot. (Sue, 20100620)

As these accounts suggested, I was quite impressed by the fact that these contemporary young women could talk about China's problems in such an open manner. In these conversations, we can see that these young women have shown a strong determination to make further changes to China in the 21st century. The open-mindedness of these young Chinese women also seems to suggest a trend of ideological change among contemporary generations of Chinese students.

Presently, although the Communist Party has retained a monopoly over key instruments of control including propaganda, personnel, military and police since its founding, the government seems to make big progress in terms of freeing the people to talk about politics and social issues in an open manner. Yet, it is also true that the small officially sanctioned minority parties cultivated by the Communist Party throughout the People's Republic of China are pledged to loyalty to the ruling party. Thus, while publications are restricted by an elaborate system of party censorship, the official ideology remains Marxism-Leninism-Mao Zedong Thought guided in practice by theories and leadership principles associated with Deng Xiaoping and his successor, Jiang Zemin. Patriotic education which is based on this official ideology still goes through the whole education system in China (see Perry and Selden 2010). For the majority of Chinese students who were born in the Mainland and are mainly educated in the Mainland, a unified national identity and a strong sense of patriotic feelings still seems to be easily observed.

By claiming this, it could also be acknowledged that in the context of China, a protest that begins as a loyalist expression of nationalism can easily evolve into a struggle, in which questions are always raised about the leadership of the Communist Party. Even Chinese authorities know that once mobilised, a patriotic fervour has the potential to work against rather than for them, and this might explain why Chinese patriotic education often finds itself working to douse as opposed to fan the flames of youthful nationalist ardor along with its social reforms (see Wang 1996). In this sense, we should see Chinese nationalism as a Janus-faced force that can and does move easily in both loyalist and oppositional directions.

During my fieldwork, I also encouraged my participants to give me their bold view and expectation of future China and also relate their career expectation to the development of the nation. Some students express their national imagination and determinations to build a democratic, wealthy and civil China with their knowledge and skills.

I think the employment of university students has become an important issue. The government needs to establish related policies to help more graduates to get a decent job. For example, employment needs to be more transparent and fairer. Chinese people like to use 'relationship' (*guanxi*) in order to get a good job. Yet, that's really unfair. We want to see democracy and justice in the process of job recruitment. (Ivy, 20100617)

Chinese people don't criticise the government because all the information we received is pro to the government. I hope that China could be more open, harmonious and wealthier in the 21st century. There are more and more Chinese students studying abroad and going to study abroad. I think they will bring new ideas and advanced knowledge to China in the future. (Fay, 20100603)

I hope that China could retain her own characteristics as well as become more internationalised. When we build up more modern buildings, we should also protect some cultural sites which are unique to China. It is Chinese traditions that are attractive. (Wendy, 20100620)

In these conversations, Ivy, Fay and Wendy mention that they hope that China could become a more democratic and civil society. As a young woman who is going to study in the West, Julie also expresses her expectation and determination of making a contribution to the country's further development in the future.

For other younger Chinese women, they discuss their expectations of China by addressing daily issues such as education and travelling. For example, in a group discussion, Dan and Lucy talked about how they imagine the future of China.

Interviewer: Can you imagine what China will be like in, say, 20 years?

Dan (20100615): I think while there will be more and more Chinese students going abroad to study, there will also be a growing number of international students from other countries coming to China to study our language and culture. I hope that more Western people would visit China and experience Chinese lives. China does not only have the Communist Party and Maoist uniform... In the future, I hope that China could be much stronger and more harmonious.

Lucy: I agree with this point. I think that there will be more Chinese brands becoming the top international brands. Many products will be labelled 'made by China' rather than 'made in China.'

Dan: Also, there will be more Chinese tourists in foreign countries since Chinese people should travel more and see how other people live. Western people are open-minded because they travel broadly. Also, people from all over the world could come to live in China so that we can enjoy each other's culture.

These interviews have reflected young people's national imagination during China's on-going modernisation in current times. At a macro level, when studying modernisation, Mouzelis (1994) points out that a society can be modern without necessarily adopting the characteristic features of Western Christian democracies. While Anglo-Saxon societies put more emphasis on democracy and economic values over social values, China and Japan may put greater weight on social values and solidarity, as the words 'stronger' and 'more harmonious' used by Dan when she imaged what China will be like in 20 years.

Truly, in China, solidarity is presented as a stronger national identity. As Esherick (2000) argued, in all developing countries (and many developed ones as well) there is an intricate dialectical relationship between modernity and national identity. On the one hand, modernity and nationalism are inseparably linked. Nationalism is very much a product of the modern age, the result of economic and political forces which have made the nation-state the social unit within which a people acquires wealth, power, and international recognition (i.e. Anderson 2006; Gellner 1983). On the other hand, there is always a certain tension between the back-looking history and the past, and the forward-looking 'demand for progress' (Geertz 1973: 258). Therefore, the forms of modernity in Asian countries present a particularly acute tension between modernity and nationalism. When modernity is defined as the mark of the imperialist powers of the West, Chinese or other Asian forms of modernity will extrude as the very powers against which the new nations have struggled for their place in the world (Esherick 2000). The two forces of modernity and nationalism dominate modern history, sometimes working in tandem but sometimes coming in conflict.

Female + Ism: Soft and Independent

In this research project, my participants not only express their preference to the term 'feminism' but also indicate a strong interest and passion to label themselves as 'feminists.' For them, the term 'feminism' is a fashionable imported product from the developed West. In their understanding, 'feminism' means 'independence, individualist and trendy.' Many of my participants relate their understandings of 'being a feminist' to a status of economically independent and professionally successful. For example, in an individual interview, a young woman told me that she supported 'feminist' because this label is so 'cool' and 'charming.' Meanwhile, these young Chinese women relate the understandings of 'citizenship' to their affiliations to dominant or subordinate groups, such as their ethnicity, origin, and urban or rural residence. Some take into consideration global and transnational positioning of these citizenships. The meanings constructed by these young women are derived from their internalisation of the cultural model of modernisation (*xiandaihua*) and modernity in Chinese context.

> I think the term "feminism" might mean that women should be financially independent... For those who can pay for their own bills, I think they are very cool. (Qian, 20100613)

> I like the idea of "feminism". It has the same meaning with "freedom" and "independence." These words seem to be posh words nowadays for describing charming modern women. I'm an independent woman who make my own decisions. So I should call myself a "feminist". (Irene, 20100618)

> I think "feminism" is something about women. Feminist women are those who are independent, adventurous and leading. They can leave others a very profound first impression... It's definitely a positive and desirable word to describe those outstanding pioneer women. (Lily, 20100622)

While Qian and Irene see 'feminism' as a newly imported concept, which means freedom and independence, Lily sees 'feminism' as a positive and desirable concept to describe leading women. They all show their interest in feminist ideas and relate the meaning of feminism and feminists to the image of outstanding pioneer women. They have provided new definitions and interpretations of 'feminism' on a popular level. As reviewed previously, on an intellectual level, when Western feminist ideas travelled to China, the English term 'feminism' has two common renditions in Chinese translation—feminism as *nuquan zhuyi* (women's rights or power-ism), which connotes the stereotype of a man-hating he-woman hungry for power; and feminism as *nuxing zhuyi* (female or feminine-ism), which is often taken to mean an ideology promoting femininity. Among the majority of Chinese women writers, the latter one appears far less threatening and therefore has been widely accepted (see Ko and Wang 2007).

In fact, in the context of China, both on an intellectual and a popular level, there remains a degree of fluidity within the relationships between women writers, female intellectuals and the general urban public when it comes to considering and debating women's and gender issues. As Zhong (2007) argued, China, since the beginning of the post-Mao era, has witnessed an increase in women's writing in literature and criticism. There has also been a rapid rise of other kinds of research activities into women's issues, including concrete social work and fieldwork carried out in different regions and theoretical debates on what it means to be a woman.

In a group discussion, some younger Chinese women discussed their understandings of feminism by emphasising women's relation with men.

Interviewer: How do you understand the term 'feminism?'

Dan (20100615): I think feminism is about women's relation with men. If a woman takes control of a man, we can say that's 'feminism.' For example, if a family is mainly led by a woman, such that it is usually the mother who makes decisions on daily issues, that is a 'feminist' family.

Lucy: Either in school or in the university, girls usually perform better than boys. So, boys listen to girls and are controlled by girls. That's feminism.

Dan: No one can control others. I think the best 'control' is to control oneself. Or, you can say you make decisions for yourself and control your own life. A woman should be responsible for herself. I think the relationship between women and men should be harmonious rather than dominant.

From the conversations presented above, it seems that these young Chinese women are suggesting a new feminist identity fostered from the grassroots. Jane further mentions that 'self-control' and 'self-responsibility' are supposed to be seen as a suitable relationship between women and men. Does this mean, then, that this younger generation of educated Chinese women is more 'enlightened' than their mothers' generation in terms of self-management and individual realisation? Or does it mean that with more younger women's acceptance of the label 'feminism,' urban Chinese women have a better understanding of what 'feminism' means and will be able to understand the workings of gender politics in society in general and in their own lives in particular? Answers to these (and other related) questions lie somewhere else. The refusal to identify with the label of feminism or to claim to be a feminist does not necessarily indicate that a woman is or is not a feminist. Rather, within the context of contemporary China, these gestures towards feminism are indicative, among others, of issues related to the changing gender politics of post-Mao China. Such gestures further reveal the global flow of feminist ideas as well as various imaginaries of what it means to be a 'modern woman.'

In other individual interviews, some young Chinese women also explained their understanding of feminism and power by mentioning the image of the 'Iron Lady' in Chinese politics.

> When you mention "feminism," the image popped up in my mind is the Iron Lady – the female Chinese politician Wu Yi. She has an absolute power in Chinese politics. She is too powerful and scares men away, so she is single. (Ivy, 20100617)

> It is a popular saying that "there are three genders in the world – male, female and female PhDs." If a woman is too strong, she will become threatening. I think a woman needs to be strong, but not too masculine. (Emily, 20100610)

> My American boyfriend is very interested in Chinese women. He said that he liked Asian girls because they are more like women. American girls are too feminist so that they lose femininity. I agree with him that Chinese women's social position is absolutely higher than American women. American women have to fight for their equal rights. But it seems that Chinese women have already had rights. (Sue, 20100620)

> There are many books writing about women nowadays. Some teach women to succeed and some teach women to obtain power. I feel that Chinese women are quite liberalised and empowered in current times, so there is no point for having any sort of movements. (Wendy, 20100620)

These conversations have indicated a complex and often contradictory association with the concept of women's liberation despite the explicit laws and consistent rhetoric in the context of China. In legal terms, contemporary anthropologist Yang (1999: 37) has stated that 'China may be better than the United States, since the Equal Rights Amendment to include a gender provision in the U.S. Constitution was never passed, despite heavy lobbying by American feminists.' Since the Chinese Communist Party has legally provided for equality in regards to gender during much of its existence, lobbying may seem not necessary in the case of China (see also Croll 1978). However, one must not assume that the state's inclusion of feminist concerns, even to the point of constitutional 'guarantees,' will automatically translate into the liberation of women.

In China, part of the lengthy historical resistance to women's exercise of power derives from notions of essential gender differences and fears for the consequences of blurring these distinctions (Edwards 2002). The public realm has traditionally been perceived as masculinising and the domestic realm feminising. Feminised male bodies or masculinised female bodies are believed to generate social instability.

As noted above, publicly powerful women symbolise the decline of the empire or family in part because they imply the weakness of men in male-coded space. Women with public political lives are regarded as becoming like men to the detriment of their essential femininity. Thus, one significant challenge for China's female political body is to ensure that in their exercise of power they do not suggest a critique of Chinese men's governance skills and do not imply a usurpation of Chinese masculinity. Fears of female arrogation of masculine domains remain strong and yet, with political power firmly located within the masculine domain, successful women political leaders like Wu Yi must strike a balance of perceived gender essences within their public persona. Wu Yi's presentation of physicality is an excellent example of an emerging new narrative for women in power—one that challenges old anxieties about women's misuse of 'male' power while simultaneously invoking gender codes sufficiently bounded to be acceptable to a broad public and to her political peers (see Perry and Selden 2010).

Following the topic of the "Iron Lady," I ask my participants to discuss the image of the female politician in Chinese context. Some young Chinese women express their ideas about women's leadership. For example, in a group discussion, Zoe and Fay discussed how women should balance masculinity and femininity when they attempted to obtain power.

Interviewer: How do you see those women in top positions, such as female politicians and female CEOs?

Zoe (20100603): It depends. Sometimes, those who look masculine and scary may be not strong per se. And those who look feminine and soft may be strong and determined. I think the real powerful women are those who take a leadership role by combining masculinity and femininity.

Fay: For me, the image of female politicians is usually too tough. but female business leaders seem to be much better. They are smart, fashionable and successful.

As Fay argued, while the image of Chinese women politicians is tough, the image of Chinese business women is more acceptable since the latter are seen as 'fashionable.' This indicates that in Chinese context, women are always corrupted by formal political power—either through the loss of their femininity or through the betrayal of their (expected) political allegiance to the mass of women. As Wang (2003), a prominent U.S.-based historian of Chinese women, argued, such views reflect a modernisation of ancient prejudices about gender boundaries that have curtailed women's formal political participation. When Chinese women enter the public political arena they have been seen as becoming unsettlingly masculinised. In this way, a delicate balance of masculinisation and essential femininity becomes more appreciated if Chinese female politicians want to gain more support from the mass of women.

At the heart of the concept of the male public civic sphere lay the tensions between power and sexuality, which is expressed in terms of anxieties about the 'bimbo' effect (sexually attractive women supporting male power) or the 'Thatcher' effect (the danger of losing femininity with power) (Ivinson et al. 2000). However, the increasing presence of fashion sense and bodily beauty in politics in the People's Republic of China has introduced a new physicality to the interpellation of female politicians in a liberalising China.

In recent years, aspiring Chinese politicians also exist in female bodies with feminine attributes. For instance, politicians in women's bodies begin to assume key positions in formal government structures and have already exercised real political power within other Chinese polities such as Taiwan and Hong Kong.

Taiwanese Vice-President Annette Lv and Hong Kong's Anson Chan and Emily Lau serve as prime examples. Owing to the ready interchange of information between the Mainland and the outside, the emergence of a legitimate space for a female political incarnation in these small but significant Chinese polities suggests the potential for denaturalising masculinist traditions of politics in the Chinese context and for legitimising the female exercise of political power. As Wang (2003) confirmed, 'female high officials' in Mainland China have begun to negotiate gendered borders with remarkable dexterity by deploying the female corporeal form in ways that are new to China in the 21st century.

Helen offers a summarised definition of 'feminism' for contemporary young Chinese women in our last meeting:

> A successful woman has various facets. In the labour market, she fights hard for her equal right. In daily life, she is considerate and soft. Those who are capable of balancing softness and strength are welcoming and desirable. (Helen, 20100628)

Clearly, for all girls who participated in this research project, although they hold different understandings and opinions on 'feminism,' the idea of feminism and feminist thought has intervened to constrain their conventional desires. For some, they believe that gender equality has been generally achieved. However, since the tropes of freedom and choice have been inextricably connected with the category of young women, feminism has been not only decisively aged but also made to seem redundant. In McRobbie's (2009: 11) words, '[f]eminism is cast into the shadows, where at best it can expect to have some afterlife, where it might be regarded ambivalently by those young women who must, in more public venues, stake a distance from it, for the sake of social and sexual recognition.

Global Citizen and China Dreams

Reading the responses of my participants for the first time, one could be forgiven for thinking that Wexler (1990) has indeed captured the meaninglessness of citizenship as a basis for political identity. It seems that the concept of citizenship means little to young people in the Chinese context as well. Despite having an appropriate word, young Chinese women initially appear to have difficulty in defining and using the term. 'Citizenship' appears to have few, if any, connotations or links to everyday life or identities. Thus, typical responses are:

> 'Maybe you can find it in the dictionary. But I don't think I understand what you mean.' (an informal chat with a first-year undergraduate student in Business)

> 'I don't know. Is it about your nationality?' (an informal chat with a third-year undergraduate student in Physics)

> 'I feel nothing about it. I think I'm a citizen. But that doesn't mean anything to me really.' (an informal chat with a final-year postgraduate student in Management)

Not surprisingly, it is hard to initiate discussions on this topic. As Jane (20100526) put, 'I think your question is quite weird. "Citizenship" is a very abstract concept to me, so I don't know how to answer this question.' Little success is had until, somewhat surprisingly, the English word 'citizenship' is used in the Chinese discussion groups when I ask my participants to relate the term 'citizenship' with the previous discussed topic of 'how to be a woman.'

Interviewer: What do you think of the term 'citizenship?' How do you think of yourself as a citizen?

Dan (20100615): I'm a bit confused about this citizenship. But I think it might be related to your origin, your country, and your location. For example, when I introduce myself to other Chinese, I would say I'm a Beijing citizen. But when I introduce myself to people from other countries, I would say I'm a Chinese citizen.

Lucy: Yes, I think the word citizen means part of the country. If you ask me about my citizenship, I would say Heinan rather than Shenzhen or Shanghai because I was born and grown up in Heinan, and I feel I'm more attached to Heinan.

Interviewer: What do you think of the term 'citizenship?' How do you think of yourself as a citizen?

Zoe (20100603): I think citizenship relates to a person's place of birth. For example, urban citizens and rural citizens definitely are quite different.

Fay: For me, citizenship seems to describe those international people who always travel abroad.

These conversations have revealed that, although citizenship has little currency in everyday discourse, it is possible to identify the different metaphors, associations and values which they call into play in trying to make sense of the term. According to Yual-Davis (1997: 4–5), the study of citizenship should consider the issue of women's citizenship not only by contrast to that of men, but also in relation to women's affiliation to dominant or subordinate groups, their ethnicity, origin, and urban or rural residence. It also should take into consideration global and transnational positionings of these citizenships. Giroux (1989: 16) also argues that citizenship is 'a form of cultural production.' The making of citizens must be understood as 'an ideological process through which we experience ourselves as well as our relations to others and the world within a complex and often contradictory system of representations and images.' (Giroux 1989: 16)

In other individual interviews, young women articulated complex relations between their moral stances and their critical interpretations of modern society.

In order to be a good citizen, a person needs to be educated, legal and making a contribution to society. What a person does reflects the kind of person you are and how people see you. Also, you should always have a positive attitude because in order to succeed you have to have this quality to begin with. (Qian, 20100613)

I don't like the older generations of local Shanghai citizens. They are arrogant, rude and naïve. They complain about immigrants for stealing their jobs. But actually, they are lazy and narrow-minded. You can see that half the population of successful people in Shanghai are not originally from Shanghai. As long as you work hard and make contributions, you are the good citizens of the place. (Beth, 20100610)

I want to return to my hometown Suzhou after I finish my studies. I feel that I could have a better personal development and a more decent life there. The case is that as long as you're a Suzhou citizen, you'll always be one. You're attached to the city and its people. Yet, it seems that there is no such a thing of "Shanghai citizen" at all. People in Shanghai are from everywhere, doing all sorts of business. There is no culture and no history. (Wendy, 20100620)

I didn't think too much about my self as a citizen before the World Expo in Shanghai. As a Shanghai citizen, I hope that my city could become a polite, green and friendly global city since this event. So, I want to work hard as a city representative. (Ivy, 20100622)

As these young women discussed their understandings of citizenship, they link a recurring series of attributes to their descriptions of legitimacy and belonging. Significant in each of these accounts is the centrality of the importance of compliance with the law and self-regulation and responsibility for personal well-being and one's behaviour within the state. Neither do they characteristically remark upon the rights and protections to which one is entitled as a Chinese citizen, or that which Hannah Arendt (see Benhabib 2004) refers to as the 'right to have rights.' Instead, these young Chinese women more commonly narrate dominant accounts of citizenship that conforms to a highly individualised moral and political order. Here, the 'good citizen' is a person who successfully utilises strategies of self-regulation and self-surveillance to contribute to the economy or to benefit from it, to become affluent and not become a 'burden' to the state.

Also, the process of classifying others as decent citizens (or not) seems here to be tied primarily to new notions of liberal individualism in Chinese context. These notions are heavily bound to exchange values, class aspirations and class status. In this understanding, citizenship is not something that a citizen negotiates with the state but is instead represented as something a citizen ought either to benefit from or feel anxious about. In other words, being a good or decent citizen may carry a high price tag in urban concentrations of fierce competition and danger when one struggles to understand the cultural frames of citizenship and their associated classifications. Such classifications are bound by urban spatial arrangements and reflect contemporary young Chinese women's disorientation of living in contemporary Chinese urban contexts where dramatic social change may seem more omnipresent than it might have in the past.

By reading through other interview transcripts, it seems that some young Chinese women construct citizenship as an abstract, but nevertheless inclusive category. They describe a sense of belonging somewhere even if 'somewhere' is vaguely defined. These descriptions have implied more than formal criteria of membership such as place of residence, place of work or place of birth. They appear to stress the 'feeling of belonging' rather than any explicit political identity. For example, Momo spoke of 'habits,' 'principles' and 'visions,' concepts closer perhaps to Bourdieu and Passeron's (1977) notion of *habitus*:

A Chinese citizen should always be proud of his/her nationality. This is because Chinese people have their own habits, principles of solving problems and visions of the world. (Momo, 20100628)

Other young women also use other benchmarks in their discussions of citizenship—namely the relationship between the individual and society. They refer less to a cultural concept of citizenship or nation and more to a new form of cosmopolitan identity. For example, in an individual interview, Lily expressed the idea of cosmopolitan when she described her imaginary self in her 50s:

> I could travel around the world and go shopping in all fashion capitals. I could have my breakfast in London and my lunch in Barcelona and then my dinner in Paris. That's my dream – become an international lady. (Lily, 20100622)

Clearly, these conversations turn to the internalised cosmopolitanism that young middle-class and affluent Chinese women embody in China in the 21st century. According to Rofel (2007), 'cosmopolitanism' serves as one of the key nodes through which sexual, material, and affective desires bind citizen-subjects to state and transnational neoliberal policies. This cosmopolitanism consists in two aspects in tension with one another: a self-conscious transcendence of locality, posited as a universal transcendence, accomplished through the formation of a consumer identity; and a domestication of cosmopolitanism by way of renegotiating China's place in the world. From the accounts provided above, we can see that some young women—especially those who are from the mass affluent family—have already begun to link their identity politics to a transnational self.

Conclusion: Toward the Future

So far, I have discussed young Chinese women's passion and expectation of the nation. The openness of contemporary young Chinese people towards political issues has suggested that some achievements have been made in Chinese political reforms in recent decades. In fact, in the first decade of the reform era, both the Chinese party-state and the elite (political and intellectual alike) struggled to depart from radical Maoist socialism, as evidenced by a number of important institutional changes, ranging from the establishment of the household responsibility system and de-collectivisation in the first half of the 1980s to a number of bold yet not necessarily successful urban reforms in the late 1980s. The rapid rise and fall of a pro-democracy students' movement in 1989 further represents a turning point, which pushed both the party-state and the elite to bid a determined farewell to Maoist socialism in the post-1989 years. Despite the persistence of political conservatism that centered around the monopoly of power by the Chinese Communist Party, Deng Xiaoping's 1992 tour to South China, the theory of a socialist market economy and Jiang Zemin's theory of the 'three represents' serve as the best examples of the official re-orientation or re-ideologicalisation toward a market economy and capitalism in China in the 21st century (Perry and Selden 2010).

By reacting to an expanding market-oriented economy, Chinese women also start their feminist adventures to 'travel' to the rest of world. Here, I hope to build up a link between the emerging forms of feminist thinking and citizenship ideas among these young Chinese women on popular level. Two decades ago, British sociologist Rose (1990) pointed out that the politics and practices of welfare, far from extending citizenship in this benign sense, in fact functioned to maintain inequality, to legitimate existing relations of power, and to extend social control over potentially troublesome sectors of society. The soul of the young citizen has become 'the object of government through expertise' by the late twentieth century (Rose 1990: 213). Today, the tension between disciplining the young citizen and the discourse of freedom, individualism, and free will/choice, may still not be resolved. This requires educational systems to increasingly promote greater freedom through neo-liberal discourses of performativity, individualisation and personalised learning, and to encourage a global collective consciousness.

In fact, educating citizens has now become a global debate. The educational system in a national context should be seen as the institution that historically shapes the relationship of male and female citizens to the state. *It is* the incorporation of gender education with the citizenship education *that* could bring direct institutional change towards a more egalitarian gender relation in modern societies. As feminist educationalists Yuval-Davis and Stoetzler (2002) argued, there is a need for an intervention of the 'gender gaze' in the citizenship education. In the Chinese context, when the dilemma between feminism and nationalism has been increasingly complicated by the powerful influences of global popular culture, it is suggested that we should further enrich feminist debate of citizenship education by adding the discussion of the changing geopolitical mapping of Chineseness into the localised educational reforms in current times.

To conclude, in the context of China, the incarnation of political power has connoted masculinity for decades. The masculinist tradition of governance has its origins in centuries of Confucian orthodoxy and deeply rooted understandings of which individuals have the legitimate right to rule. It is an educated body, not an aesthetic, sporty, or stylish one that signifies potential for public politics. Under Confucian orthodoxy, men have ruled the People's Republic of China since its establishment and female participation in government has been corralled within the narrow scope of 'women's work'[2] or discredited by the ideological machinery of a resilient patriarchal tradition. Class divisions, along with gender, also naturalise an educated male as the political body (see Louie 2002). By putting my data within this broader social and cultural context in which these women belong, this chapter presents fourteen promising young Chinese women's civic obligations and their feminist adventures in the 21st century. In my analysis, I do not hold the essentialist notion that feminism and nationalism are inherently contradictory. Rather, the feminist–nationalist tension is always located within specific historical contexts, in which both feminism and nationalism are constructed in such ways as to contradict

---

[2] 'Women's work' refers to those areas of governance that specifically pertain to the mobilisation of women. See Judd (2002) and Edwards (2004) for a discussion of the problems this concept has caused for women's political aspirations.

each other. In other words, the tension is a nonstop negotiation between feminism and nationalism, and between feminist desires and national imaginations.

If a national identity is how a nation defines itself in the world, what it thinks is an appropriate role and actions for itself and others, such development of global citizen awareness among the younger generation of people will be more and more important for China. Powell (2004: 231) sees a national identity as 'a relatively stable understanding and expectation about self and others.' It is constituted through two basic means: current interactions between countries, and the narratives that nations tell about their national pasts (Wendt 1994). For China, Chinese national identity is not fixed, but rather has changed as both China and the world have changed. Lessons of the past, and narratives about the past, do have an influence on Chinese outlooks, as they do on any country. Therefore, in this research project, although the most recent social changes brought about by the reform and opening-up policy in 1979 are the basis of my analysis of young Chinese women's national identity and sense of citizenship, one should not be taking this period out of the context of China's historical development in order to fully understand Chinese people in contemporary times.

As a young Chinese woman who has experienced the dramatic social change of Mainland China myself, I believe that the most important lesson China learnt from the past should be that the norm of sovereignty is a key part of modern international relations instead of the resentment that China feels for past wrongs. Coupled with a historical lack of territorial aggrandisement, this has led to a focus on pragmatic and cooperative interactions with the rest of the world, so long as China's national interests are not threatened. Thus, when writing this chapter, it is my sincere hope that China has passed the stage of depending on a big-R revolution to achieve its nationalist goals for modernisation in the 21st century. The two-part Revolution of 1911 and 1949 has brought to the surface what is possible and what is not, what can be fruitful and what is not (see Wang 1996). The experiences have been so rich and varied, and so much has been learnt by so many millions both inside and outside, that we can now hope that China will remain open to the world. I believe that the majority of the younger generation of educated Chinese in the Mainland nowadays realise that only through this openness, and the trials and changes which that would bring, can China fulfill the nationalist expectations her peoples have had for so long for the Chinese revolutions. If there is a message here by interpreting the national imagination amongst these young women student representatives, I think the message could be like this: be open to the world and then be as Chinese as you like.

Chapter 8
Scenarios

New Feminism in China

> Gender ought not to be constructed as a stable identity or locus of agency from which various acts follows; rather, gender is an identity tenuously constituted in time, instituted in an exterior space through a *styli[s]ed repetition of acts*. (Butler 1990: 140)
>
> Education for global citizenship will require a radical change in values, epistemologies, structures and mechanisms whereby we regulate our interactions as members of local communities, nation state and international society. (Lynch 1992: 20–21)

The last four decades have witnessed tremendous upheavals and transformations in every aspect of Chinese culture and society, from national politics to everyday life. At the level of everyday life, some of the most obvious and remarkable of these transformations have affected, or occurred in, the realm of gender. In this book, I am always having the ambition to understand contemporary urban young women's lives and to predict the further change of gender relations in future China under the current external forces, such as globalisation, marketisation and individualisation. Although I do not intend my analysis to be comparative or comprehensive as soon as I write 'young Chinese women',[1] I do hope that my claims could make some implications on the national trend of the gender transformation in future China.

Scenario 1: The Ambivalent 'Post' Condition

During my fieldwork in Shanghai, I was always deeply impressed by the landscape of the Pudong district, where some of the world's tallest skyscrapers are rising. In fact, the Pudong district of Shanghai is one of the paradigmatic geographical settings dramatising the recent rise of Mainland China as a world power. On the west

---

[1] I acknowledge that it was always problematic to define the experiences of categories of young women by simply using national classification. In other words, the voice of Han-ethnic, city-dwelling and middle-class educated young Chinese women presented in this thesis would be very different with the lived experiences of poor, rural, not-university-educated or ethnic-minority Chinese girls and young women. Thus, I have tried to be very specific about Chinese young women I describe.

© Foreign Language Teaching and Research Publishing Co., Ltd
and Springer Science+Business Media Singapore 2016
J. Zheng, *New Feminism in China*, DOI 10.1007/978-981-10-0777-4_8

Fig. 8.1 Daytime and nighttime of Shanghai Pudong district. *Source* Jiaran Zheng

side of the Huangpu River, there are the neoclassical and art deco buildings of Shanghai's former colonial occupiers from the late nineteenth to early twentieth centuries; on the east side, there are 21st-century high-rises and the fanciful futuristic design of the Pearl Tower pointing the way for China to march towards modernity (see Fig. 8.1). This setting might be the best point where we see how China's past and future meet. Implied in the comparison of this setting is also the idea that China has finally 'stood up' (*zhanqilaile*), first by shaking off its imperialist occupiers through the anti-Japanese war and the Communist Revolution, and then by advancing to the forefront of the world economy during the post-Mao economic miracle. Clearly, we can see China's official dream of a strong and prosperous future in the party-state's three centrally orchestrated mega-events: the 2008 Beijing Olympics presented China as a soft superpower; the National Day military parade in 2009 reminded everyone that China also has hard power; and the Shanghai World Expo in 2010 was billed as the 'Olympics for Culture, Economy and Technology' (see Fig. 8.2). Just by the time of finishing this book, China has won the bid for the Winter Olympics in 2022, which undoubtedly indicates a further development of China in all aspects including infrastructure and environment.

In any sense, we are living through a new and radical form of globalisation where economic prospects are changing, not just in the emerging nations but also in the Western world. However, I am not convinced we have understood the full implications.

Many contemporary Western postmodern theorists argue that the very same post-Enlightenment legacy has infused the expansionist projects of the colonial empires, particularly those of England, and that one of its political by-products is the modern nation-state (see McGrath 2008). However, once transplanted into China, the legacy served to add a new dimension to Chinese semantics: in fact, the very word 'new' (*xin*) became the crucial component of a cluster of new word compounds denoting a qualitative change in all spheres of life: from a series of the late Qing reform movements (Hundred-Day Reform in particular), with its institutional designations such as new policies (*xinzheng*), to new schools (*xinxue*) to Liang Qichao's celebrated notion of new people (*xinmin*) and the May Fourth slogans such as new culture (*xin wenhua*) and new literature (*xin wenxue*). Two terms that gained wide popularity in the 1920s were *shidai* (time or epoch) and *xin shidai* (new epoch),

Fig. 8.2 The 2010 Shanghai World Expo at night. *Source* Jiaran Zheng

based on the Japanese word *jidai*. This sense of living in a new epoch, as advocated by May Fourth leaders such as Chen Duxiu, was what defined the ethos of a Chinese modernity. By the 1900s, another Japanese term was adopted: *wenming* (*bunmei*), or civilisation, which came to be used with words like *dongfang* (East) and *xifang* (West) to form the common May Fourth vocabulary of 'Eastern' and 'Western' civilisations as dichotomous and contrasting categories (Rofel 1999).

By the early 1990s, in the face of all the changes sweeping the Chinese economy and cultural scene, some Chinese critics began to distinguish the 'new era' (*xin shiqi*) of 1978–89 from the 'post-new era' (*hou xin shiqi*) that was dawning.[2] The 'post' of this post-new era was also linked to the suggestion that China was entering a postmodern phase in its cultural life, as the essentially modern intellectual ideologies of the 1980s, and the modernist works of art that accompanied them, were felt to have been surpassed and discredited. While postmodernism as an aesthetic or critical pose may have been adopted by various Chinese artists and writers, its meaning in relation to modernism and modernity is very different than in the Western discourse on postmodernity. Much English scholarship on Chinese culture

---

[2]The term post-new era was coined by Beijing-based critic Zhang Yiwu in his article 'Post-new era literature: a new cultural space' ('*Houxinshiqi wenxue: Xinde wenhua kongjian*'), Literary Debate (*wenyi zhengming*), 1992, (06): 9–10.

since 1989 takes a similar view, with postmodernism as the guiding theoretical approach to study the Chinese approach to modernity or the postmodern condition (see, for example, Rofel 1999; Dirlik and Zhang 2000; Lu 2001).

Thus, the concept of postmodernism is often useful in the analysis of contemporary Chinese culture. McGreth (2008) argues in his book that there is a fundamental sense in which contemporary China is intrinsically postmodern, insofar as it closed the door on the particular vision of modernity offered by the Cultural Revolution in Mao's era. By the turn of the century, it becomes even more obvious that the sort of globalised society of superficial media spectacle which we often associate with postmodernity is very much in evidence in China, particularly in its largest and richest cities. Yet, it is also true that in the context of China, postmodernity can only be perceived as an alternative version of modernity, or at most to say, a newer version of modernity proper, instead of 'an essential critique of' or 'a break with' it (Gao 2003: 247–248). In this sense, terms of 'postsocialist modernity' or 'refracted modernity' coined by McGrath (2008) maybe are the best way to describe China's search for modernity.

By claiming this, it has to be acknowledged that there has been very real ambivalence about the meaning of the precocious prefix 'post' used in previous pages, such as 'postmodern,' 'postsocialist' and 'post-feminist.' This ambivalence is even more apparent when the prefix 'post' meets the suffix '-ism' in a singular term.[3] While recognising the multiple meanings of 'post'—after, beyond, neo, I have further built upon its very deep ambivalence in my arguments throughout this book. In other words, for me, either 'postsocialism' or 'post-feminism' which I associate with this research project is just a periodisation and a political aspiration. I work with these concepts as aspirational in both their theoretical and political senses and attempt to build connections between these 'post' conditions in the context of China to study the changing life experiences of her young people.

For example, I point out the significant role of the flourishing global popular culture in the cultural production of young Chinese femininity. While acknowledging the positive impact of popular culture that often challenges the rigidity of authoritarian nationalist discourses, particularly on the issue of sexuality, I argue that these young Chinese women's revolution (if it can be called revolution) is rather limited, since it is motivated not by political commitment to social change but by the desire to profit.

Moreover, I put my efforts on studying some fundamental elements in Chinese civilisation and give my emphasis on the uniqueness of Chinese cultural context when I try to explain the continuities and changes of Chinese people's mentality

---

[3]Many contemporary scholars have argued for such ambivalence. Lingard and Jn Pierre (2006), for example, work with the ambivalence of postcolonialism. By drawing on a number of postcolonial theorists, they provide a postcolonial policy analysis of the *Education Sector Development Plan: 2000–2005 and Beyond* in the small Caribbean island nation of St Lucia. Their analysis demonstrates the way a postcolonial politics, manifest as strengthening national capital, worked in relation to the production of the Plan in its consultative mode of production and in its extensive cross-sector coverage.

under the current social change. This is because I believe that most of the civilisations are ancient, and have long-standing traditions of learning and knowledge. Each social context is unique in its multi-dimensionality and so is it in terms of the breadth and nature of challenges faced by the region. If we make a general comparison between the Chinese and Western contexts, their values, traditions and the very worldview of the two contexts—they are different and, often quite opposite. For example, while we see a very strong sense of individual liberty, freedom, and free will prevailing in the different contexts in West, we also see harmony, friendship and family are valued more in the Chinese context in place of the idea of each person's being in charge of his or her own life and having freedom to act accordingly (see Nisbett 2003). In other words, in contrast to the Western debate to discover the truth, preserving a harmonious interdependent social life is prioritised in many contexts in the Eastern part of the world. Such socio-cultural factors have their impact on behaviour, performance, the learning and leadership styles, whose outcomes cannot be simply ignored by taking a simplistic universal or general Western approach in any social science research. Otherwise, '[w]e are prone to constantly misunderstanding one another' (Pascoe[4] 2011).

Scenario 2: 'Chinese Modernity' and 'China Dreams'

In this research, I make my investigation of 'China Dreams' by focusing on the individual dreams of young middle-class women living in urban Shanghai. During my fieldwork, I found that there are two strategies which these young Chinese women employ in order to achieve their individual liberation—traditional strategies that emphasise accommodation to mainstream social norms for female attractiveness and gender roles, and non-traditional strategies that emphasise resistance to those norms. Although the forms of resistance being adopted by each young Chinese woman vary, the understanding of subject formation among these young women is more generative at the discursive level, touching on important issues related to agency, such as the material and the symbolic, identity and the self and the relation between the psychological and the social (see McNay 2000: 14–21).

Besides, I found that young Chinese women's identity construction and understandings of young womanhood is closely related to a new form of modernity in Chinese context. For example, my analysis has revealed that 'do-it-yourself' (Beck 2002) or 'choice' (du Bois Raymond 1998) biographies convincingly indicates that the emerging Chinese middle-class young women have also begun to be individually responsible for their own choices and destiny, and begun to construct these life trajectories against declining social norms and traditional cultural frames. Detradtionalisation, disembedment, the creation of a life of one's own by DIY biographic work, and the irresistible pressure to be more independent and

---

[4]Richard Pascoe is the former director of Nottingham University's China Policy Institute.

individualistic which are used to be all indicators of individualisation in Western Europe can also be observed from Chinese individuals nowadays.

However, there are also important differences between the process of individualisation promoted by institutional changes and identity politics in the context of China and in the West. For example, in Western Europe, Giddens (1992) uses 'disembedment' to refer to the change whereby social groups no longer define the identity of the individual, who, by breaking away from the previously encompassing social categories, remakes herself or himself through institutional mechanisms, such as an education, career or lifestyle. Yet, breaking away from the social in identity construction does not mean cutting off interactions with other individuals in everyday life or abandoning sociality; on the contrary, it only redefines relationships by recognising the full autonomy of the individual in the face of the social and with one another, such as the new type of pure relationship of intimacy (see Giddens 1992). This is an equally important part of the indivdualisation process, which is refereed to as 're-embedment' by Beck and Beck-Gernsheim (2002). Nevertheless, both 'disembedement' and 're-embedment' take place at the level of life politics, the everyday politics of lifestyle and personal identity.

In contrast, disembedment in Chinese context manifests itself mainly in the domain of emancipatory politics, such as the everyday politics of life chances, and social status, as revealed in the biographic account presented above. The individual effort of DIY biography is first and foremost about the improvement of living standards and social status. Personal identity does matter, but it matters mainly because it affects one's life chances. As a result, mobility, which seems to be merely one of many factors in many Western European contexts, plays a pivotal role in Chinese context of individualisation. Identity, the core of the politics of recognition, relates more to the claim of individual rights and the redefinition of the individual-group-institution relationship than to the search of the self (see also Yan 2009).

By claiming this, evidence collected in this research also suggests that urban middle-class young women in China do actively engage with contemporary global feminisms and activism through acquiring First World identifications. Indeed, while the media has become the key site for redefining alternative lifestyles and ways of thinking in current times, it also casts new judgments and re-establishes the rules of play in the realm of gender. Particularly for young Chinese women, evidence from this research project in contemporary Shanghai has suggested that the younger generation of Chinese women have also gained tremendous success in education and have begun to serve as a vital labour force within the restructured and globalised market. They make up the ranks of those part-time, flexible workers required by emerging and changing industries and become the latest models of overachieving professionals. In the words of Walkerdine et al. (2001: 3), they are experiencing a remaking process 'as the modern neoliberal subject; a subject of self-invention and transformation who is capable of surviving within the new social, economic and political system.' Success and self-invention has become the full project for them. However, while the discourse of the successful girls is operating so powerfully in the re-conceptualisation of the work of gender study in current times, it should also be noted that feminism is routinely disparaged across many channels of communication (see McRobbie 2009), especially in contemporary Chinese society.

Certainly, there has been virtually no contact between China and the world for 2000 years and then, as soon as there is, it quickly becomes a clash of civilisations in which, as the Chinese see it, the warlike Europeans get the upper hand and start to colonise chunks of Chinese cities such as Shanghai, Tianjin and Guangzhou (Pascoe 2011). Thus, in the 21st century, both of us need to make a real effort to understand the other side and to take the trouble to work out why the other side thinks what they think. The Guardian (2011) reporter claims that such commitment requires the EU to tap in more to this reservoir of goodwill. Meanwhile, it is required the Chinese to keep open to the world. In this sense, my ambition to achieve some cross-cultural understandings through investigating into the life experience of urban middle-class young Chinese women in this single research project has to end in a mode of 'ambition.'

Scenario 3: Troubling Gender in Higher Education

There is no doubt that a general upward trend of women's participation in the current Chinese higher education has reflected feminists' success in improving women's social status and firming beliefs and expectations society holds for women in the Chinese context. For example, while young Chinese women's success in school education has further enabled those who are diligent and focused enough to enroll in reputed urban universities for an advanced higher education degree, this seems to promise a rosy picture for the future of university-educated young Chinese women in terms of the income, respect and occupations that they are able to obtain after their graduation. However, it should also be noted that while an expanding and meritorcratic system at universities could increase opportunities for these women, an expanding patriarchal university system more closely linked to power structures may further marginalise them. As Arnot et al. (1999) have confirmed, while there have certainly been significant gains for girls in the education arena, the decline in gender inequality at university, there has been no reduction in social class inequality and higher education remains socially stratified (Reay et al. 2001).

Therefore, in order to further formulate the 'gendered citizenship education' (see Arnot 2009) in future China, we need to re-examine the relationship between women and Chinese higher education in the wake of higher education expansion, marketisation and internationalisation. Specifically, it is equally important for Chinese educationalists and policy-makers to ensure that the current educational arena for female students could *indeed* cultivate them a higher degree of self-expectations and self-responsibility as individualised and self-perfecting cosmopolitans through posing challenges and questions, such as how far the 'male-stream' curriculum has been permeated and transformed in the current educational system in China; whether the functions of Chinese universities have changed themselves as 'protected spaces' for women; and what role participation in university plays in constructions of class, race, age, disability and sexuality and in the lives of women outside in Chinese context.

For example, during my interviews with contemporary university-educated women in this research, I have always been frustrated by tensions and contradictions in their presentations of feminist efforts. Perhaps, it is such a redistribution of opportunity and a blurring of class and gender distinctions that characterises this new form of young Chinese feminism in today's China. Yet, I also find myself with a renewed excitement about the possibilities of this field of study in the context of China. I feel we have really only scratched the surface of what women can and should know, and the implications of academic feminism for a *transformative* higher education and a *transformable* society. As Quinn (2009: 340) argued, 'we have barely begun to make connections and relations and to engage in mutual learning with women across the globe.'

Admittedly, this book is a result of my firm belief that feminist knowledge production is a form of activism. In other words, I believe that power, opportunities, and success are all modelled by the 'future girl'—a kind of young woman celebrated for her 'desire, determination and confidence' to take charge of her life, seize chances, and achieve her goals (see Baker 2010). Since my commitments are at all times consciously present in this project, such an explicit inscription of commitment may also carry a risk—of dismissal as yet another 'biased' product, too subjective, irrational and emotional. This would provide a neat means for a reader not to take its points seriously. However, 'feminism *is* serious: the question of (the suppression of) sexual difference is one of the most crucial questions in contemporary society' (Young 1995: 128).

Also, this book is my subjective production of one of the differently located Chinese feminisms and nationalisms in the hope to accentuate the flexibility of both terms and to illuminate the critical development of feminist criticism. Throughout the book, I present my personal negotiation of my own in-betweenness by being given the space to reflect upon my cross-cultural experiences, and my own feminist intervention as a young feminist activist who is writing about the cultural reproduction of that nation and her women inside and outside China. In this sense, I hope to make clear that the feminist agenda of China has been fraught with perhaps the same problem as has come to be associated with China's attempts at modernity, namely a contextual barrier that encompasses China's own uniqueness in historical and cultural terms.

Last but not the least, by making efforts on integrating the concepts of Western feminism, Chinese culturalism and the development of individual autonomy into a new theoretical framework, it is my sincere hope that this book could encourage more cross-cultural feminist research in the future so that we could increase our understanding and appreciation of other ways of thinking and living, and therefore conduct a more inclusive cultural conversation rather than an exclusive debate.

Conclusion: Doing Feminism in China

Modernisation is not gender neutral. In the modernisation process women are 'developed' differently, and often inadvertently, from men. By actively participating in the social production and civic activities, young women in present China are establishing dynamic new conceptions of cultural practice. In this process, they deem to encounter not only new opportunities but also new challenges.

When studying the current social change and its impact on young people, Australian feminist youth theorist Harris (2004) put it best—for her, if young people living in the West in the post-war period could be seen as active yet ultimately dependent members of the twentieth-century democratic state, then those who living at the turn of the twenty-first century might be seen, in contrast, as highly individualised and self-perfecting cosmopolitans, who no longer require state-bounded support or recognise traditional national boundaries. Yet, although contemporary neoliberal discourses are continually working to convince us that we can shape the conditions of our lives, the nature of late modern autonomy is illusory or at least limited (Baker 2010). Still, people can only be governed *through* their freedoms and desires rather than *in spite of* them (Rose 1990).

In the gender realm, although contemporary social theorists have increasingly agreed that theorising about greater detachment from social norms and constraints has particular implications for girls and young women (Baker 2010), many reflexive modernisation work, such as Beck's and Giddens', have not yet engaged significantly with feminism (see also Jamieson 1999; McRobbie 2004). Thus, we still need to cultivate an awareness of the danger of conflating de-traditionalisation with emancipation for women in feminist analysis of individualisation. Adkins (2002) holds a similar stance, arguing that individualisation does not *necessarily* transgress gender categories, and social changes are still more likely to be simultaneously produced or co-constructed with traditions.

In the West, the circumstances and characteristics of late modernity have given rise to anxieties about the direction of social and economic life. As Furlong and Cartmel (2007: 15) keenly pointed out in their book *Young People and Social Change*, 'young people today are growing up in a different world to that experienced by previous generations—changes which are significant enough to merit a re-conceptualisation of youth transitions and processes of social reproduction.' This 'different world' is marked by both social and economic characteristics that have forced a fundamental reassessment of the material with which young people are able to craft their identities and forge their livelihoods.

Similarly, in the context of China, it is also much expected that there will be more and more young Chinese women benefit from the dynamic economic modernisation and become 'international', 'global' and 'mobile' cosmopolitans. Yet, it also deserves our attentions and continuous feminist efforts to emancipate younger generations of Chinese female citizens since the extent to which these individuals are *actually* free to choose remained to be disputed, as revealed from the life experience of these young urban middle-class women in this research.

Appendix 1
A Brief Note on Romanisation of Chinese Names and Pronunciation

Small things matter. In this book I choose not to use romanised Chinese name since there is no wholly satisfactory way of using Roman letters to represent the sounds of Chinese. For example, with a few exceptions such as Sun Yat-sen and Yuan Shih-kai, who remain much better known by other forms of translation, Chinese terms and names mainly adopts the pinyin system used in the People's Republic of China.

During most of the nineteenth and twentieth centuries, English speakers used the so-called Wade-Giles system, devised by British Sinologue Sir Thomas Wade in 1859 and then modified by another British Sinologue, Herbert Giles, in 1912. It is in this system of romanisation that English speakers first met Mao Tse-tung, Teng Hsiao-p'ing, and the rest of the dramatis personae of China's long history. However, in the early 1980s things changed. 'Mao Tse-tung' became 'Mao Zedong,' and "Teng Hsiao-p'ing" became 'Deng Xiaoping.' Another important Chinese name is 'Fei Hsiao-tung,' who is a well-known Chinese sociologist in Western scholarship, becoming 'Fei Xiaotong' now.

This new system was called *hanyu pinyin* (*pinyin*, to be precise), a system first put into use in 1958 in the People's Republic of China and officially adopted there in 1979. Since then, *pinyin* has been adopted by the Library of Congress, the American Library Association, and the International Organisation for Standardisation. Even so, the system is still not universal within the Chinese-speaking world. The Republic of China on Taiwan devised a close cousin of *hanyu pinyin* called *tongyong pinyin* and adopted it in 2002, but local jurisdictions still retain the right to adopt the romanisation system of their choice, and some have exercised it.

None of this would matter to the ordinary English reader, except that the *hanyu pinyin* system often uses the letters of alphabet in confusing ways, which in turn misleads the uninitiated about which sound is being represented. For example, different letters are used to represent the same sound. Thus, Chou En-lai, who signed the Geneva Accords of 1954 and who famously shook the hand of Richard Nixon in 1972, is now Zhou Enlai. His surname comes first and is pronounced 'Joe' either way. But 'zh' is not the only way alphabet 'j' sound is represented to English readers. When the 'j' sound is followed by a long 'e' sound, then the syllable is

© Foreign Language Teaching and Research Publishing Co., Ltd
and Springer Science+Business Media Singapore 2016
J. Zheng, *New Feminism in China*, DOI 10.1007/978-981-10-0777-4

written 'ji' (as in 'gee whiz'). And just when you think you have learned that an 'i' represents the long 'e' sound, you will come across the syllable 'zhi'—which is to be pronounced as if it had an 'r' tacked on, as in 'Ger' in 'Germany'. The same rule applies to 'shi' (as in 'shirred') and to 'chi' (as in 'church'). But when the 'ch' sound is followed by English long 'e' sound, it is represented by a 'q' so that 'qi' is pronounced 'chee,' as in 'cheesecake,' and 'qu' is the 'choo' in 'choo-choo train.' This is how the Ch'ing (rhymes with 'ring') dynasty, which ended in 1912, and which figures prominently in this thesis, became the Qing dynasty.

Appendix 2
Problems of Using Ethnographic Methods in China

Assumptions of Western ethnographic research methods	Cultural differences in China
1. Relying on Chinese local language translators to interpret information	Local Mainland Chinese translators with a communist upbringing might not be familiar with the Western or capitalist ways of working and concepts. Translators outside the domain of design and ethnographic research might misinterpret information and important concepts
2. Recruit respondents randomly from a market segmentation database to ensure objectivity	As China is a relationship-oriented society, research teams might encounter difficulty in recruiting when 'knocking on the door cold.' Chinese people do not respond well to strangers as the social structure differentiates 'in-groups' (friends/family) from the 'out-groups' (strangers) (Blackman 1997)
3. Ask questions in an objective or scientific way, inquiring about the 'truth'	Chinese people are more interested in maintaining a harmonious relationship when interacting with each other. Researchers asking a similar question repeatedly in multiple ways with an inquisitive attitude might come through as an offensive interrogation to the Chinese
4. Treat respondents as 'subjects' of study (users). Keeping emotionally distant from respondents to maintain objective results	The separation between 'friendship' and 'business' dealings in the U.S. might come through as an insincere gesture and create distrustful feelings in the Chinese towards Westerners. In China, friendship is a prerequisite to dealing with business and money

(continued)

© Foreign Language Teaching and Research Publishing Co., Ltd and Springer Science+Business Media Singapore 2016
J. Zheng, *New Feminism in China*, DOI 10.1007/978-981-10-0777-4

(continued)

5. Assume respondents will verbally express themselves communicating truthful feelings or opinions	Chinese traditional education is dogmatic and requires the young to be obedient and silent to show respect for teachers, elderly and superiors. This upbringing discourages openness in verbal communication. Chinese will refrain from giving criticisms openly in public especially to strangers and say 'appropriate thing' so as not to offend, giving the opposite party 'face'
6. Assume respondents will participate creatively in the making of artifacts revealing deeper inner thoughts	Chinese education traditionally does not encourage the expression of individual creativity but to excel in imitating the master of classics. Chinese thinking also tend not to challenge the norm but to conform to social expectations and benefits of the group, therefore stifling individual ideas and expressions

Resource Ann (undated). The original research report has been attached at the end of the study

Appendix 3
Categorisation of Chinese 'Class' in the Book

China's rapid economic growth during the past two decades has been accompanied by an equally impressive increase of personal income for urban residents. According to the National Bureau of Statistics of China (2001), per capita annual disposable income of urban households had increased from RMB 343.4 (GDP 33) in 1978 to RMB 6859.6 (GDP 684) in 2001. Even after adjusting for the inflation, the magnitude of increase is still a remarkable 225 %, corresponding to an average annual growth of 6.4 %. To put these numbers into perspective, we note that in the same time period, the annual growth rate of real wage for employees in the US averaged merely 0.54 % (calculated from figures at the US Department of Labour's Bureau of Labour Statistics website at http://www.bls.gov).

Therefore, in urban areas, their population and income characteristics are so different and changing so rapidly that the concept of 'middle-class' has always been confusing and misleading (see Watson 1984). In this thesis I use the standard created by the world leading management and strategic consulting firm McKinsey & Company (see McKinsey 2011) in my categorising of my participants' family background. Generally speaking, according to Chinese household annual income, there have been six classes in contemporary Chinese society:

1. Very wealthy (>RMB 10 million in income or assets) (>GBP 1 million)
2. Wealthy (RMB 300 thousand–RMB 10 million) (GBP 30,000–GBP 1 million)
3. Mass affluent (RMB 200 thousand–RMB 300 thousand) (GBP 20,000–GBP 30,000)
4. Upper middle class (RMB 100 thousand–RMB 200 thousand) (GBP 10,000–GBP 20,000)
5. Lower middle class (RMB 55 thousand–RMB 100 thousand) (GBP 5400–GBP 10,000)
6. Aspirants (<RMB 55 thousand) (<GBP 5400).

© Foreign Language Teaching and Research Publishing Co., Ltd and Springer Science+Business Media Singapore 2016
J. Zheng, *New Feminism in China*, DOI 10.1007/978-981-10-0777-4

Appendix 4
A Brief Introduction of China's Tiered City System and City Geography of Shanghai

As mentioned in the book, my participants in this research project were born and grown up in different inland Chinese cities. Here, I first provide a brief introduction of Chinese city system and the recent structural change. In the 1980s, instead of opening up the whole of China, China decided to develop Special Economic Zones (SEZs) and to open up cities near the coast for foreign investments as part of an economic risk reduction strategy. Since then, resources from western China were drawn and consolidated to support these strategically positioned coastal cities prominently for Beijing in the north, Shanghai in the midst, and Guangzhou in the south, with Shenzhen acting as a gateway from Hong Kong. As such, cities begin their economic reform at different stages and thus with time, this became known as the Chinese tiered city system with cities given the connotation as first, second, third or fourth tier cities (Nee and Cao 2005).

Presently, first tier cities, such as Beijing, Shanghai and Guangzhou, are fuelled by their own domestic demand and consumption, providing the platform for improved living standards, better business and job opportunities and an international showcase to the rest of the world. Yet, we can also see that more of the second tier cities (with over 20 cities in this category) are also taking action to develop as the backbone of China's future economy. For example, already armed with a relatively medium to high disposable incomes and an average GDP per capita of RMB 30,000, these second tiered cities provide a lucrative option for firms to apply blue ocean strategy on Chinese domestic markets (see Nee and Cao 2005).

Then, I sketch out the city geography of Shanghai—where this research project takes place—and the dramatic change experience by Shanghai in recent decades. Located at the mouth of the Yangtze River, Shanghai has been considered as 'China's most Westernised city' (Hayhoe 1988). As a result of the Nanjing Treaty in 1842, Shanghai was forced to be one of five Chinese trading ports open to foreign countries. Since then, Shanghai became a semi-colony with settlements dominated by world powers (including Britain, French, Japan, the USA, and the former Soviet Union) until the return of settlement rights to China in 1945 (Goto-Shibata 1995; Lu 2001a). After the implementation of the economic reform and opening up policy in the 1980s, Shanghai had been given strategic priority for its economic development by the state. Deng Xiaoping, the patriarch of China's economic reform, argued that if China wanted to acquire international status in finance, it needed to depend primarily on Shanghai (Sung 1996). Presently, Shanghai has been viewed as an aspiring international city in the twenty-first century, serving as an economic engine in leading mainland China to transform from a secondary player in the Second (or Third) world to a central force in the global capitalist system.

Now Shanghai spreads across 6300 km^2 (10 times larger than in the 1840s) and is one of China's 33 administrative regions. Demographically, Shanghai is also widely known as a migrant society in China. According to the statistic, the population of Shanghai comprised 13.2 million people with Shanghai resident status (64 % of the population) in 2000, whilst the rest of the population were mainly Chinese migrants (36 %) (Shanghai Municipal Statistical Bureau 2001). In Shanghai, Mandarin is the national common oral language of communication for public occasions and in schools, whilst the major local dialect is Shanghainese, which has no standard written form.

Particularly in recent decades, Shanghai has made serious efforts to achieve its economic goal of becoming an aspiring global city in mainland China, sharing the same fame as other international centers, such as London and Tokyo. For example, since the 1990s Shanghai local government has committed more resources to education by expanding higher education, promoting continuing education for adults and learning in the workplace to improve the quality of its workforce (Chan et al. 2004). It also introduced a series of initiatives to improve students' transnational skills, particularly information technology and English proficiency (Hills and Fleisher 1997). In 1998 Shanghai launched a pilot scheme for bilingual teaching beginning with key point primary or secondary schools and foreign language schools. It is expected to establish about 100 (about 5 %) schools in bilingual teaching in the early 2000s, and to extend the bilingual teaching to more subjects from previous elective ones (Xiao and Lo 2003). This English strategy taken by the Shanghai Municipal Education Commission enables Shanghai to go ahead of Beijing in this respect for three years.

The year 2002 witnessed Shanghai winning the bid to host the 2010 World Expo. In 2004 Shanghai was ranked as the leading mainland Chinese city in terms of general production, growth in GDP and general urban competitiveness (Ni 2005). The existing national competitive edge gives the Shanghai Municipal Government sufficient confidence to achieve its goal to become an international metropolis, the third regional tourist centre in Asia (after Hong Kong and Tokyo), an international cyber port as well as one of the world's international economic, financial, trading and shipping centres through every available means (Gu and Tang 2002). Moreover, the Shanghai Garment Trade Association (SGTA) has formalised its efforts of promoting Shanghai as the new fashion capital of world by forming a new federation that would bring representative organisations from the five major fashion capitals (New York, London, Milan, Paris and Tokyo) together.

In the education arena, Shanghai has also carried out a series of education reforms for its citizens since the late 1970s as a response to social change including globalisation and marketisation. For example, many scholars (Price 1992; Lee 1996; Hawkins et al. 2001; Wan 2004) have identified significant ideological changes in Shanghai, in which the local government has shifted its attention away from socialist revolution to the use of capitalist means for modernisation and international competition. Accordingly, there has been an increased tension between the domination of the CCP-oriented collectivism and the recognition of individual rights and responsibilities. Mak and Lo (1996) observe that education in Shanghai is caught between economic task and moral demand, arguing that this tension is difficult to solve because political and market spirits are antithetical. By examining the citizenship education in Shanghai, Goodman (2002), Zhang (2002) and O'Brien (2001, 2002) have also expressed their new concerns for urban China from the perspectives of the rise of localism (He 2005), the internal local identity struggles between native residents and migrants, and students' weak global citizen identity as a result of lacking global education provision (Lee and Gu 2004; Law 2007).

Appendix 5
Participant Demographics

No.	Name	Age	Studying subject	Status*	Family category	Place of birth	Years in SH	Father's job	Mother's job	Degree of trust***
1	Qian	24	Chinese literature	PG	Lower middle class	Yunman	6	Teacher	Teacher	High
2	Ivy	20	Information technology	UG	Mass affluent	Shanghai	20	Engineer	Civil servant	High
3	Rain	25	Education	PG	Lower middle class	Sichuan	8	Civil servant	Retired	Lower
4	Nancy	23	Psychology	PG	Lower middle class	Hunan	6	Civil servant	Teacher	Lower
5	Lily	23	Media study	UG	Mass affluent	Guangdong	5	Self-employed	Accountant	High
6	Dan	20	Foreign language	UG	Upper middle class	Beijing	2	Engineer	Doctor	Medium
7	Lucy	21	Foreign language	UG	Upper middle class	Shenzhen	3	Company employee	Teacher	Medium
8	Jane	22	Finance	UG	Lower middle class	Hunan	4	Company employee	Retired	Medium
9	Helen	24	Physics	PG	Upper middle class	Hubei	6	Doctor	Doctor	High
10	Fay	25	Psychology	PG	Upper middle class	Shenzhen	3	Self-employed	Accountant	High
11	Julie	23	Finance	UG	Mass affluent	Shaanxi	5	Banker	Accountant	Medium
12	Pearl**	18	Language course	Pre-Uni.	Mass affluent	Shaanxi	5	Banker	Accountant	Medium
13	Ning	26	Chemistry	M.Sc.	Upper middle class	Beijing	1	Civil servant	Engineer	Lower
14	Wendy	24	Business	PG	Upper middle class	Jiangsu	2	Company employee	Teacher	Medium

(continued)

(continued)

15	Sue	24	Business	B.Sc.	Mass affluent	Zhejiang	20	Self-employed	Self-employed	Medium
16	Zoe	19	Management	UG	Upper middle class	Fujian	1	Self-employed	Company employee	High
17	Irene	19	Human resources	UG	Lower middle class	Hunan	1	Company employee	Teacher	Medium
18	Momo	22	Sociology	UG	Lower middle class	Shanghai	22	Civil servant	Company employee	High
19	Beth	22	Management	UG	Upper middle class	Zhejiang	18	Self-employed	Self-employed	Medium
20	Emily	23	Management	UG	Upper middle class	Fujian	16	Self-employed	Accountant	Medium

*UG: current undergraduate student; PG: current postgraduate student; Pre-Uni.: pre-university

B.Sc.: Bachelor of Science degree holder; M.Sc.: Master of Science degree holder

**Julie and Pearl are sisters

***Degree of trust is measured by the times of interviews. For example, once interview with the participant produces lower degree of trust; twice interviews with the participant produces medium degree of trust; interviews with the same participant for three or more times produce high degree of trust

Appendix 6a
Participant Information Sheet

The Impact of Contemporary Social Change in China on Urban Young Chinese Women's Life

The purpose of this project is to develop an in-depth understanding of contemporary urban young Chinese women students' life experience and their perceptions and concerns about gender-related issues in their study and future career. It will provide insight into the strategies used by young Chinese women to achieve equality in both public and private spheres. From this I will develop materials and strategies that support Chinese women in their self-realisation and personal improvement, including further education progression, career development and so on.

The research is co-funded by the Cambridge Overseas Trust (COT) and the China Scholarship Council (CSC), and it will be conducted by Ms. Jiaran ZHENG at the University of Cambridge. The results of the study will be written up and published in a variety of formats in the public domain.

You have been invited to take part in this project as you are a young Chinese woman currently living and studying in Shanghai. Participation is entirely voluntary and you are not obliged to participate. Should you initially decide to take part and then later change your mind, you are free to withdraw from the project at any time. Information collected will be anonymised and safely stored. Further permission will be sought from you regarding using your photos. Otherwise, no reference, either direct or indirect, will be made to you as an individual in any publications of any kind.

If you have any queries, please do not hesitate to contact:

Ms. Jiaran Zheng
Faculty of Education
184 Hills Road
University of Cambridge
Cambridge
CB2 8PQ, UK

Email: jbz21@cam.ac.uk

YOU WILL BE GIVEN A COPY OF THIS TO KEEP,
TOGETHER WITH A COPY OF YOUR CONSENT FORM

© Foreign Language Teaching and Research Publishing Co., Ltd
and Springer Science+Business Media Singapore 2016
J. Zheng, *New Feminism in China*, DOI 10.1007/978-981-10-0777-4

Appendix 6b
Participant Consent Form

The Impact of Contemporary Social Change in China on Urban Young Chinese Women's Life

- I agree to take part in this research which is to investigate the impact of contemporary social changes in China on my life as a young woman.
- The researcher has explained to my satisfaction the purpose of the study and the possible risks involved.
- I have had the principles and the procedure explained to me and I have also read the information sheet. I understand the principles and procedures fully.
- I am aware that I will be required to answer questions about my experience of being a young woman in the family, school, university, and workplace. I am also aware that I will be asked about my attitudes towards sex and personal opinion on Chinese politics, and I feel comfortable to express my opinion as much honestly and freely as I can.
- I understand that any confidential information will be seen only by the researchers and will not be revealed to anyone else.
- I understand that the results of this project will be published in the form of reports, conference papers, journal articles and other academic outputs, although all data provided by myself and other participants will be anonymised as much as possible.
- I understand that I am free to withdraw from the investigation at any time*.

  * However, in the event that I withdraw from the investigation, I give permission for data to continue to be used in an anonymous form.
  Name (please print): ....
  Signed: ....
  Date: ....
  If you have any queries, please do not hesitate to contact:

© Foreign Language Teaching and Research Publishing Co., Ltd
and Springer Science+Business Media Singapore 2016
J. Zheng, *New Feminism in China*, DOI 10.1007/978-981-10-0777-4

Ms. Jiaran Zheng
184 Hills Road
Faculty of Education
University of Cambridge
CB2 8PQ, UK
Email: jbz21@cam.ac.uk

Appendix 7
Samples of Interview Questions

Opening Statement: The purpose of this research is to learn more about the impact of China's social changes (i.e. higher education expansion, urbanisation and economic transformation) on the post-reform generation of young women's lives. I want to know more about your values and beliefs concerning family, education and work. I'm seeking to listen to your life stories, opinions, and concerns as a young woman in today's China. I plan to use the information I collect to write my dissertation and possibly published papers or books. A pseudonym will be used to protect your confidentiality, as stated on the consent form. In exchange I will offer my assistance to you in regard to providing any information I can which may help you solve the problems and difficulties you are confronting with. I would also like to provide you copies of what I write about your experiences for your review for accuracy, additional information, or concerns you may have. I am requesting to record the interview and if you would like the MP3 recorder to be turned off at any time during the interview, please let me know. Do you have any questions before we begin?

Topic 1: Female Body, Beauty and Fashion

1. How would you like to describe yourself? In other words, if you were to think to yourself 'who am I?' then describe yourself, what would you say? Please use one or two sentences.
2. If you had to choose one primary or centralising characteristic concerning your identity, what would it be? Could you say a little more about why you chose this particular aspect of your identity?
3. How do you think of the saying 'a man is mainly assessed by his talent and ability whereas a woman is purely judged by her appearance' (*Langcai Numao*)?
4. How do you think women express their beauty? How do you think Chinese women express their beauty?
5. Do you think your hairstyle matters in your daily life?
6. How do you think hair, especially naturally black straight long, means to Chinese women?
7. Why you choose this hairstyle?
8. Which hairstyle do you think is a 'good' hairstyle for you?

© Foreign Language Teaching and Research Publishing Co., Ltd
and Springer Science+Business Media Singapore 2016
J. Zheng, *New Feminism in China*, DOI 10.1007/978-981-10-0777-4

9. How often do you change your hairstyle? And for what reasons do you think you will change your hairstyle?
10. How do you see fashion? Do you think clothes are associated with power in any way?
11. What do you think of Western brand clothes and Chinese brand clothes?
12. How do you see luxurious goods?
13. Which kind of lifestyle are you dreaming for?
14. Do you think women in China have achieved gender equality in employment nowadays?

Topic 2: Education Goal, Work Expectations and Marriage Expectations

1. Why have you come to this university, in other words, what or who influenced your decision? And why do feel it is important for you to attend university?
2. What concerns, if any, do you have about your success in university?
3. Could you foresee a situation in which you would graduate from this university?
4. Thinking about your experiences with this university thus far, what encounters, relationships, or experiences have been positive, negative, or particularly memorable?
5. Could you tell me about some of your experiences thus far with university faculty?
6. Could you tell me about some of your experiences thus far related with other students?
7. What is your career goal?
8. Have you changed your goals or done any more investigation of your major or career path?
9. What is a 'good job' for you? What is your ideal job?
10. How do you think the gender issue in the labour market in general?
11. Do you have any working experience? Tell me more about your previous experience.
12. Which one do you think is more important: work and marriage?
13. Do you think marriage is important for women?
14. What do you think is the most important factor for women to get married well?
15. How do you define a 'good marriage' and a 'good husband?'
16. How do you think of campus lovers? What do you think cohabitation before marriage?
17. Whether you would consider cohabitation in your relationship?
18. What is your expectation of your future family? For example, do you want to get married? If yes, what is your ideal husband? When do you plan to get married?
19. How do you think of 'leftover women?' Will you feel worried if you are still single in your 30?

Topic 3: Family and Off-Campus Life

1. Can you talk more about your family, such as your family relation, the closeness between you and your parents, and who plays a more authoritative role in family matters?
2. Can you talk more about your parents? You can say anything about them, such as their marriage, their family philosophy, and how you feel about your relation with them?
3. What do you think of being a 'good' daughter?
4. How do you describe yourself in your family?
5. Do your parents have some expectations for you? What are their expectations?
6. Will your parents push you to do something which you don't like to do?
7. If so, will you try to argue with your parents and to persuade them to change their minds and listen to you?
8. Could you say more about your family life? For example, which things leave a deep impression on you?
9. How much control do you feel you have in regard to your financial situation and choices about your life in general?
10. What are some things you do with any free-time you may have?
11. What involvement, if any, do you have in out-of-class activities, programmes, or organisations? Can you tell me more about the experiences you've had in any of these?
12. Which other women would you take as role models, or have influenced you?

Topic 4: Politics and National Identity

1. How do you think of joining the Party in the university?
2. When and why you joined the Communist Party?
3. What other social activities do you prefer to attend in the campus?
4. In terms of your own participation in the social life on campus, do you feel very connected, somewhat connected, or isolated? And, could you share with me a little more about how important social life on campus is for you?
5. Taking the 2010 Work Expo as an example, to what extent do you get involved with this event? What do you think of China hosting the 2008 Olympic Games in Beijing and the on-going World Expo in Shanghai?
6. How do you feel about these events?
7. How do you see contemporary China's position in the world?
8. Can you imagine what China will be like in, say, 20 years?
9. What expectations do you have for the future of China?
10. What do you want to do in the future in order to contribute more to the wider society?
11. What do you think of some social problems in contemporary Chinese society, such as the wealth gap between urbanites and rural people, and any other issues which you can think of?
12. In your specific discipline and at university in general, what opportunities and constraints do you think are important for you to achieve your aims?

13. In the wider social and political context, what opportunities and constraints do you think could influence you to achieve your aims?
14. How do you understand the term 'feminism? What is your definition of 'feminism?'
15. What do you think of the term 'citizenship?' How do you think of yourself as a citizen?
16. This question relates to gender in Chinese society. What do your think on what the media, politicians, educators or others say about what women should like, act like, or do?
17. How do you introduce China (and Shanghai) to foreigners?

Bibliography

Aapola, S., Gonick, M., & Harris, A. (2005). *Young femininity. Girlhood, power and social change*. New York: Palgrave Macmillan.

Abbott, P., & Wallace, C. (1990). *An introduction to sociology: Feminist perspectives*. London and New York: Routledge.

Abbott, P., & Wallace, C. (1992). *The family and the new right*. London: Pluto Press.

ACWF. (1986). *Historical materials of Chinese women's movement: 1921–1927 (Zhongguo funu yundong lishi ziliao: 1921–1927)*. Beijing, China: People's Press.

ACWF. (1988). *Cai Chang, Deng Yingchao, Kang Keqing: Selected works on issues of women's liberation (Cai Chang, Deng Yingchao, Kang Keqing: funu jiefang wenti wenxuan)*. Beijing, China: Pepole's Press.

ACWF. (1989). *History of Chinese women's movement: New democratic revolution period (Zhongguo funu yundongshi: xin minzhuzhuyi geming shiqi)*. Beijing, China: Chunqiu. All-China Women's Federation, Women's Studies Institute.

ACWF Research Group. (2001). Statistics on Chinese women's wage. *Collection of Women's Studies, 5*.

Adkins, L. (2002). *Revisions: Gender and sexuality in late modernity*. Milton Keynes, UK: Open University Press.

Anderson, B. (2006). *Imagined communities: Reflections on the origin and spread of nationalism*. London, New York: Verso.

Andrews, M., Squire, C., & Tamboukou, M. (2008). *Doing narrative research*. London: Sage.

Arnot, M. (2009). *Educating the gendered citizen: Sociological engagements with national and global agendas*. London: Routledge.

Arnot, M., David, M., & Weiner, G. (1999). *Closing the gender gap: Post-war education and social change*. Cambridge: Polity Press.

Arnot, M., & Dillabourgh, J.-A. (Eds.). (2000). *Challenging democracy: International perspectives on gender, education and citizenship*. London, New York: Routledge.

Arnot, M., & Ghaill, M. M. A. (Eds.). (2006). *The RoutledgeFalmer reader in gender and education*. Cornwell: Routledge.

Arnot, M., & Marshall, H. (2008). *Globalising the school curriculum: Gender, EFA and Global Citizenship Education*. RECOUP working paper no. 17. Retrieved February 23, 2009 from http://recoup.educ.cam.ac.uk/publications/WP17-MA.pdf

Baker, H. D. R. (1979). *Chinese family and kinship*. London: Macmillan.

Baker, J. (2010). Great expectations and post-feminist accountability: Young women living up to the 'successful girls' discourse. *Gender and Education, 22*(1), 1–15.

Banks, I. (2000). *Hair mattes: Beauty, power and black women's consciousness*. New York: New York University Press.

Bao, X. L. (1995). *An introduction to western feminist scholarship (Xifang niixingzhuyi yanjiu pingjie)*. Beijing, China: Sanlian Bookstore.

Barker, C. (2008). *Cultural studies. Theory and practice* (3rd ed.). London: Sage.

Barmé, G. R. (1999). *In the red: On contemporary Chinese culture*. New York: Columbia University Press.

Bartky, S. (1988). Foucault, femininity, and the modernisation of patriarchal power. In I. Diamond & L. Quinby (Eds.), *Feminism and foucault: Reflections on resistance*. Boston: Northeastern University Press.

Basit, T. (1996). I'd hate to be just a housewife: Career aspirations of British Muslim girls. *British Journal of Guidance and Counselling, 24*(2), 227–242.

Bateson, G. (1972). *Steps to an ecology of mind: Collected essays in anthropology, psychiatry, evolution and epistemology*. London: Intertext Books.

Baumgardner, J., & Richards, A. (Eds.). (2000). *Manifesta: Young women, feminism, and the future*. New York: Farrar, Straus and Giroux.

Beck, U. (2002). From 'living for others' to 'a life of one's own': Individualisation and women. In U. Beck & E. Beck-Gernsheim (Eds.), *Individualisation: Institutionalised individualism and its social and political consequences* (pp. 54–84). London: Sage.

Beck, U., & Beck-Gernsheim, E. (1995). *The normal chaos of love*. Cambridge: Polity Press.

Beck, U., & Beck-Gernsheim, E. (2002). *Individualisation: Institutionalised individualism and its social and political consequences*. London: Sage.

Benhabib, S. (2004). *The rights of others: Aliens, residents and citizens*. Cambridge: Cambridge University Press.

Bianco, L. (1971:28). *Origins of the Chinese revolution: 1915–1949*. Stanford, California: Stanford University Press.

Blackman, C. (1997). *Negotiating China: Case studies and strategies*. Australia: Allen & Unwin Pty Ltd.

Bordo, S. (1989). *Gender/body/knowledge: Feminist reconstructions of knowing*. Newark, NJ: Rutgers University Press.

Bordo, S. (1993). *Unbearable weight: Feminism, western culture, and the body*. Berkeley: University of California Press.

Bourdieu, P., & Passeron, J.-C. (1977). *Reproduction in education, society and culture*. London, Beverly Hills: Sage.

Boyatzis, E. R. (1998). *Thematic analysis and code development: Transforming qualitative information*. London: Sage.

Buckingham, D. (2000). *The making of citizens: Young people, news and politics*. London: Routledge.

Budgeon, S. (2001). Young women and the practice of micropolitics. *The European Journal of Women's Studies, 8*(1), 7–28.

Bulbeck, C. (2001). *Young women's imagined lives in 1970 and 2000*. Unpublished presentation in Casting New Shadows: Australian Women's Studies Association Conference, Institute for Women's Studies, Macquarie University, Sydney, 31 January–2 February.

Butler, J. (1990). *Gender trouble: Feminism and the subversion of identity*. New York: Routledge.

Butler, J. (1993). *Bodies that matter: On the discursive limits of 'sex'*. New York: Routledge.

Bynner, J., Ferri, E., & Wadsworth, M. (Eds.). (2003). *Changing Britain, changing lives: Three generations at the turn of the century*. London: Institute of Education, University of London.

Chan, D., Mok, K. H., & Tang, A. (2004). Education. In L. Wong, L. T. White, & S. X. Gui (Eds.), *Social policy reform in Hong Kong and Shanghai: A tale of two cities* (pp. 85–126). M. E. Sharpe: Armonk, London.

Charmaz, K. (2003). Grounded theory, objectivist and constructivist methods. In N. Denzin & Y. Lincoln (Eds.), *Strategies of qualitative inquiry* (2nd ed., pp. 249–291). London: Sage.

Charmaz, K. (2006). *Constructing grounded theory*. London: Sage.

China Daily. (2005). *China to be top luxury goods consumer*. Retrieved December 12, 2005 from http://www.chinadaily.com.cn/english/doc/2005-12/12/content_502708.htm

Chow, E. N. L. (2003, August). *Gendered migration, human security, and citizenship: The case of factory workers in South China*. Paper presented at the Annual Meeting of the American Sociological Association, Atlanta, GA.

Chow, E. N. L., & Chen, K. (1994). The impact of the one-child policy on women and the patriarchy family in the People's Republic of China. In E. N. L. Chow & C. W. Berheide (Eds.), *Women, the family, and policy: A global perspective*. Albany: State University of New York Press.

Chow, E. N. L., Zhang, N. H., & Wang, J. L. (2004). Promising and contested fields: Women's studies and sociology of women/gender in contemporary China. *Gender and Society, 18*(2), 161–188.

CNN Report. (2010). *China love report: 'Leftover women' look for younger men*. Retrieved September 10, 2011 from http://www.cnngo.com/shanghai/none/china-love-report-989133

Coles, R. (1989). *The call of stories*. Boston, MA: Houghton Mifflin.

Coles, B. (1995). *Youth and social policy*. London: UCL Press.

Cooper, W. (1971). *Hair: Sex, society and symbolism*. New York: Stein and Day.

Creswell, J. W. (2007). *Qualitative inquiry and research design* (2nd ed.). Thousand Oaks, CA: Sage.

Croll, E. (1978). *Feminism and socialism in China*. London: Routledge and Kegan Paul.

Croll, E. (1995). *Changing identity of Chinese women: Rhetoric, experience and self-perception in the twentieth-century China*. Hong Kong: Hong Kong University Press.

Croll, E. (2000). *Endangered daughters: Discrimination and development in Asia*. London: Routledge.

Crotty, M. (2003). *The foundations of social research meaning and perspective in the research process*. London: Sage.

de Beauvoir, S. (2009). *The second sex* (C. Borde & S. Malovany-Chevallier, Trans.). London: Jonathan Cape.

de Certeau, M. (1984). *The practice of everyday life*. Berkeley: University of California Press.

de Marrais, K. B., & Lapan, S. D. (Eds.). (2004). *Foundations for research: Methods of inquiry in education and the social sciences*. Mahwah, NJ: Lawrence Erlbaum.

Deloitte. (2009). *China's consumer market: What next?* Retrieved May 10, 2010 from http://www.deloitte.com/view/en_GX/global/insights/deloitte-research/consumer-business-research/2d5a17149b6b4210VgnVCM100000ba42f00aRCRD.htm

Denfeld, R. (1995). *The new victorians*. Sydney: Allen and Unwin.

Deng, X. P. (1987). *Deng Xiao-ping: Speeches and writings* (Central Committee of the CCP, Trans.). Oxford: Pergamon Press.

Denzin, N. K. (1989). *Interpretive biography*. Newbury Park, CA: Sage.

Denzin, N. K. (2001). *Interpretive interactionism*. London: Sage.

Denzin, N. K., & Lincoln, Y. S. (Eds.). (1998). *Strategies of qualitative inquiry*. Thousand Oaks, CA: Sage.

Denzin, N. K., & Lincoln, Y. S. (2003). Introduction: The discipline and practice of qualitative research. In N. K. Denzin & Y. S. Lincoln (Eds.), *Strategies of qualitative inquiry* (2nd ed., pp. 1–45). London: Sage.

Denzin, N. K., & Lincoln, Y. S. (2005). *The Sage handbook of qualitative research* (3rd ed.). Thousand Oaks, CA: Sage.

Dirlik, A., & Zhang, X. D. (Eds.). (2000). *Postmodernism and China*. Durham, NC: Duke University Press.

Doctoroff, T. (2007). *Billions: Selling to the new Chinese consumer*. Basingstoke, New York: Palgrave Macmillan.

Du, F. Q. (1993). Introduction. In The Women's Studies Centre of the Tianjin Normal University (Ed.), *Chinese women and development: Status, health, and employment (Zhongguo funu yu fazhan: diwei, jiankong, jiuye)*. Zhengzhou, China: Henan People's.

Du, F. Q. (1998). *Historical and cultural exploration of gender in China (Zhongguo shehui xingbei de lishi wenhua xunzong)*. Tianjin, China: Tianjin Academy of Social Sciences Press.

Du, F. Q. (2000). *Opportunities and mission: Paths and prospects of women's studies centres in universities (Yunming yu shiming: gaoxiao funu yanjiu zhongxin de licheng he qianjin)*. [Reprinted Materials from Newspapers and Journals *Women's Studies* (Baokan fuyin ziliao: funu yanjiu) (Vol. 3, pp. 16–20)].

Du, F. Q. (2001). *Local women's studies reflected in a global perspective—China's experience: An unfinished process (Quanqiu shiye zhong de bentu funuxue: zhongguo dejingyan: yi ge wei wancheng de guocheng)*. [Reprinted Materials from Newspapers and Journals: *Women's Studies* (Baokan fuyin ziliao: funu yanjiu)].

du Bois Raymond, M. (1998). I don't want to commit myself yet: Young people's life concepts. *Journal of Youth Studies, 1*, 63–79.

Durkheim, E. (1984). *The division of labour in society* (W. D. Halls and with an introduction by L. Coser, Trans.). London: Macmillan.

Dwyer, P., & Wyn, J. (2001). *Youth, education and risk: Facing the future*. London: Routledge/Falmer.

Dyhouse, C. (2013). *Girl trouble: panic and progress in the history of young women*. Zed books.

Edwards, L. (2002). Narratives of race and nation in China: Women's suffrage in the early twentieth century. *Women's Studies International Forum, 25*(6), 619–630.

Edwards, L. (2004). Constraining women's political work with "women's work". In A. McLaren (Ed.), *Chinese women, working and living*. London: RoutledgeCurzon.

Eisenhardt, K. M. (1989). Building theories from case study research. *Academy of Management Review, 14*(4), 532–550.

Ely, M., Vinz, R., Downing, M., & Anzul, M. (1997). *On writing qualitative research: Living by words*. London: Falmer.

Entwistle, J. (2000). *The fashioned body: Fashion, dress and modern social theory*. Cambridge: Polity Press.

Erikson, E. H. (1968). *Identity, youth and crisis*. New York: W.W. Norton.

Ermisch, J. F., & Francesconi, M. (2000). Cohabitation in Great Britain: Not for long, but here to stay. *Journal of the Royal Statistical Society, Series A, 163*, 153–171.

Esherick, J. (2000). *Remaking the Chinese city: Modernity and national identity, 1900–1950*. Honolulu: University of Hawai'i Press.

Esherick, J., & Rankin, M. (1990). *Chinese local elites and patterns of dominance*. Berkeley: University of California Press.

European Group for Integrated Social Research. (2001). Misleading trajectories: Transition dilemmas of young adults in Europe. *Journal of Youth Studies, 4*(1), 101–118.

Evans, H. (2002). Past, perfect or imperfect: Changing images of the ideal wife. In S. Brownell & J. N. Wasserstrom (Eds.), *Chinese femininities/Chinese masculinities: A reader*. London: University of California Press.

Fei, X. T. (1983). On Chinese familism. In Y. H. Lin (Ed.), *The golden wing: A sociological study of Chinese familism*. London: Kegan Paul.

Fetterman, D. M. (1989). *Ethnography: Step by step*. London, New Delhi: Sage Publications.

Fine, G. A., & Mechling, J. (1991). Minor difficulties: Changing children in the late twentieth century. In A. Wolfe (Ed.), *America at century's end*. Berkeley: University of California Press.

Firth, R. (1973). *Symbols: Public and private*. Ithaca, NY: Cornell University Press.

Fong, V. L. (2004). *Only hope: Coming of age under China's one-child policy*. Stanford, CA: Stanford University Press.

Foucault, M. (1979). *The history of sexuality* (Translated from the French by Robert Hurley, An Introduction), (Vol. 1). London: Allen Lane.

Frader, L. L. (2003). Labor history after the gender turn: Transatlantic cross currents and research agendas. *International Labor and Working-Class History, 63*, 21–31.

Frost, L. (2001). *Young women and the body. A feminist sociology*. London: Palgrave.

Furlong, A., & Carmel, F. (1997). *Young people and social change*. Buckingham: Open University Press.

Furlong, A., & Carmel, F. (2007). *Young people and social change: New perspectives* (2nd ed.). Maidenhead: McGraw-Hill/Open University Press.

Ganetz, H. (1995). The shop, the home and femininity as a masquerade. In J. Fornas & G. Bolin (Eds.), *Youth culture in late modernity*. London: Sage.

Gao, M. L. (2003). Post-utopian avant-garde art in China. In A. Erjavec (Ed.), *Postmodernism and the postsocialist condition: Politicised art under late socialism*. Berkeley: University of California Press.

Garner, H. (1995). *The first stone: Some questions about sex and power*. Sydney: Pan Macmillan.

Gaskell, J., Eichler, M., Pan, J., Xu, J. Y., & Zhang, X. M. (2004). The participation of women faculty in Chinese universities: Paradoxes of globalisation. *Gender and Education,16*(4), 511–529.

Gasster, M. (1969). Reform and revolution in China's political modernization. In M. C. Wright (Ed.), *China in revolution: The first phase* (pp. 1900–1913). New Haven: Yale University Press.

Gauthier, M. (2003). The inadequacy of concepts: The rise of youth interest in civic participation in Quebec. *Journal of Youth Studies,6*, 265–277.

Geertz, C. (1973). *The interpretation of cultures: Selected essays*. New York: Hutchinson.

Gellner, E. (1983). *Nations and nationalism*. Ithaca: Cornell University Press.

Gemzoe, L. (2003). *Bildas Ismer, feminism*. Stockholm: Bilda Forlag.

Geronimus, A. T. (1997). Teenage childbearing and personal responsibility: An alternative view. *Political Science Quarterly,112*(3), 405–430.

Gerson, K. (1991). Coping with commitment: Dilemmas and conflicts of family life. In A. Wolfe (Ed.), *America at century's end*. Berkeley: University of California Press.

Ghaill, M. M. A., & Haywood, C. (2007). *Gender, culture and society: Contemporary femininities and masculinities*. New York: Palgrave Macmillan.

Gibson, R. (1986). *Critical theory and education*. London: Hodder and Stoughton.

Giddens, A. (1992). *The transformation of intimacy: Love, sexuality and eroticism in modern societies*. Oxford: Polity Press.

Gilbert, S. (1973). The emancipation of Chinese women. *World Politics,26*(1), 55–79.

Gillham, B. (2005). *Research interviewing: The range of techniques*. England: Open University Press.

Gilmartin, C. K. (1995). *Engendering the Chinese revolution: Radical women, communist politics, and mass movements in the 1920s*. Berkeley: University of California Press.

Gilmartin, C. K., Hershatt, G., Rofel, L., & White, T. (1994). *Engendering China: Women, culture and the state*. London: Harvard University Press.

Giorgi, A. (1995). Phenomenological psychology. In J. A. Smith, R. Harre, & L. Van Langenhove (Eds.), *Handbook of qualitative research methods*. Leicester: BPS Books.

Giroux, H. A. (1989). *Schooling for democracy: Critical pedagogy in the modern age*. London: Routledge.

Glaser, B. G., & Strauss, A. (1967). *The discovery of grounded theory*. Chicago: Aldine.

Global Citizenship Project. (2003). *Global citizenship: The newsletter of the global citizenship project*. Winter. Global Citizenship Project, Faculty of Education, University of Glasgow. Available on http://www.global-citizenship.org

Goodman, D. S. G. (2002). Structuring local identity: Nation, province and country in Shanxi during the 1990s. *China Quarterly,172*, 837–862.

Gordon, T. (1990). *Feminist mothers*. London: Macmillan.

Gordon, T. (1994). *Single women—On the margins?*. London: Macmillan.

Goto-Shibata, H. (1995). *Japan and Britain in Shanghai*. Basingstoke: MacMillan.

Grbich, C. (2007). *Qualitative data analysis: An introduction*. London: Sage.

Griffin, C. (2001). The young women are having a great time: Representations of young women and feminism. *Feminism and Psychology,11*(2), 182–186.

Gu, X. L. (2001). Have a clear view of the situation, make clear the tasks, strive to open up a new prospect for women's federation's work in education and training (Renqing xingshi, mingque renwu, nuli kaichuang fulian jiaoyu peixun gongzuo de xin jumian). *Chinese Women's Movement (Zhongguo fuyun),9,* 9–15.

Gu, F. R., & Tang, Z. L. (2002). Shanghai: Reconnecting to the global economy. In S. Sassen (Ed.), *Global networks, linked cities*. London: Routledge.

Guba, E. G., & Lincoln, Y. S. (1994). Competing paradigms in qualitative research. In N. K. Denzin & Y. S. Lincoln (Eds.), *Handbook of qualitative research* (pp. 105–117). London: Sage.

Guo, F. (2000). The historical track of the Chinese ancient female personality. *Chinese Education and Society,33*(6), 6–14.

Haerpfer, C. W., & Wallace, C. (2002). Pattern of participation in the informal economy in east-central Europe, 1991–199. In R. Neef & M. Stanculescu (Eds.), *The social impact of informal economies in eastern Europe* (pp. 28–45). Hants and Burlington: Ashgate.

Hakim, C. (2000). *Work-lifestyle choices in the 21st century: Preference theory*. Oxford: Oxford University Press.

Hakim, C. (2011). *Honey money: The power of erotic capital*. London: Allen Lane.

Hamel, J. (1993). *Case study methods*. Thousand Oaks, CA: Sage.

Hansen, L. (2000). *Gendered communities: The ambiguous attraction of Europe. International relations theory and the politics of the European Union* (pp. 131–148). London: Routledge.

Harris, A. (2001, May 27–31). Riding my own tidal wave: Young women's feminist work [Special issue: Young women: Feminist, activists, grrrls]. *Canadian Women's Studies Journal*.

Harris, A. (2004). *Future girl: Young women in the twenty-first century*. New York: Routledge.

Harris, A. (2008). *Next wave cultures: Feminism, subcultures, activism*. London: Routledge.

Harvey, L. (1990). *Critical social research*. London: Unwin Hyman.

Haskey, J. (2001). Cohabitation in Great Britain: Past, present and future trends—and attitudes. *Population Trends,103,* 4–25.

Haskey, J. (2005). Living arrangements in contemporary Britain: Having a partner who usually lives elsewhere and living apart together (LAT). *Population Trends,122,* 35–45.

Haste, H. (2005). Moral responsibility, moral creativity and citizenship education. In D. Wallace (Ed.), *Art, science and morality: Creative journeys*. New York: Plenum Press.

Hawkins, J. N., Zhou, N. Z., & Lee, J. (2001). China: Balancing the collective and the individual. In W. K. Cummings, M. T. Tatto, & J. N. Hawkins (Eds.), *Values education for dynamic societies: Individualism or collectivism* (pp. 191–206). Hong Kong: The University of Hong Kong, Comparative Education Research Centre.

Hayhoe, R. (1988). Shanghai as a mediator of the educational open door. *Pacific Affairs,61,* 253–284.

Hays, S. (1996). *The cultural contradictions of motherhood*. New Haven and London: Yale University Press.

He, B. G. (2005). Village citizenship in China: A case study of Zhejiang. *Citizenship Studies,9,* 205–219.

Health, S., & Cleaver, E. (2003). *Young, free and single*. Basingstoke: Palgrave.

Helve, H. (1997). Perspectives on social exclusion, citizenship and youth. In J. Bynner, L. Chisholm, & A. Furlong (Eds.), *Youth, citizenship and change in a European context*. Aldershot: Ashgate.

Hesse-Biber, N., & Leavy, P. (2006). *The practice of qualitative research*. London: Sage.

Hills, S., & Fleisher, B. M. (1997). Education and regional economic development in China: The case of Shanghai. *Comparative Economic Studies,39,* 25–52.

Hiltebeitel, A., & Miller, B. D. (1998). *Hair: Its power and meaning in Asian cultures*. Albany: State University of New York Press.

Hite, S. (1987). *The Hite report: Women and love: A cultural revolution in progress*. London: Penguin.

Hom, S. K., & Xin, C. Y. (1995). *English–Chinese lexicon of women and law*. Beijing, China: CTPC and UNESCO.

Hu, Z. P. (2001). *How the trend of girls achieving better results than boys emerges in China's schooling*. Presented in AARE 2001 International Education Research Conference, Fremantle, Australia, 2–6 December 2001.

Huang, Q. Z. (1996). *Incorporate gender perspective into mainstream decision making (Xingbei guandian naru juece zhuliu)*. [Reprinted Materials from Newspapers and Journals: *Women's Studies* (Baokan fuyin ziliao: Funu yanjiu) (Vol. 4, p. 14)].

Hughes-Bond, L. (1998). Standing alone, working together: Tensions surrounding young Canadian women's views of the workplace. *Gender and Education,10*(3), 281–297.

Iacovou, M., & Berthoud, R. (2001). *Young people's lives: A map of Europe*. Colchester: University of Essex, Institute for Social and Economic Research.

Ivinson, G., Arnot, M., Araujo, H., Deliyanni-Kouimtzi, K., Rowe, G., & Tome, A. (2000). Student teachers' representations of citizenship: A comparative perspective. In M. Arnot & J. Dillabough (Eds.), *Challenging democracy: Feminist perspectives on gender, education and citizenship*. London: RoutledgeFalmer.

Jacka, T. (1997). *Women's work in rural China: Change and continuity in an era of reform*. Cambridge: Cambridge University Press.

Jacobs, J. (2003). *Women, violence and memory: The ethics of feminist ethnography in holocaust research*. Paper presented at the Annual Meeting of the American Sociological Association. Atlanta, GA: Atlanta Hilton Hotel (Online). Retrieved May 26, 2009 from http://www.allacademic.com/meta/p106944_index.html

Jamieson, L. (1999). Intimacy transformed? A critical look at the 'pure relationship'. *Sociology,33*, 477–494.

Janesick, V. (2000). The choreography of qualitative research design: Minuets, improvisation and crystallisation. In N. Denzin & Y. Lincoln (Eds.), *Handbook of qualitative research* (2nd ed., pp. 379–399). London: Sage.

Jiang, Z. M. (1990, March 8). The whole party and society should have Marxist perspectives on women (Quandang quanshehui douyao shuli Marxist funuguan). *People's Daily*.

Jin, Y. H. (2000). *The decline of patriarchy: Gender in the modernisation process of rural areas in southern Jiangsu province (Fuquan de shiwei: jiangnan nongcun xiandaihua jincheng zhong de xingbei yanjiu)*. Chengdu, China: Sichuan People's Press.

Jin, Y. H. (2007). Rethinking the 'iron girls': Gender and labour during the Chinese cultural revolution. In D. Ko & Z. Wang (Eds.), *Translating feminisms in China: A special issue of gender and history*. Oxford: Blackwell Publishing Ltd.

Jones, G. (1995). *Leaving home*. Buckingham: Open University Press.

Jones, G., & Bell, R. (2000). *Balancing acts: Youth, parenting and public policy*. York: Joseph Rowntree Foundation.

Jordan, J. V. J., Kaplan, A. G., Miller, J. B., Stiver, I. P., & Surrey, J. L. (1991). *Women's growth in connection: Writings from the stone centre*. New York: The Guilford Press.

Jordan, S., & Yeomans, D. (1995). Critical ethnography in contemporary theory and practice. *British Journal of Sociology of Education,16*(3), 389–408.

Judd, E. R. (2002). *The Chinese women's movement: Between state and market*. Stanford: Stanford University Press.

Kang, K. Q. (1978). Noble tasks for the Chinese women's movement in the new era (Xin shiqi zhongguo funu yundong de chonggao renwu). In All-China Women's Federation (Ed.), *Mobilizing women of all ethnic groups to carry out the new long march (Ge zu funu dongyuan qilai jinxing xin de changzheng)*. Beijing, China: People's Press.

Kenway, J., & Langmead, D. (2000). Cyberfeminism and citizenship? Challenging the political imaginary. In M. Arnot & J.-A. Dillabourgh (Eds.), *Challenging democracy: International perspectives on gender, education and citizenship*. London, New York: Routledge.

Kettley, N., Whitehead, J. M., & Raffan, J. (2008). Worried women, complacent men? Gendered responses to differential funding in higher education. *Oxford Review of Education,34*(1), 111–129.

Kiernan, K. (2001). The rise of cohabitation and childbearing outside marriage in western Europe. *International Journal of Law, Policy and the Family,15*(1), 1–21.

Kiernan, K. (2004). Unmarried cohabitation and parenthood in Britain and Europe. *Law and Policy,26*(1), 33–56.

Kincheloe, J. L., & McLaren, P. (2000). Rethinking critical theory and qualitative research. In N. Denzin & Y. Lincoln (Eds.), *Handbook of qualitative research* (2nd ed., pp. 279–314). London: Sage.

Kleinman, A. (1988). *The illness narratives*. New York: Basic Books.

Ko, D., & Zheng, W. (Eds.). (2007). *Translating feminisms in China*. Oxford: Blackwell Publishing.

KPMG. (2007). *Luxury brands in China*. Retrieved March 10, 2010 from http://www.kpmg.com/cn/en/issuesandinsights/articlespublications/pages/luxury-brands-china-200703.aspx

Kvale, S. (1989). *Issues of validity in qualitative research*. Lund: Studentlitteratur.

Law, W. W. (2007). Globalisation, city development and citizenship education in China's Shanghai. *International Journal of Educational Development,27*, 18–38.

LeCompte, M. D., Millroy, W. L., & Preissle, J. (Eds.). (1992). *The handbook of qualitative research in education*. San Diego: Academic Press.

LeCompte, M. D., Preissle, J., & Tesch, R. (1993). *Ethnography and qualitative design in educational research* (2nd ed.). San Diego, London: Academic Press.

Lee, W. O. (1996). Guest editor's introduction to the special issue on moral education policy: Developments since 1978. *Chinese Education and Society,29*, 5–12.

Lee, W. O., & Gu, R. F. (Eds.). (2004). *Global citizenship education: A survey on secondary schools in Hong Kong and Shanghai (Guoji Shhiye Yu Gongmin Jiaoyu: Xianggang Ji Shanghai Zhongxue Zhuangkuang Diaocha)*. Shanghai: Academy of Social Sciences Press.

Lees, S. (2000). Sexuality and citizenship education. In M. Arnot & J.-A. Dillabourgh (Eds.), *Challenging democracy: International perspectives on gender, education and citizenship*. London, New York: Routledge.

Leonard, M. (1998). Paper planes: Travelling the new grrrl geographies. In T. Skelton & G. Valentine (Eds.), *Cool places: Geographies of youth cultures*. London: Routledge.

Li, X. J. (1988). *The exploration of eve (Xiawa de tansuo)*. Zhengzhou, China: Henan People's Press.

Li, X. J. (1989). *Gender gap (Xing gou)*. Beijing, China: SanLian.

Li, X. J. (1995). *Toward women: Report of women's studies in the new era (Zou xiang nuren: xinshiqi funu yanjiu jishi)*. Zhengzhou, China: Henan People's Press.

Li, X. J. (2000). Moving in-between the margin and the centre (Youli yu bianyuan yu zhuliu zhijian). *Chinese Female Culture (Zhongguo nuxing wenhua),1*, 43–54.

Li, Y. H. (2005). *Nuxing zhuyi*. Jinan: Shandong People's Press.

Li, H. L., & Wang, Q. (1996). *Research on the Chinese work unit society*. Frankfurt am Main: Peter Lang.

Lin, J. L. (2000). Evolution of the confucian concept of women's value in recent times. *Chinese Education and Society,33*(6), 15–23.

Lin, C., Liu, B. H., & Jin, Y. H. (1998). Women's studies in China. In A. Jagger & I. Young (Eds.), *A companion to feminist philosophy*. Oxford, UK: Basil Blackwell.

Lingard, B., & Jn Pierre, K. D. (2006). Strengthening national capital: A postcolonial analysis of lifelong learning policy in St Lucia, Caribbean. *Pedagogy, Culture and Society,14*(3), 295–314.

Lingard, B., Martino, W., & Mills, M. (2009). *Boys and schooling: Beyond structural reform*. Basingstoke: Palgrave Macmillan.

Lister, R. (2003). *Citizenship: Feminist perspectives* (2nd ed.). New York: New York University Press.

Liu, L. (1995). The female body and nationalist discourse: The field of life and death revisited. In I. Grewal & C. Kaplan (Eds.), *Scattered hegemonies: Postmodernity and transnational feminist practices*. Minneapolis, London: University of Minnesota Press.

Liu, B. H. (1999). *'95 world conference on women and Chinese women's studies. (Shijie funu dahui he zhongguo funu yanjiu)*. [Reprinted Materials from Newspapers and Journals: *Women's Studies* (Baokan fuyin ziliao: funu yanjiu) (Vol. 2, pp. 13–18)].

Liu, F. S. (2006). Boys as only-children and girls as only-children—Parental gendered expectations of the only-child in the nuclear Chinese family in present-day China. *Gender and Education, 18*(5), 491–505.

Liu, D. L., Ng, M. L., Zhou, L. P., & Haeberle, E. (1997). *Sexual behaviour in modern China*. New York: Continuum Publishing Company.

Liu, Y. S., & Wang, Z. M. (2009). Women entering the elite group: A limited progress. *Frontiers of Education in China, 4*(1), 27–55.

Lloyd, M. (1996). Feminism, aerobics and the politics of the body. *Body and Society, 2*(2), 79–98.

Looker, E., & Magee, P. (2000). Gender and work: The occupational experience of young women and men in the 1990s. *Gender Issue, 18*(2), 74–88.

Louie, K. (2002). *Theorising Chinese masculinity: Society and gender in China*. Cambridge: Cambridge University Press.

Lu, J. G. (2001a). *Abnormal prosperity: Shanghai ruled by foreign powers between the Mid-1800s and Early 1990s*. Shanghai: Baijia Press.

Lu, S. H. (2001b). *China, transnational visuality, global postmodernity*. Stanford, CA: Stanford University Press.

Lu, M. Y. (2004). The awakening of Chinese women and the women's movement in the early twentieth century. In J. Tao, B. J. Zheng, & S. L. Mow (Eds.), *Holding up half the sky*. New York: The Feminist Press.

Lynch, J. (1992). *Education for citizenship in a multi-cultural society*. London: Cassell.

Mak, G. C. L., & Lo, L. N. K. (1996). Education. In Y. M. Yeung & Y. M. Sung (Eds.), *Shanghai: Transformation and modernisation under China's open policy* (pp. 375–398). Hong Kong: Chinese University Press.

Marder, E. (1992). Disarticulated voices: Feminism and Philomela. *Hypatia, 7*(2), 148–166.

Marshall, T. H. (1950). *Citizenship and social class*. Cambridge: Cambridge University Press.

Martin, F. (2003). *Interpreting everyday culture*. London: Hodder Arnold.

Marx, K. (1968). *Capital: A critique of political economy*. New York: Vintage Books.

Mason, J. (2002). *Qualitative researching* (2nd ed.). London: Sage.

Maxwell, J. A. (1998). Designing a qualitative study. In L. Bickman & D. J. Rog (Eds.), *Handbook of applied research methods* (pp. 69–100). London: Sage.

Maynard, M. (2004). *Dress and globalisation*. Manchester: Manchester University Press.

McClelland, S. I., & Fine, M. (2008). Rescuing a theory of adolescent sexual excess. Young women and wanting. In A. Harris (Ed.), *Next wave cultures. Feminism, subcultures, activism*. New York: Routledge.

McGrath, J. (2008). *Postsocialist modernity: Chinese cinema, literature, and criticism in the market age*. Stanford: Stanford University Press.

McGregor, J. (2005). *One billion customers*. London: Nicholas Brealey Publishing.

McKinsey, I. (2009). *The coming of age: China's new class of wealthy consumers*. Retrieved May 10, 2010 from http://bx.businessweek.com/china-marketing/view?url=http%3A%2F%2Fwww.mckinsey.com%2Flocations%2Fgreaterchina%2Fmckonchina%2Freports%2Fchina_wealthy_household.aspx

McKinsey Quarterly. (2011, April). *Tapping China's luxury-goods market*. Retrieved December 18, 2011 from http://www.asia.udp.cl/Informes/2011/china_luxury.pdf?mod=WSJASIA_hps_MIDDLEThirdNews

McNay, L. (2000). *Gender and agency: Reconfiguring the subject in feminist and social theory*. Cambridge: Polity Press.

McRobbie, A. (2000). *Feminism and youth culture* (2nd ed.). Basingstoke: Macmillan.

McRobbie, A. (2004). Post-feminism and popular culture. *Feminist Media Studies,4*, 255–264.

McRobbie, A. (2009). *The aftermath of feminism: Gender, culture and social change*. London: Sage.

Merriam, S. B. (1998). *Qualitative research and case study applications in education*. San Francisco, CA: Jossey-Bass Publishers.

Merriam, S. B. (2009). *Qualitative research: A guide to design and implementation*. San Francisco: Jossey-Bass.

Meskill, J. (Ed.). (1973). *An introduction to Chinese civilisation*. New York: Columbia University Press.

Miles, S. (2000). *Youth lifestyles in a changing world*. Buckingham: Open University Press.

Mirza, H. S. (1992). *Young, female and black*. London: Routledge.

Mishler, E. (1991). *Research interviewing: Context and narrative*. Cambridge, MA: Harvard University Press.

Mohanty, C. (2003). Under western eyes. Revisited: Feminist solidarity through anti-capitalist struggles. *Signs: Journal of Women in Culture and Society,28*(1), 499–535.

MORI. (2005). *Being young in Scotland 2005*. Retrieved July 14, 2009 from www.scotland.gov. uk/publications/2005/09/02151404/14051

Mouzelis, N. P. (1994). *Back to sociological theory: The construction of social orders*. Basingstoke: Macmillan.

Musil, C. (2000). Women's studies: Overview. In C. Kramarae & D. Spender (Eds.), *Routledge international encyclopedia of women: Global women's issues and knowledge*. New York: Routledge.

Narayan, U. (2008). 'Westernisation', respect for cultures and third-world feminists. In S. Deidman & J. C. Alexander (Eds.), *New social theory reader* (2nd ed.). New York: Routledge.

Nee, V., & Cao, Y. (2005). Institutional change and income inequality in urban China. In H. D. Assmann & K. M. Filseck (Eds.), *China's new role in the international community: Challenges and expectations for the 21st century*. Switzerland: Peter Lang.

News Report. (2007). *The 100 most powerful women*. Retrieved January, 2010 from http://www. forbes.com/lists/2007/11/biz-07women_The-100-Most-Powerful-Women_Rank.html

Ni, P. F. (Ed.). (2005). *Annual report on urban competitiveness—industrial cluster: The engine of China economy (Zhongguo Chengshi Jingzhengli Baogao 3 – Jiti: Zhongguo Jingji De Longmai)*. Beijing: Social Sciences Academy Press.

Nicoletti, C., & Tanturri, M. L. (2005). *Differences in delaying motherhood across European countries: Empirical evidence from the ECHP*. Colchester: Institute for Social and Economic, Research University of Essex.

Nisbett, R. E. (2003). *The geography of thought: How Asians and Westerners think differently and why*. New York: Free Press.

North-eastern Normal University, Centre for Female Research. (2002). Summary of seminar on women's studies curriculum and teaching in Chinese Universities (Zhongguo gaoxiao nuxingxue kecheng jianshe yujiaoxue yantaohui zongshu). *Collection of Women's Studies (Funu yanjiu luncong),11*, 62–68.

O'Brien, S. (1999). Is the future of Australian feminism feral? In R. White (Ed.), *Australian youth subcultures: On the margins and in the mainstream*. Hobart: National Clearinghouse for Youth Studies.

O'Brien, K. J. (2001). Villagers, elections, and citizenship in contemporary China. *Modern China,27*, 407–435.

O'Brien, K. J. (2002). Villagers, elections, and citizenship. In M. Goldman & E. J. Perry (Eds.), *Changing meanings of citizenship in modern China* (pp. 212–231). Cambridge, Mass: Harvard University Press.

Oakley, A. (1981). *Subject women*. Oxford: Robinson.

One plus One. (2004). *Relationships Today, 5 May*. Retrieved May 19, 2007 from www. oneplusone.org.uk

Ong, A. (1999). *Flexible citizenship: The cultural logic of transnationality*. Durha, NC: Duke University Press.

Ono, K. (1978). *Chinese women in a century of revolution, 1850–1950*. Stanford, CA: Stanford University Press.

Pallotta-Chiarolli, M. (1999). Coming out/going home: Australian girls and young women interrogating racism and heterosexism [Special issue: Girl trouble? Feminist inquiry into the lives of young women]. *Women's Studies Journal15*(2), 71–88.

Papic, Z. (1992). In A. Ward, J. Gregory, & N. Yuval-Davis (Eds.), *Women and citizenship in Europe: Borders, rights and duties*. Stoke-on-Trent: Trentham Books and EFSF.

Pateman, C. (1988). *The sexual contract*. Oxford: Polity.

Patton, M. Q. (1985, April). Quality in qualitative research: Methodological principles and recent developments. *Invited Address to Division J of the American Educational Research Association, Chicago*.

Patton, M. Q. (2002). *Qualitative research and evaluation methods* (3rd ed.). Thousand Oaks, CA: Sage.

Pepper, S. (1996). *Radicalism and education reform in 20th-century China: The search for an ideal development model*. Cambridge: Cambridge University Press.

Perry, E. J., & Selden, M. (2010). *Chinese society: Change, conflict and resistance* (3rd ed.). London: Routledge.

Peshkin, A. (1988). In search of subjectivity—one's own. *Educational Researcher,17*(7), 17–22.

Peshkin, A. (1990). *Qualitative inquiry in education: The continuing debate*. New York, London: Teachers College Press.

Philo, G. (2007). *Cultural transfer: The impact of direct experience on evaluation of British and Chinese societies*. A report on cultural transfer between Britain and China for the British Council. Retrieved October 29, 2008 from http://www.gla.ac.uk/centres/mediagroup/Philo%20China%20article%20Guardian290307.pdf

Powell, R. (2004). The inefficient use of power: Costly conflict with complete information. *American Political Science Review,98*(2), 229–239.

Price, R. F. (1992). Moral-political education and modernisation. In R. Hayhoe (Ed.), *Education and modernisation: The Chinese experience* (pp. 211–237). Oxford: Pergamon Press.

Print, M., Saha, L., & Edwards, K. (2004). *Youth electoral study: Enrolment and voting*. Retrieved December 10, 2008 from www.aec.gov.au/_content/What/publications/youth_study_1/index.htm

Probert, B., & Macdonald, F. (1999). *Young women: Poles of experience in work and parenting. Australia's young adults: The deepening divide*. Sydney: Dusseldorp Skills Forum.

Punch, M. (1994). Politics and ethics in qualitative research. In N. K. Denzin & Y. S. Lincoln (Eds.), *Handbook of qualitative research*. Thousand Oaks: Sage.

Pye, L. W. (1992). *The spirit of Chinese politics*. Harvard: Harvard University Press.

Quinn, J. (2009). Many more rivers to cross: Women and higher education. Review essay. *Gender and Education,21*(3), 337–341.

Ragin, C. C. (1992). 'Casing' and the process of social inquiry. In C. C. Ragin & H. S. Becker (Eds.), *What is a case? Exploring the foundations of social inquiry* (pp. 217–226). Cambridge: Cambridge University Press.

Ragin, C. C., & Byrne, D. (2009). *The Sage handbook of case-based methods*. London: Sage.

Rattansi, A., & Phoenix, A. (1997). Rethinking youth identities: Modernist and postmodernist frameworks. In J. Bynner, L. Chisholm, & A. Furlong (Eds.), *Youth, citizenship and change in a European context*. Aldershot: Ashgate.

Reay, D., Davies, J., David, M., & Ball, S. J. (2001). Choices of degrees or degrees of choice? Class, 'race' and the higher education choice process. *Sociology,35*, 855–877.

Reissman, C. (1993). *Narrative analysis*. London: Sage.

Rich, E. (2005). Young women, feminist identities and neo-liberalism. *Women's Studies International Forum,28*, 495–508.

Richardson, D. (1998, February). Sexuality and citizenship. *Sociology, 32*(1).

Robson, C. (2002). *Real world research*. Oxford: Blackwell.

Roces, M., & Edwards, L. (2000). *Women in Asia: Tradition, modernity and globalisation*. Michigan: The University of Michigan Press.

Rofel, L. (1999). *Other modernities: Gendered yearnings in China after socialism*. Berkeley: University of California Press.

Rofel, L. (2007). *Desiring China: Experiments in neoliberalism, sexuality, and public culture*. Durham and London: Duke University Press.

Roiphe, K. (1995). *The morning after*. Boston: Little Brown.

Rose, N. (1990). *Governing the soul: The shaping of the private self*. London: Routledge.

Rossiter, M. (1999). Understanding adult development as narrative. In M. C. Clark & R. S. Caffarella (Eds.), *An update on adult development theory: New ways of thinking about the life course. New directions for adult and continuing education. No. 84*. San Francisco: Jossey-Bass.

Rudd, P., & Evans, K. (1998). Structure and agency in youth transitions: Student experiences of vocational further education. *Journal of Youth Studies,1*(1), 39–62.

Sagger, S. (2000). *Race and representation: Electoral politics and ethnic pluralism in Britain*. Manchester: Manchester University Press.

Schirokauer, C. (1991). *A brief history of Chinese civilisation*. San Diego: Harcourt Brace Jovanovich.

Schwandt, T. A. (2000). Three epistemological stances for qualitative inquiry. In N. Denzin & Y. Lincoln (Eds.), *Handbook of qualitative research* (2nd ed., pp. 189–213). London: Sage.

Scott, J. W. (1996). *Feminism and history*. Oxford: Oxford University Press.

Selman, P. (2003). Scapegoating and moral panics: Teenage pregnancy in Britain and the United States. In S. Cunningham-Burley & L. Jamieson (Eds.), *Families and the state: Changing relationships*. Palgrave: Basingstoke.

Shanghai Municipal Education Commission. (2001). *An opinion concerning the implementation of the strengthening of bilingual teaching in primary and secondary schools in Shanghai provisional (Guanyu Jinyibu Jiaqiang Benshi Zhongxiaoxue Waiyu Jiaoxue De Shishi Yijian Shixing)*. Shanghai: Shanghai Municipal Education Commission.

Shanghai Municipal Statistical Bureau. (2001). Retrieved August 10, 2010 from http://www.shanghai.gov.cn/shanghai/node17256/node17432/node17435/userobject22ai17.html

Shkedi, A. (2005). *Multiple case narrative: A qualitative approach to studying multiple populations*. Amsterdam: John Benjamins.

Si, X. S., & Bruton, G. (1999). Knowledge transfer in international joint ventures in transitional economies: The Chinese experience. *The Academy of Management Executive,13*(1), 83–90.

Silva, E. B., & Smart, C. (Eds.). (1999). *The new family?*. London: Sage.

Silverman, D. (2001). *Interpreting qualitative data: Methods for analysing talk, text and interaction*. London: Sage.

Siu, B. (1982). *Women of China: Imperialism and women's resistance 1900–1949*. London: Zed Press.

Skeggs, B. (1997). *Formations of class and gender: Becoming respectable*. London: Sage.

Social Exclusion Unit. (1999). *Teenage pregnancy*. London: HMSO.

Spivak, G. C. (1988). *In other worlds: Essays in cultural politics*. New York: Routledge.

Spivak, G. C. (2010). Can the subaltern speak? In R. Morris (Ed.), *Reflections on the history of an idea*. New York; Chichester: Columbia University Press.

Stake, R. E. (1995). *The art of case study research: Perspectives on practice*. London: Sage.

Stocking, G. W. (1983). *Observers observed: Essays on ethnographic fieldwork*. Madison, London: University of Wisconsin Press.

Stockyard, J. E. (2002). *Marriage in culture: Practice and meaning across diverse societies*. London: Harcourt College Publishers.

Stranahan, P. (1981). Changes in policy for Yanan women, 1935–1947. *Modern China,7*(1), 95.

Strauss, A., & Corbin, J. (1998). *Basics of qualitative research, techniques and procedures for developing grounded theory*. London: Sage.

Summers, A. (1994). *The future of feminism—a letter to the next generation. Damned whores and god's police*. Harmondsworth: Penguin.

Sung, Y. W. (1996). Dragon head of China's economy? In Y. M. Yeung & Y. W. Sung (Eds.), *Shanghai: Transformation and modernisation under China's open policy* (pp. 171–198). Hong Kong: Chinese University Press.

Synnott, A. (1987). Shame and glory: A sociology of hair. *The British Journal of Sociology,38*(3), 381–413.

Tao, C. F. (1991). *Introduction to marxist perspective on women (Marxist funuguan gailun)*. Beijing: Chinese Women's Press.

The Analects. (2014). *Authored by Confucius and translated by Annping Chin*. Penguin Classics.

The Guardian. (2011, April 18). *European football, cars and fashion seduce China*. Retrieved April 19, 2011 from http://www.guardian.co.uk/education/2011/apr/18/china-european-culture

The Independent. (2011, January 1). *Consumer predictions for 2011: 'Urbanomics', 'Made for China,' 'Wellthy'* .... Retrieved April 05, 2011 from http://www.independent.co.uk/life-style/consumer-predictions-for-2011-urbanomics-made-for-china-wellthy-2173488.html

Thogersen, S., & Heimer, M. (2006). *Doing fieldwork in China*. Honolulu: University of Hawaii Press.

Thomson, R., Henderson, S., & Holland, J. (2003). Making the most of what you've got? Resources, values and inequalities in young women's transition to adulthood. *Educational Review,55*(1), 33–46.

Thorne, B. (1982). Feminist rethinking of the family: An overview. In B. Thorne & M. Yalom (Eds.), *Rethinking the family: Some feminist questions*. New York: Longman.

Turner, B. S. (1999). The possibility of primitiveness: Towards a sociology of body marks in cool societies. *Body and Society,2–3*, 39–50.

Unger, J. (1982). *Education under Mao*. New York: Columbia University Press.

Unger, J. (Ed.). (1996). *Chinese nationalism*. New York: M.E. Sharpe.

Van Maanen, J. (1982). Fieldwork on the beat. In J. Van Mannen, J. M. Dabbs, & R. R. Faulkner (Eds.), *Varieties of qualitative research* (pp. 103–151). Beverly Hills, CA: Sage.

Veteran Cadres of Weinan Women's Federation. (1996). Discussion transcribed by Gao Xiaoxian and Gail Hershatter.

Walkerdine, V., Lucey, H., & Melody, J. (2001). *Growing up girl: Psychosocial explorations of gender and class*. Basingstoke: Palgrave.

Wallace, C., & Kovatcheva, S. (1999). *Youth in society: The construction and deconstruction of youth in east and west Europe*. London: Macmillan.

Wan, M. G. (2004). Ethnic diversity and citizenship education in the People's Republic of China. In J. A. Banks (Ed.), *Diversity and citizenship education: Global perspectives* (pp. 355–371). San Francisco, CA: Jossey-Bass Publishers.

Wang, G. W. (1996). Openness and nationalism: Outside the Chinese revolution. In J. Unger (Ed.), *Chinese nationalism*. London: M.E. Sharpe.

Wang, Z. (1998). Research on women in contemporary China. In G. Hershatter, E. Honig, S. Mann, & L. Rofel (Eds.), *Guide to women's studies in China*. Berkeley: Institute of East Asian Studies, University of California.

Wang, Z. (1999). *Women in the Chinese enlightenment: Oral and textual histories*. London: University of California Press.

Wang, J. L. (2001). Summary of 'gender and sociology' reading seminar ('shehui xingbei yu shehuixue' dushu yantao ban zongshu). *Collection of Women's Studies (Funu yanjiu luncong),2*, 63–67.

Wang, Z. (2003). Gender, employment and women's resistance. In E. J. Perry & M. Selden (Eds.), *Chinese society: Change, conflict and resistance* (2nd ed.). London, New York: RoutledgeCurzon.

Wang, F. L. (2005). *Organising through division and exclusion: China's Hukou system*. Stanford, CA: Stanford University Press.

Warner-Smith, P., & Lee, C. (2001). Hopes and fears: The life choices, aspirations and well-being of young rural women. *Youth Studies Australia,20*, 32–37.

Watson, J. L. (Ed.). (1984). *Class and social stratification in post-revolution China.* Cambridge: Cambridge University Press.

Watson, R. (1996). Chinese bridal laments: The claims of a dutiful daughter. In B. Yung, E. S. Rawski, & R. S. Watson (Eds.), *Harmony and counterpoint: Ritual music in Chinese context.* Stanford, California: Stanford University Press.

Watson, J. L. (2000). Food as lens: The past, present and future of family life in China. In J. Jing (Ed.), *Feeding China's little emperors* (pp. 1–26). Stanford: Stanford University Press.

Weiner, G. (2006). Out of the ruins: Feminist pedagogy in recovery. In B. Francis, L. Smulyan, & C. Skelton (Eds.), *International handbook of gender and education* (pp. 79–92). London: Sage.

Weitz, R. (Ed.). (1998a). *The politics of women's bodies: Sexuality, appearance, and behaviour.* New York, Oxford: Oxford University Press.

Weitz, R. (1998b). *The politics of women's bodies.* New York: Oxford University Press.

Weitz, R. (2001). Women and their hair: Seeking power through resistance and accommodation. *Gender and Society,15*(5), 667–686.

Wendt, A. (1994). Collective identity formation and the international state. *American Political Science Review,88*(2), 384–396.

Wesoky, S. (2002). *Chinese feminism faces globalisation.* New York, London: Routledge.

Wexler, P. (1990). Citizenship in the semiotic society. In B. Turner (Ed.), *Theories of modernity and postmodernity.* London: Sage.

White, T. (2003). *China's longest campaign: Birth planning in the People's Republic 1949–2005.* London: Cornell University Press.

Whorton, J. (2001). Looking back: The solitary vice. *Western Journal of Medicine,175*(1), 66–68.

Wyn, J., & White, R. (1997). *Rethinking youth.* London: Sage.

White Paper. (1994, June). The situation of Chinese women. Released by the information office of the State Council of the People's Republic of China, Beijing, China.

Wicks, D., & Mishra, G. (1998). Young Australian women and their aspirations for work, education and relationships. In E. Carson, A. Jamrozicz, & T. Winefield (Eds.), *Unemployment: Economic promise and political will.* Brisbane: Australian Academic Press.

Wilkinson, H., Howard, M., Gregory, S., Hayes, H., & Young, R. (1997). *Tomorrow's women.* London: Demos.

Willis, E. (1992). *Lust horizons: Is the women's movement pro-sex? In no more nice girls: Countercultural essays.* Middletown, CT: Wesleyan University Press.

Wolf, M. (1987). *Revolution postponed: Women in contemporary China.* London: Methuen.

Wolf, N. (1993). *Fire with fire: The new female power and how it will change the 21st century.* London: Chatto and Windus.

Woolf, V. (1938). *Three guineas.* New York: Harcourt, Brace and Company.

Woollett, A., & Marshall, H. (1996). Reading the body: Young women's accounts of the meanings of the body in relation to independence, responsibility and maturity. *European Journal of Women's Studies,3*(2), 199–214.

Wu, J. J. (2009). *Chinese fashion: From Mao to Now.* New York: Oxford International Publishers.

Wyn, J., & White, R. (1997). *Rethinking youth.* London: Sage.

Xiao, J., & Lo, L. N. K. (2003). Human capital development in Shanghai: Lessons and prospects. *International Journal of Educational Development,23*, 411–427.

Xiong, Y. M., Liu, X. C., & Qu, W. (1992). *A decade of women's theoretic studies in China: 1981–1990 (Zhongguo funu lilun yanjiu shinian).* Beijing: Chinese Women's Press.

Yakaboski, T. (2009). Book review of Harris's next wave cultures: Feminism, subcultures, activism. *Comparative Education Review,53*(3), 468.

Yan, Y. X. (2009). *The individualisation of Chinese society.* Oxford, New York: Berg.

Yang, M. (1999). *Spaces of their own: Women's public sphere in transnational China.* Minneapolis, MN, London: University of Minnesota Press.

Yang, X. Y. (2010, July 18). *China's censors rein in 'vulgar' reality TV show.* Retrieved December 11, 2010 from http://www.nytimes.com/2010/07/19/world/asia/19chinatv.html

Yi, Y. (2000). Preliminary review of women's studies organizations in modern China (Dangdai zhongguo funu yanjiu zuzhi chutan). *Collection of Women's Studies (Funu yanjiu luncong),2,* 34–38.

Yin, R. K. (1994). *Case study research design and methods.* London: Sage.

Young, A. (1995). Writing femininity in dissent. In B. Skeggs (Ed.), *Feminist cultural theory: Process and production.* Manchester: Manchester University Press.

Yual-Davis, N. (1997). Women, citizenship and difference. *Feminist Review,57,* 4–27.

Yuval-Davis, N., & Stoetzler, M. (2002). Imagined boundaries and borders: A gendered gaze. *The European Journal of Women's Studies,9*(3), 329–344.

Zha, Q. (2009). Diversification or homogenisation: How governments and markets have combined to (re)shape Chinese higher education in its recent massification process. *Higher Education,58* (1), 41–58.

Zhang, L. (2002). Spatiality and urban citizenship in late socialist China. *Popular Culture,14,* 311–334.

Zhang, N., & Wu, X. (1995). Discovering the positive within the negative: The women's movement in a changing China. In A. Basu (Ed.), *The challenge of local feminisms: Women's movements in global perspective.* Boulder, CO: Westview Press.

Zhong, X. P. (2007). In Z. Zhang (Ed.), *The urban generation: Chinese cinema and society at the turn of the 21st century.* London: Duke University Press.

Zhou, J. H. (2006). *Remaking China's republic philosophy and Chinese women's liberation: The volatile mixing of confucianism, marxism and feminism.* New York: The Edwin Mellen Press.

Zizek, S. (2005). *The metastases of enjoyment: On women and causality.* London: Verso.

Zweig, D., Chang, G. C., & Rosen, S. (2004). Globalisation and transnational human capital: Overseas and returnee scholars to China. *The China Quarterly,179,* 735–757.

CPSIA information can be obtained
at www.ICGtesting.com
Printed in the USA
LVOW02*1614290416

485947LV00002B/8/P